T0306049

PETER DRUCKER AND MANAGEMENT

Peter Drucker is arguably the world's most influential management writer, but his contributions as a social theorist and philosopher are also notable. This book presents Drucker as a key thinker, whose work encompasses ideas beyond management practice.

Illuminating Drucker as a complex figure, this book highlights how his work draws upon, impacts, and intersects fields such as technology, sociology, philosophy, and theology. The book presents and contextualizes Drucker as an important historical figure, whose work resonates in a contemporary world where moderation between extremes is an essential ingredient in interpreting and navigating complex events and processes.

Combining deep insights into Peter Drucker's life and work, this unique book is valuable reading for scholars, students, and reflective practitioners of management as well as those with an interest in intellectual history more broadly.

Karen E. Linkletter is the Director of the Management as a Liberal Art Research Institute, USA.

Routledge Key Thinkers in Business and Management
Series Editor: David Collins, *Northumbria University, UK*

Students of business often emerge from their years of business school training without having had the benefit of seeing how its ideas have evolved. A black hole is developing in management education, and the intellectual vacuum needs to be addressed. The solution is to look at the major intellectual figures in the development of business, management and organisation thinking and practice. In short, who are the makers of modern management? And why should we care?

This series provides authoritative accounts of the key thinkers across the business disciplines. Critical, contextual and comprehensive, books in the series will include figures who've made significant impacts to management thought and practice.

Tom Peters and Management
A History of Organizational Storytelling
David Collins

Peter Drucker and Management
Karen E. Linkletter

For more information on this series please visit: www.routledge.com/Key-Thinkers-in-Business-and-Management/book-series/THINKBUS

PETER DRUCKER AND MANAGEMENT

Karen E. Linkletter

Routledge
Taylor & Francis Group

LONDON AND NEW YORK

Designed cover image: Drucker Archives, Special Collections and Archives,
The Claremont Colleges Library Claremont, CA USA

First published 2024
by Routledge
4 Park Square, Milton Park, Abingdon, Oxon OX14 4RN

and by Routledge
605 Third Avenue, New York, NY 10158

Routledge is an imprint of the Taylor & Francis Group, an informa business

British Library Cataloguing-in-Publication Data
A catalogue record for this book is available from the British Library

Library of Congress Cataloging-in-Publication Data
Names: Linkletter, Karen E., author.
Title: Peter Drucker and management / Karen E. Linkletter.
Description: Abingdon, Oxon ; New York, NY : Routledge, 2024. |
Series: Routledge key thinkers in business & management |
Includes bibliographical references and index. |
Identifiers: LCCN 2023055501 (print) | LCCN 2023055502 (ebook) |
ISBN 9781032531335 (hardback) | ISBN 9781032531328 (paperback) |
ISBN 9781003410485 (ebook)
Subjects: LCSH: Drucker, Peter F. (Peter Ferdinand), 1909–2005. | Management.
Classification: LCC HD31.D776 L56 2024 (print) |
LCC HD31.D776 (ebook) | DDC 658–dc23/eng/20240119
LC record available at https://lccn.loc.gov/2023055501
LC ebook record available at https://lccn.loc.gov/2023055502

ISBN: 9781032531335 (hbk)
ISBN: 9781032531328 (pbk)
ISBN: 9781003410485 (ebk)

DOI: 10.4324/9781003410485

Typeset in Sabon
by Newgen Publishing UK

CONTENTS

ACKNOWLEDGMENTS

I am indebted to Terry Clague, Senior Publisher with Routledge Books, and Naomi Round Cahalin, Senior Editorial Assistant with the Taylor and Francis Group at Routledge. They have been a joy to work with. I must acknowledge Bridget Lawlor, who brought this opportunity to my attention.

Sourcing for this project was challenging, as Peter Drucker did not leave much material about his early life other than his memoir. I was fortunate to have copies of archival material in my possession dating back to my work establishing the Drucker Archives 20 years ago and now was able to dig into digital sources to find more information. I am thankful for personal conversations with Peter Paschek, a longtime friend of Drucker. Our Zoom meetings were delightful and enlightening. He has an intimate knowledge of Drucker through lengthy correspondence and relationship and has become a friend of mine. Michael Kelly, Executive Director of the Drucker Archives, was instrumental in finding photos that I thought were important to supply context to the text.

Colleagues are always important in the editing and writing process. I submitted chapters to many of my peers for comment and review to help expedite the publication process. Many thanks to Rick Johnson, Timo Meynhardt, Pooya Tabesh, Franco Gandolfi, Peter Paschek, Byron Ramirez, Rob Kirkland, and Nina Murayama for their review and comment on chapters. I'm also thankful for patient friends who listened to me prattle on about Peter Drucker as I worked on this project.

I am thankful to have connected with Peter and Doris's daughters, Joan and Cecily about this book. I have strived to present their father and mother in a truthful and respectful manner.

Finally, I would like to thank the people that supported me to think about Drucker as more than a management person. Joe Maciariello was on my dissertation committee 20 years ago; "Drucker Redux: Management as Intellectual and Philosophical Product" was an early venture in transdisciplinary scholarship back in 2004, and I appreciate the support of Maciariello, Elazar Barkan, Robert Dawidoff, and Bill Jones during this early work, some of which is incorporated into this book.

INTRODUCTION

No society can function as a society unless it gives the individual member social status and function, and unless the decisive social power is legitimate power. The former establishes the basic frame of social life, the purpose and meaning of society. The latter shapes the space within the frame; it makes society concrete and creates its institutions. If the individual is not given social status and function, there can be no society but only a mass of social atoms flying through space without aim or purpose. And unless power is legitimate, there can be no social fabric; there is only a social vacuum held together by mere slavery or inertia.

(Drucker, 2003, pp. xvi–xvii)

Peter Drucker is known for being the "father of modern management." To many, he is an archaic figure from the past whose name may be recognizable but whose work and contributions may be unknown. While he remains well-known and read in Japan and other places, the former "guru" of management in America and much of Europe has been displaced by newer practitioners and authors. Yet, to characterize Drucker as simply a management expert does not begin to do him or his work justice. Drucker was, first and foremost, a social theorist who wrote about management by accident of his time and place in history.

Born in 1909 in Austria, Drucker moved to Germany to attend university and work just as Germany was experiencing the social and economic turmoil of the years after World War I. As a journalist, he covered the rise of Hitler and the National Socialist Party and participated in political

DOI: 10.4324/9781003410485-1

activities aimed at subverting Hitler's success. With the Nazi's eventual victory, Drucker fled first to England and then to the United States. Landing in the United States during the Great Depression, shortly before that country's entry into World War II, Drucker witnessed the dramatic changes happening in the American economy, as it transformed into an industrial manufacturing powerhouse (first for armament production, and, after the war, for a vast array of consumer goods). By sheer accident of timing and history, Drucker was catapulted from world to world. First, Drucker's youth in a placid upper-middle-class neighborhood in Vienna, the crown of the Austro-Hungarian Empire, was marred by the upheaval of World War I and its aftermath. As a young man starting an independent life, he was shattered by the rise of the Nazis and the threat to his family, career, and personal safety. Landing in America on the cusp of that country's entry into World War II, Drucker experienced the subsequent massive economic and cultural shifts and disruptions that the war created in the United States. Given that Drucker experienced all of these discontinuities in his first some 35 years of life, it is not surprising that his work focused on his primary project: how to find a path to a functioning society, and one that would balance change and continuity.

For Drucker, the key to avoid another totalitarian or fascist disaster such as that he witnessed in Europe in the 1930s was to provide people with a society that made sense. When rational explanations for events broke down, people lost all hope and turned to authoritarianism—a strong leader who made promises that, even if they made no sense, would at least offer a way out of misery. The only recompense was to create a society that gave individuals social status and function. Everyone needs to feel that they are important somewhere in society, that they matter and are recognized and valued. They also need to feel that they contribute and have a purpose (a job). Additionally, society needs to be held together by an agreed-upon power that is deemed legitimate. How do we create this functioning society?

In mid-twentieth-century America, as business and other organizations began to become more important than the traditional dominance of government as the primary institution, Drucker was naturally drawn to management as he sought to shore up the institutions of society. If the new institutions of society—first corporations, and later non-profits and other institutions—were well-managed, they could provide individuals with status and function and also represent a legitimate form of authority and power. Ultimately, a pluralistic society of organizations that were well-managed could prevent the rise of totalitarianism and, while not creating an ideal society, at least provide the opportunity for a tolerable one. The fact that Drucker witnessed such incredible change in his life only reinforces the recurring theme of continuity and discontinuity in his work.

That Drucker would focus on management was merely a byproduct of this larger social vision of a tolerable, bearable society of many institutions and organizations all working toward their own goals and objectives, yet collectively keeping an eye on the common good. Readers of Drucker have complained of his lack of specificity, citations, simplicity of tone, and tendency toward generalization. Those readers are looking to Drucker to be an orthodox *management* writer. Drucker was never that. He was, by his own admission, a social observer and a journalist. It is our hope that this text presents Peter Drucker as not merely a social observer but also a social theorist who impacted the world of management.

This book is organized into chapters that can be read independently from one another but also present a logical thematic approach to Drucker's work. Chapter 1 gives the reader an in-depth biographical evaluation of Drucker's life focusing on his European roots and how that background informed his later work and life. Chapter 2 lays out Drucker's social theory in detail, tracing how his concept of a functioning society worked its way into his writings. Chapter 3 delves into the detail of Drucker's work on the actual practice of management, as he moved from his theoretical work to his efforts to make management a profession. Chapter 4 takes up the subject of leadership, a topic of much interest today that Drucker was, frankly, lukewarm to. Drucker came late to the leadership conversation, and this chapter explains why, with some takeaways as to what we might learn from Drucker on this today. Chapter 5 addresses Drucker's signature term, the knowledge society, and addresses some of our current concerns with new developments in this area. Chapter 6 takes up Drucker's work on innovation and entrepreneurship, including his early thinking on that topic before his 1985 book, as well as how we might use his ideas today. In Chapter 7, we confront the controversial topic of Drucker's work on government and how he has been misinterpreted by some politically; Drucker was intentionally an apolitical figure, and we hope to show that efforts to recruit him as a political icon are misconstrued. The current topic of technology and society is related to discussion of artificial intelligence and other emerging developments. Chapter 8 shows that Drucker was a pioneer in thinking about how such advances are part of historical context and larger processes, and thus need to be viewed carefully in terms of threats and potential. Lastly, Chapter 9 looks at Drucker as he characterized himself: a social ecologist. We begin the book looking at Drucker as a theorist. Social ecology is the way Drucker put his theory into practice, not just for individual organizations but also for society as a whole.

I knew Peter Drucker. He was a brilliant man with whom I had many wonderful conversations, and with whom I laughed and shared personal experiences. He was also a complicated person with a history we cannot begin to understand or imagine. I hope that I have captured something of his life and work in these pages.

Bibliography

Drucker, P.F. (2003) *A functioning society*. New Brunswick, NJ: Transaction.

1

DRUCKER THE EUROPEAN

Introduction

Warren Bennis wrote that Drucker had much in common with another "foreign visitor" to America: Alexis de Tocqueville: "Drucker and Tocqueville have made more sweeping and readable generalizations about this country and its institutions than any of our native sons or daughters" (Bennis, 1985, p. 27). Like Tocqueville, Drucker was a bystander, an observer of American culture. His education and upbringing in the intellectual world of Austria before World War I, coupled with his experience seeing the rise of National Socialism in Germany and the failure of social institutions in that country, prepared him to be the architect of a social theory that placed management at the center. Landing in industrial America by accident of history, Drucker's search for a functioning society of institutions led him to use America as a blueprint for avoiding the breakdown of social structures that occurred in Europe. Steeped in a wealth of knowledge in political philosophy, literature, economics, sociology, and many other disciplines, Drucker's unique perspective as a European émigré allowed him to see the world in the context of larger patterns of change and continuity. His experience with the massive disruptions of two world wars, economic upheaval, and totalitarian government gave Drucker an early education in the need to balance change with continuity. Driven by his experiences in Austria as a teenager and in Germany as a young man, Drucker's life project was the search for a tolerable society of institutions that would provide meaning to people and prevent a repeat of the history he witnessed.

DOI: 10.4324/9781003410485-2

Drucker the Bystander

In his interviews and memoir, Drucker told a consistent story of his life and career development, one that emphasizes his role as an observer or bystander in American society. He often used a quotation from Goethe's *Faust* to describe himself: "Born to see, meant to look" (Drucker, 1995). By deliberately fashioning himself as a bystander, not a participant, Drucker distanced himself from the very culture he also claimed as his own. Austrian-born and German educated, Drucker, like many other émigrés, was drawn to America because it in so many ways contrasted with Old World Europe. Yet, at the same time, he sought to lose his European identity, to become American, he created his own identity as an outsider rather than an insider. As a self-made bystander, Peter Drucker wrote for himself an identity that placed him between identities; he was neither fully American nor European. Although he retained his Austrian accent, he wrote as an American bystander, taking title to American society and culture. However, as someone who fled Europe around the same time as Hannah Arendt, Ludwig von Mises, Erich Fromm, and Herbert Marcuse, Drucker could not help but write from the perspective of an émigré. He crafted an identity that selectively blurred his status as a European immigrant, yet, at the same time, prevented him from complete immersion and assimilation in American life.

Drucker's bystander identity was useful to him as a means of negotiating the virtual impossibility of complete assimilation. Other fellow émigrés experienced similar difficulties with becoming American, and, like Drucker, constructed outsider identities. Theologian Paul Tillich entitled his autobiography "On the Boundary," conveying his bystander status along the outskirts of American society. Others, such as Theodore Adorno and Berthold Brecht, established a Tocquevillian stance, as the outsider looking in to critique American culture for its homogeneity and mind-numbing effect (Heilbut, 1983). Drucker, however, used his bystander identity for its practical applications in his role as a consultant; by maintaining his distance from his clients' organizations, he retained his objectivity. USC management professor Warren Bennis stated that Drucker told him this was one of the secrets of consulting: "be an outsider" (Bennis, 1985, p. 25). But it served another important function as well. It allowed him to find his own place of meaning and status in society, a topic which is of great importance to him, while still protecting his own individuality and uniqueness. As management professor Warren Bennis has commented, "It is not clear where Peter Drucker does belong." He clearly did not fit into the corporate world; he never worked for one of the large organizations, business or non-profit, that he analyzed. He was never at home in the academic realm, which he himself acknowledged: "...I am not a scholar and I have always had a very large part of my life outside the university." In terms of his functional identity, the bystander persona allowed Drucker to carve out his own place and position of status in American society, one that let him serve as a writer and observer who expounds "strange views from the rooftops...for it is his [the bystander's] lot to see things differently" (Drucker, 1978, p. 6).

Childhood in Austria

Drucker's management theories cannot be appreciated without an understanding of the context of his early life in Austria and Germany. Born in 1909, he was raised in an upper-middle-class family in Vienna. His father, Adolph, was an economist and government official, serving as the director of the Department of Foreign Trade in the Imperial Austro-Hungarian government. Adolph founded the Salzburg Music Festival and later became an international lawyer. His mother, Caroline, studied medicine and was a talented musician (see Photo 1.1). His uncle (married to Caroline's younger sister) was Hans Kelsen, an important legal theorist and philosopher who was the architect of Austria's post-war constitution (see Chapter 2 for a more extensive discussion of Drucker's thoughts on Kelsen's theories). Drucker later described Kelsen as "a typical political scientist...He was an abstract philosopher concerned with the nature of the law and the nature of punishment..." (Arnn, Masugi, and Schramm, 1984). Young Peter was raised in an intellectual environment, privy to wide-ranging discussions about literature, philosophy, and science, in something of a haven from the turmoil of interwar Austria (Tarrant, 1976; Drucker, 1978). Drucker's upbringing was, in many ways, more typical of the Austrian-Hungarian monarchy before the war. Hermann Simon, an expert on pricing strategies who long corresponded with Drucker from Germany, remarks that Drucker was "a man of the past," a product of this unique environment in Vienna, where "great emphasis was placed on culture, art, music, historical consciousness, urbanity, and international openness...Another famous Venetian [sic], the writer Stefan Zweig (1881–1942), calls this 'yesterday's world'" (Simon, 2002, p. 1).

Zweig's memoirs, *The World of Yesterday*, describe Habsburg Vienna as a lost world of stability, culture, and order. The sheer range of intellectual production to come out of pre-war Vienna is staggering: Schoenberg's twelve-tone scale, Freud and psychoanalysis, Adolf Loos and modern architecture, Wittgenstein's reinvention of the discipline of philosophy, Klimt and the Secession movement in painting—the list goes on. The Hofmannsthal salon in which Drucker spent considerable time was a microcosm of this early Viennese society, where government officials, Habsburgs, artists, philosophers, and other such luminaries all traveled in very close circles. This was not a mass industrial society by any stretch of the imagination, but a tightly knit city with a distinctive cultural and intellectual identity as the "City of Dreams."

Drucker was only nine years old when the Habsburg monarchy fell in 1918 and Austria began its post-World War I decline. His memory of the war's outbreak is dim—he remembers having a beach vacation but not that it was cut short by the assassination of the Archduke (Drucker, 1978, pp. 34–35). Drucker does have memories of the immediate post-war years and the effects of the fall of the empire. Most of the high culture of pre-war Austria had been subsidized by the monarchy and the upper classes, so with their demise came considerable social as well as economic changes. Inflationary pressures alone caused remarkable stress. In 1919, six Austrian crowns equaled one dollar; by August of 1922, it took 83,000 crowns to equal the same amount (Large, 1990). Adolph Drucker's mother, who had inherited a considerable fortune when her husband, Ferdinand Bond, died, lost nearly all of it to post-war inflation. According to Drucker, his grandmother's quality of life suffered substantially, as she became "poor as a churchmouse" [sic] (Drucker, 1978, pp. 10–13).

Religious Background

Drucker was always private about the role of faith and religion in his own life. As Tim Stafford notes, although Drucker was a Christian, he seemed "determined to keep his faith a secondary characteristic for his readers. Drucker hardly ever uses theological or biblical terminology to express himself, even if he is writing about something that easily fits theological categories." As Stafford points out, this is a conscious choice (Stafford, 1999, p. 44).

Jewish Cultural Roots

Drucker's religious status has been the subject of much speculation and investigation. It seems evident that the Drucker family, like many in Austria and Germany during the late nineteenth and early twentieth centuries, had members who were ethnically Jewish. Drucker told author Andrea Gabor that virtually every Austrian of his era and class had Jewish relations (Gabor, 2000, p. 300). While Austrian society was quite cosmopolitan in this era, anti-Semitism existed, and it was not uncommon for non-practicing ethnic Jews to convert to Christianity to make life easier.

According to author Peter Starbuck, Drucker's parents were Jewish by birth but converted to Lutheranism before Drucker was born. They were not married in a synagogue, which indicates that they were not religiously practicing Jews. Drucker's parents moved from a Jewish area of Vienna to a protestant area (19th District, Doblinger, Haupstrasse). The Druckers received a *Heimatschein* (certificate of family origin) which gave permission for the Jewish family to reside in this part of the city. The Doblinger location was affluent, with larger homes that were individually designed. Drucker was baptized into the Lutheran church shortly after birth (Starbuck, 2012, pp. 9–10).

Starbuck does not source his work but claims that there are Austrian documents to evidence his assertions. Drucker's uncle, Hans Kelsen, was Jewish, born into a middle-class family in Prague. Yet, like many Jews in this era, Kelsen was not religious; however, his ancestry caused him problems throughout his career. He converted to Catholicism in 1905 to avoid persecution and the loss of job opportunities (Lieblich, 2015). Doris Drucker, Peter's wife, discusses the world of ethnic Jews and their progeny in her own memoir. According to Doris, she had "non-Jewish Jews" in her family, including her grandmother. Such non-observant Jews were not considered Jewish by their Orthodox neighbors; Drucker's family celebrated Christmas and Easter rather than Hanukah or Passover. Her town of Koenigstein was ethnically and religiously diverse, consisting of Roman Catholics, Lutheran Protestants, and a few Jewish families (Drucker, 2004, pp. 70–71).

This history is important, because it establishes the relative unimportance of religion for Drucker and others in his circle during his formative years. Germany and Austria of the interwar period, at least in the more affluent regions, hosted a range of ethnicities that co-existed. While anti-Semitism certainly existed, it was not experienced to the degree it would be a few years later under the Nazi regime. In her memoir, Doris states that, even though she had finished her law degree, she could not practice once the Nazis came into power because of her Jewish ancestry (Drucker, 2004, pp. 178–179). Doris's details allow us to understand the dilemma faced by Peter and his family when the Nazis came to power. Even though they were Christians, they had relatives who were ethnically Jewish, and thus potential targets of the Nazi Regime.

Drucker's Christianity

While Drucker's status as a Christian is no longer a topic for debate, the nature of his Christianity is. Stafford's observations, as an evangelical Christian, are astute. Drucker held faith to be a personal matter and considered individual spiritual matters to be private. In *The End of Economic Man*, Drucker postulated that the churches could not have prevented fascism from taking hold in Europe, because religion could not provide meaning to one's life in society:

> Personal religious experience may be invaluable to the individual; it may restore his peace, may give him a personal God and a rational understanding of his own function and nature. But it cannot re-create society and cannot make social and community life sensible.
>
> *(Drucker, 1939a, p. 102)*

This tension between living in the material world and the understanding of its ultimate meaningless was, to Drucker, "the essence of why nobody can be a Christian. You can only hope to become a Christian. You know, whenever any of you people talk of me as a Christian, I wince" (Buford, 1991, p. 9). The personal nature of religion, apart from life in society, explains the impact of Kierkegaard on Drucker when he was faced with what seemed to be a hopeless society after World War II. It also explains why he never explicitly discussed religion or religious influences in his work.

Scholars have explored the possible Christian influences on or origins of Drucker's work (see Bonaparte and Flaherty, 1970; Tarrant, 1976; Beatty, 1998; Linkletter and Maciariello, 2009). Others have taken a stronger position on Drucker's own personal religiosity. Timo Meynhardt argues that the very essence of Drucker's work is "his non-compromising urge for moral purpose, deeply rooted in the Christian tradition, and the relationship with practical wisdom as a key virtue for the manager" (Meynhardt, 2010, p. 618). Conversely, Toubiana and Yair posit that "Drucker's moral work is latched to the latent theological motives which run through German social theory," and that he was a "secularized German theologian" (Toubiana and Yair, 2012, p. 170). Lastly, Fernandez positions Drucker as a "spiritual philosopher" driven by an internal moral compass that permeates his work on management (Fernandez, 2009).

It seems clear that, while Drucker may have personally been a spiritual individual with his own private religious beliefs, his work was informed more by his insistence on moral purpose rather than theology or specific religious beliefs. Drucker was disdainful of theology as a discipline (although he certainly valued religious philosophy). In terms of theology, he thought that

> people are dreadfully bored with theology…and I sympathize with them. I've always felt that quite clearly the good Lord loves diversity. He created 25,000 species of flies. If he had been like some theologians I know, there would have been only one right specie of fly.
>
> *(Steinfels, 2005)*

Peter Paschek, Drucker's friend for over 20 years, reports that in the many conversations they had, religion only came up once, and that is when Drucker defined himself. Referencing Henry Adams, Drucker referred to himself as a Christian Conservative Anarchist:

> A conservative Christian anarchist—yes, that's me, more or less! The older I get, the more skeptical I am that society can satisfy all of the promises that humanity hopes to realize. I think one of the quintessential experiences of the last 50 years has been our growing disillusionment with "Volksvergluckung" [rabble rousing] and our gradual recognition that a

society can at best be tolerable, but never perfect...This is a conservative concept, yet also a Christian one, since it emphasizes the individual and his or her belief, while seeking a perfect state of affairs not in the temporal world but in another. I am a conservative Christian and an anarchist in the sense that I am increasingly wary of governments—no, that is the wrong word—of power...I have always regarded power as the central problem and the yearning for power—not sex—as mankind's greatest sin...So, in this sense, I am an anarchist, but unlike traditional anarchists, I accept the necessity of governance and government.

(Paschek, 2020, p. 57)

As Paschek related to this author, Drucker stated that he saw himself as Christian in the sense that there was something beyond society, and that every human being was deserving of dignity and respect. For Drucker, spirituality was something integrated into one's whole personality rather than a separate part of one's identity as a religious person (Paschek, 2023a, 2023b).

Adventures of a Bystander

Drucker's 1978 memoir is composed as more of a collection of stories or vignettes rather than an autobiographical narrative. Casting himself in the role of the observer, Drucker crafts a work that aims to capture the spirit and emotion of the interwar years in Europe. The work has been enjoyed by many readers familiar with Drucker's work on management and society. However, it has come under criticism, in some cases blistering, particularly from the academic community, who fault the book for its many inaccuracies and historical errors. Kenneth McRobbie, a poet and historian who worked with the Hungarian economist and sociologist Karl Polanyi, devoted an entire essay to Drucker's chapter on Polanyi, in which he takes Drucker to task for his numerous factual errors and lack of truth and objectivity (McRobbie, 1999). McRobbie criticizes Drucker for bending facts to fit Polanyi into a larger narrative that serves Drucker's purpose in the book. In this sense, McRobbie's complaint, as an historian, is valid; Drucker's presentation of Polanyi's life and career is not historically accurate by any stretch of the imagination. It does make one think twice about other characterizations (and even the real existence) of people in Drucker's memoir.

Yet, Drucker himself tips us off that this is no ordinary autobiography. In the Preface, he states:

A historian can, of course, get the *facts* about the past. A good many historians have done that—some successfully—in respect to the years between 1918 and the end of the 1940s and 1950s. Yet only a great novelist could give us these years as the present—the way Balzac gave us France of the early 19th century; Dickens gave us England of the mid 19th century; and Twain gave us America of the second half of the 19th century. I am not a novelist—certainly not a 'great' one. But no one else has attempted to do what this book attempts: a self portrait of these vital inter-war years by venue [sic] of their *human, emotional, and mental* qualities.

(Drucker, 1978, p. vii)

Reader, you have duly been warned, albeit slyly, by your author that, as he told his friend Peter Paschek, "Never forget, there is a lot of fiction in it" (Paschek, 2020, p. 196). It is not surprising that Drucker would go on to publish two novels not long after writing *Adventures of a Bystander*: *The Last of All Possible Worlds* (1982) and *The Temptation to do Good* (1984). Drucker was always interested in using material to make a point, to tell a story. He found the obsession with historical accuracy and detail to be tedious and pointless. During a conversation with this author, he referred to my insistence on historical accuracy as a "hang up" (Drucker, 2005a). In the case of *Adventures of a Bystander*, the point was to convey the essence and mood of the years between the two world wars. His bending of the truth (and, in some cases, creation of entirely fictional characters who are presented as historical personages) is unnerving for those seeking an accurate description of Drucker's early life. But readers of Drucker should never look to facts or evidence as the heart of his work. Rather, it is his use of concepts, ideas, and broad trends that conveys his points; detail is not used for evidence for an argument but rather to shape a story or pattern.

Doris Drucker

In contrast to Peter Drucker, Doris Drucker had vivid memories of World War I's impact on her life, conveyed through a conventional memoir (Drucker, 2004). A product of the same generation in Europe, Doris Drucker herself is an interesting personage, an entrepreneur and scientist (see Photo 1.2). Not surprisingly, she had her own significant intellectual influence on Drucker's work, although she denied this (Drucker, 1999). Nevertheless, her descriptions of historical events provide at times an interesting contrast to Drucker's; at other times, her comments reinforce Drucker's observations.

Doris Drucker describes her childhood as "stultifying," as she was raised under the rigid discipline of her Prussian mother, Clara. While the Drucker family entertained one fascinating guest after another, Doris Schmitz had "no encouragement to explore, only a constant insistence on fitting in, being inconspicuous, and above all, doing our mother proud" (Drucker, 2004). Like the Druckers, however, the Schmitz family emphasized the importance of learning, particularly literature, and the children were well schooled in Goethe and Schiller, as well as the Iliad and the Odyssey. The personal, reflective nature of this memoir is such a striking contrast to Peter Drucker's *Adventures of a Bystander*, where Drucker himself is virtually absent; it bears comment. Mrs. Drucker is extremely candid in her discussions of her mother, her strict upbringing, and her own personal attitudes and actions. Such details of Peter Drucker's early years are notably missing. Drucker's "memoir" is not that; it is a semi-fictional work that attempts to recreate a mood and feeling of a time rather than to convey factual events. It thus confounds historians and others concerned with factual details about Drucker's early life and makes a recounting of Drucker's early life a challenge in terms of conveying accurate information.

When Doris's father was called to serve in the war, the rest of the family moved to the maternal grandparents' home in Mainz for the war's duration. The images and sounds of warfare became commonplace for her:

> We stood by the window and watched a small plane circle lazily over the rooftops. Suddenly it dropped a dark object; there was a loud bang, and my mother came into the room and said we should get away from the window.
>
> *(Drucker, 2004, p. 8)*

Doris remembers that the economic conditions in Germany were equally dire to those in Austria, if not more so. She remembers using million-mark bills as scratch paper in school because the currency was worthless a week after it had been issued (Drucker, 2004, p. 63).

After the war Doris' father came back to the home in Mainz, which was part of French-occupied Germany. Following a long period of unemployment, he finally found a position in Frankfurt, working as a sales manager. Unfortunately, Frankfurt was on the German side of the checkpoint, so he was unable to cross over for fear of being stuck in occupied France. Once again, Doris' father lived away from the family, this time in a rented apartment in Frankfurt. Eventually the border was suspended, allowing him to rejoin the family, now in Konigstein (Drucker, 2004). But the post-war inflation, along with the "stultifying" life under her controlling mother, made Doris, like Drucker, long for an escape from her own miasma.

"Pre-War Nostalgia" and Escape

Back in Peter Drucker's own Austria, with the fall of the monarchy and subsequent socioeconomic upheaval came the rise of the industrial working-class party, the Social Democrats, in Vienna. As Vienna became an increasingly industrial city, the socialist government instituted a number of reforms aimed at redressing the social problems borne by a growing population of factory workers. During the 1920s, Vienna saw a boom in the construction of hospitals, schools, housing, and libraries, all of which were funded through fairly heavy taxation on the upper and middle classes. While Vienna served as a model of social reform for industrial societies, the rest of Austria was not as progressive. The national government, headed by Chancellor Seipel, was conservative, Catholic, and anti-socialist. Thus, Austria was a small country characterized by sharp contrasts between "Red" Vienna and the socialists and the "Black" conservatives of the national government. This tension came to a head when the paramilitary forces from both sides clashed on 15 July, 1927, on what is known as Bloody Friday. In a violent confrontation, 57 socialists, 28 bystanders, and four policemen were killed.

In 1927, then, the streets of Vienna were anything but calm scenes of intellectual discourse. Although Drucker found Vienna a most interesting "social laboratory," it is not surprising that a 17-year-old Drucker decided to leave Austria for Germany immediately after high school (gymnasium), the same year as Bloody Friday (Lenzner and John, 1997, p. 127). Raised in an intellectual salon, to Drucker, the crowded streets of socialist Vienna were uncomfortable, which is clear in his memoirs, *Adventures of a Bystander*. The book begins with him reflecting on his decision at the age of 14 not to participate in a Republic Day march in 1923. Republic Day in socialist Austria was a day of mass celebration, and in Drucker's description, we get a sense as to his discomfort with being one of the crowd:

> ...the rhythmic pounding of the feet of my followers behind me, the press of mass man, the physical coercion of mass movement overpowered me...I thrust the banner, without saying a word, into the arms of the hefty medical student in back of me, dropped out of the ranks, and turned toward home...the massed ranks of Viennese Socialists, marching twelve abreast and carrying their banners, passed me going the other way. I felt terribly lonely and yearned to join them. But I also was lightheaded and elated beyond words.
>
> *(Drucker, 1978, pp. 3–4)*

It is at this moment, Drucker tells us, that he "found out that I don't belong" (Drucker, 1978, p. 4). His description of the march as "physical coercion" reveals his reverence for individualism. Yet, in this moment of individual choice, he realized that such a choice could result in loneliness. This tension between the individual and the group is one of the prominent themes in Drucker's writings; although this passage is his way of establishing his bystander identity early on in his memoir, it also reflects this prevalent thread. As a writer, Drucker is well aware of the ways in which literary structure can be used to convey a message, to persuade, or to argue; thus, it is appropriate to pay special attention to the ways in which he begins and ends books and chapters. This opening anecdote from *Adventures* is quite self-revealing from a man who essentially devoted his life to studying organizations, groups, and the ways in which individuals can become fulfilled within them. It is simultaneously conscious artifice—a statement of individual identity through choice—and self-revelation—a testimonial of individual despair at isolation and the powerful pull of group identity and mass movements.

Escape from Austria meant escape from the crowd, from lack of identity. In addition, leaving Austria also reflected another theme that would become a thread throughout his later work: his disdain for nostalgia. The paroxysm of World War I, so shockingly violent and long, gave birth to a collective yearning for life before the war, as well as a sense of fear of the unknown future. Intellectuals such as music critic Max Graf reflected on the impact of the war and its unexpectedness:

> We who were born in Vienna, and grew up there, had no idea, during the city's brilliant period before the first world war that this epoch was to be the end...and still less did we suspect that the Habsburg Monarchy...was destined to decline...We enjoyed the splendid city which was so elegantly beautiful, and never thought that the light which shone over it could ever be that of a colorful sunset.
>
> *(Graf, 1945, p. 65)*

Doris Drucker also comments on this obsession with pre-war but from the perspective of one who was a child during the war. For her, "pre-war" was something adults wistfully described as a dream world: "'Before the war' meant for us an unfathomable past. Was it then that giants lurked in the hills, Red Riding Hood went to visit her grandmother, and the animals in Aesop's fables talked to one another?" (Drucker, 2004, p. 12).

Peter Drucker was clearly steeped in the longing for "pre-war" days. He writes that his grandmother "held fast to 'prewar'" (Drucker, 1978, p. 15). Like the "physical coercion" of the march, pre-war nostalgia "was like a miasmic smog pervading everything, paralyzing everybody, stifling all thought and imagination" (Drucker, 1978, p. 59). Wishing for the "good old days" of pre-war represented a backward vision of society for Drucker, and one from which he knew he had to escape. The structure of *Adventures of a Bystander* illustrates his preoccupation with this notion of escape. Drucker sketches a picture of pre-war Austria through America before the onset of World War II. Drucker's experiences in "Atlantis" and the "Old World" are contrasted with the "Indian Summer" of America. In the United States, there was no "pre-war," although, as Drucker notes, there was "pre-Depression." Interestingly, Drucker comments that America lost her innocence with her entry into World War II (Drucker, 1978, p. 335). Drucker's choice of structure for his memoirs signals to us that we should believe this sense of escape from first Vienna and later Europe as a whole was prominent in his thinking both early and later in his life. In the same work, he indicates that "I had known since I was fourteen that I was not going to live there [Vienna]," and that

> As a youngster, I knew intuitively that I had to escape 'prewar.' This was, I am convinced, the reason why I knew very early that I would leave Vienna as soon as I could...It was not until I came to the United States in 1937 that I escaped it.
>
> *(Drucker, 1978, pp. 25, 60)*

Again, Drucker carefully frames his childhood in the context of his chosen identity as an American bystander.

After Peter's death, Doris Drucker discussed his feelings for Austria as an older man. She explained that he only returned to visit on Christmas and New Years, and, that after his parents left, he never returned. Why did he have no desire to return? Doris states that she relates what he told her, "which may have been the truth or not, I don't know" (Drucker, 2009). Evidently, Drucker felt like a tourist in his own country, which, after World War I, had gone from the sprawling Austro-Hungarian Empire to a nation the size of the small American state of Maine. Drucker had nostalgic memories of wildflowers and landscapes; he would practice yodeling on hikes with Doris. Drucker was, at heart, a rural man; as she said, "You can't take the country out of the boy" (Drucker, 2009). Drucker's friend Peter Paschek recalls meeting the Druckers in Claremont for dinner. Peter asked Paschek if he had been to the Mojave Desert, telling him about the beautiful landscapes and variety of flowers. Paschek remembers Doris rolling her eyes and elbowing Peter to talk about something else (Paschek, 2023b). So, perhaps, for Drucker, the pre-war nostalgia of his elders was annoying and stultifying. But it seems he had his own version of nostalgia: one for a lost country that no longer existed after he escaped.

Weimar Germany

Drucker's first escape at age 17 took him to Hamburg, where he served as an apprentice at an export firm and enrolled in law university to appease his father. Neither law studies nor his apprenticeship demanded much of his time, which afforded him the opportunity to read history, novels, and, most importantly, to discover Kierkegaard, the philosopher Drucker claims was the most important intellectual influence on his ideas (Drucker, 1999). He also began his career as a writer, publishing a university thesis on the Panama Canal in a German economic journal. While back in Vienna for Christmas vacation, he met Karl Polanyi at an editorial conference for the Austrian Economist, beginning an important friendship. In 1929, Drucker moved to Frankfurt, where he worked as a securities analyst and enrolled as a student of international law at Frankfurt University. When the investment bank he worked for went under following the stock market crash of 1929, Drucker went to work as a financial writer for a regional newspaper, the *Frankenfurter General-Anzeiger*. Two years later, the paper promoted him to one of the top editors, where he covered politics, foreign, and economic news (Drucker, 1978).

The news in the 1929 Weimar Republic was anything but good. The inflation that wracked Austria was equally bad or worse in Germany. Unemployment was horrendous. In September 1929, 1.32 million people were out of work; by 1931, the figure was over 4.35 million. In Drucker's own words, "All around me society, economy, and government—indeed civilization—were collapsing. There was a total lack of continuity" (Drucker, 1993a, p. 442).

Politically, the fragile Weimar coalition was crumbling. Save for a few fringe factions, the prominent political parties in the 1920s were the three Republican center parties: the Social Democrats, the Democratic Party, and the Catholic Center. On the left were the Communists (KPD) and on the right were two monarchist parties, the German People's and German Nationalist (DNVP) parties. Prior to 1930, the DNVP was the primary right-wing opposition to the Weimar coalition. They embraced a monarchist platform, and during the turbulent 1920s, had a marginal rise in electoral support. Party members were split over the Dawes plan and the Treaty of Locarno, however, and these policy differences were exacerbated by social differences along class lines. The Dawes Plan fixed the amount of German reparations from 1925 to 1929. Following World War I, Germany was required to pay reparations to the victors of the war; in 1921, the Allies set the reparations amount at 132 billion marks to be paid in annual installments of 2 billion marks, which amounted to nearly $500 million in annual payments. Germany felt forced to sign this arrangement and later balked at making the payments. The Dawes Plan, which was a compromise worked out by Great Britain, France, and the United States, advanced Germany a large loan to aid in rebuilding the nation's economy. As the German economy improved, the reparations payments were to increase. The right-wing parties in Germany, including the DNVP, saw the payment of reparations as a national disgrace and opposed any such agreements. An adjunct agreement to the issue of reparations was the Treaty of Locarno, signed in 1925, which addressed more political concerns. This treaty required Germany to recognize its western borders; any attack on France (or by France on Germany) would engender the response of all Allied powers, including Great Britain and Italy. Germany was also admitted to the League of Nations under the Locarno Treaty. Conservative parties were upset over the concession of Germany's right to the territory of Alsace-Lorraine in the West (Gilbert and Large, 1991, pp. 208–210).

In 1928, the DVNP took a more radical course after its significant electoral defeat (Peukert, 1987). The right turn of the DVNP meant that they were edging perilously closer to the Nazis. Although, according to Drucker, few people believed the National Socialists would actually come into power, he claims he took them as a serious threat and put his political weight behind the People's Conservative Union, which split from the National People's Party in 1929 (Brem, 1999). The Conservative Union (*Volkskonservative Veriniguing*) centered around a leader named Gottfried Treviranus, who was a submarine captain and World War I hero, as well as a minister in Heinrich Bruning's Catholic Center party cabinet. According to Drucker, the Union was the brainchild of Konrad Adenauer, who at that time was mayor of Cologne, and was an attempt to attract conservative Protestants, who were losing interest in affiliating with the Catholic Center party. The underlying fear was, of course, that these conservatives would side with the National Socialists. The Protestant areas of Germany had lost their traditional institutions of authority during the 1920s, whereas these institutions had remained intact in Catholic regions. Thus, the Protestant areas were more susceptible to left- and right-of-center influences. Furthermore, the more the DNVP moved to the right, the more they convinced people to vote for the Nazis, who were perceived as the younger, more dynamic party (Peukert, 1987).

Drucker's job was to recruit prominent conservatives and to win them away from the Nazi cause. His potential recruits included Ernst Junger and Carl Schmitt, two prominent intellectuals. Junger was not an academic but a World War I soldier, a devotee of Nietzsche, and the architect of an early example of fascist theory. Junger envisioned a new civilization that would revolve around the "Soldier/worker" as an archetype of man-as-hero, a man engaged in "total war" (Peukert, 1987; Gleason, 1995). Schmitt belonged more to Drucker's circle, although he was a Catholic. Trained in law, he believed in the establishment of a strong state to preserve domestic order. Not surprisingly, Schmitt expressed interest in Drucker's graduate thesis, which was to be on three conservative parliamentary figures who had created the concept of the *Rechtsstaat*: Wilhelm von Humboldt (1767–1835), Joseph von Radowitz (1797–1853), and Friedrich Julius Stahl (1802–1861). Schmitt offered to be Drucker's thesis adviser in Cologne; but, as Drucker observed, "it was naturally very clear to Schmitt that my world view and convictions did not agree with his" (Brem, 1999). Schmitt eventually joined the Nazi party in 1933 (Jones, 1999; Gleason, 1995).

Ultimately, Drucker's Conservative Union failed in its mission, losing a number of key recruits to the National Socialists. Furthermore, the party they left behind, the DVNP, joined with the Nazis, ensuring that Hitler now had their bourgeois industrial connections and financial backing. His political activities ending in disarray, Drucker turned his attention again to journalism and academia. After graduating with his Doctorate in International Public

Law, he began work on his thesis, writing on one of the three subjects, Stahl. Drucker planned on publishing his treatise on Stahl, a Jewish jurist, as a way of making his stand against the Nazis clear before he left the country. But the Nazi's rise to power in 1933 led Drucker to act quickly.

Nazi Germany and Escape

The details of Drucker's last weeks in Germany are unclear as he gave conflicting accounts as to why he left when he did. In one telling, shortly after the Nazis assumed power, they took over control of Frankfurt University, where Drucker was working as a teaching assistant. During a faculty meeting, the Nazi representative to the university announced that all Jewish personnel would be dismissed at once. Drucker decided he would leave Germany within the next two days. That evening, he tendered his resignation to the paper. Later that night, a fellow editor knocked on his door, wearing a Nazi uniform. Drucker's colleague offered him the opportunity to replace the editor in chief, who was being let go because of his marriage to a Jewish woman. Drucker finally persuaded the man to leave (Drucker, 2005b). In another account, as a conservative, Drucker appealed enough to the Nazis that they offered him a position within the National Socialist government in 1933, with the Ministry of Information (Drucker, 1978). At this point, Drucker took the portion of his thesis on Friedrich Julius Stahl to J.C.B. Mohr, one of Germany's most prominent publishing houses. Mohr published the Stahl article in March 1933, and several weeks later, the Nazi party banned the work. Drucker has stated that he managed to publish the article before he left, in part as a reminder to the elites that they had betrayed the ideals of their parliamentary forefathers (Brem, 1999). Drucker noted that his father was a Freemason and thus a target of the Nazis. In this account, the National Socialists came to arrest Adolph but had an old address for him, thus giving him time to escape (Drucker, 1978). The senior Drucker did not emigrate to the United States until 1938, the year of the *anschluss*. Gerhart, Peter's younger brother, arrived in New York with a medical degree from the University of Vienna six months before Peter arrived and found an internship position at a hospital. According to this account, Drucker's parents arrived the following year, with his father obtaining a position teaching international economics at the University of North Carolina at Chapel Hill (Drucker, 2005b). Drucker's penchant for storytelling leads us to skepticism regarding the details of the family's escape from Nazi Germany and Austria. At any rate, as many other intellectuals did, Drucker left the country for London in 1933.

Drucker was one of a long list of German and Austrian academics, artists, and intellectuals to escape during the 1930s (Kent, 1953; Fleming and Bailyn, 1969). The sheer number of talented and brilliant individuals who escaped is staggering: among them include Hannah Arendt, Billy Wilder, Edward Teller,

Kurt Weill, Alfred Eisenstaedt, Claude Levi-Strauss, and Thomas Mann (Heilbut, 1983; Brinkmann and Wolff, 1991). Most of these émigrés were Jewish; Thomas and Heinrich Mann and Berthold Brecht were not but had married women who were (Heilbut, 1983, p. 25). And, for many, escape was the operative word. The Nazi program against Jewish intellectuals in particular was not limited to simply denying them jobs or burning their publications. Hannah Arendt was imprisoned for hiding communists, as well as for studying the working class's use of antisemitic language (Heilbut, 1983, pp. 400–401). Novelist Leonhard Frank climbed over the barbed wire fence of a detention center in order to make his escape (Heilbut, 1983, p. 27). Not every case involved such dramatic circumstances; nevertheless, the intellectual flight from Nazi Germany and, later, Austria represented a massive brain-drain that shifted the intellectual capital from Europe to the United States during World War II.

The impetus behind that migration was National Socialism's brand of anti-Semitism, and our modern understanding of exile, emigration, or escape during this time cannot avoid the ultimate horror of the Holocaust. That Jewish intellectuals, imprisoned or otherwise threatened, would seek escape is self-evident. Yet, as Peter Gay notes, Gentiles left as well, including Paul Hindemith and Adolf Busch (Gay, 1991). Drucker's friend, Berthold Freyberg, chose to stay and become a leader of the Protestant opposition to Hitler. Drucker, a Lutheran, however, told Freyberg that he could not live under a system that did not abide by the tenets of Christianity or constitutional law (Tarrant, 1976, pp. 4–5). Drucker's reasons for leaving, then, had to do with the very same fundamental philosophical and moral beliefs that, as we shall see, underlie his management and social writings.

Intellectual Émigré in London

Like many émigrés, Drucker did not immediately head toward the United States but rather moved to London. The majority of those who fled Nazi Germany remained in Europe, assuming that they would eventually return to their home (Heilbut, 1983). In England, Drucker became reacquainted with Doris Schmitz. Like Peter, Doris had made her own initial escape from pre-war, although hers took a different route. Reaching a compromise with her mother, who had plans for her to work as a trainee for a Parisian bank and "marry a Rothchild," Doris instead was permitted to attend university with the caveat that she study law. As European students were allowed to travel and attend any university they wished, Doris attended the London School of Economics for a year, then lived several months in Paris, primarily spending her time with a young painter with whom she had fallen in love. Returning to Germany, she returned to her law studies, ending up in a number of classes with senior classman Peter Drucker. The two saw each other as friends but, as

Doris says, "our interest in one other never developed into a serious, or even unserious, attachment" (Drucker, 2004, pp. 176–177). Neither the Schmitz's nor the Druckers were particularly interested in having their child seriously involved with the other; Doris' mother wanted her to marry someone in the Rothchild's class, and Caroline Drucker was "determined that he marry the daughter of an immensely wealthy British nobleman." Nevertheless, the two connected in London, finding themselves "drawn together by shared apprehensions" about the future (Drucker, 2004, p. 181).

Depression-era London was a difficult place to find employment. The couple did not marry, as Depression-era laws prevented married women from working, as they were perceived as taking breadwinning positions away from men. Doris worked as a buyer for the department store Marks and Spencer and Drucker worked as an insurance trainee and in banking. He also attended the famous Keynes seminars, where he was exposed to the economist's novel ideas. Drucker remained unconvinced, however, referring to Keynesianism as "Economics as a Magical System":

> Keynes' work was built on the realization that the fundamental assumptions of nineteenth-century laissez-faire economics no longer hold true in an industrial society and a credit economy. But it aimed at the restoration and preservation of the basic beliefs, the basic institutions of nineteenth-century laissez-faire politics; above all, it aimed at the preservation of the autonomy and automatism of the market. The two could no longer be brought together in a rational system; Keynes's policies are magic—spells, formulae, and incantations, to make the admittedly irrational behave rationally.
>
> *(Drucker, 1946/1993, p. 119)*

Although this is a later observation (the essay was first published shortly after Keynes' death in 1946), Drucker retained his Austrian view of economics as an organic system composed of human beings rather than mathematically described fixed markets. Economist Jay Prag, Professor at the Peter Drucker School of Management since 1986, referred to Drucker as a humanist economist (Prag, 2010).

Drucker went home to Vienna for Christmas in 1933 and was tempted to remain by several offers of lucrative government positions (Drucker, 1978, pp. 25–26). Nevertheless, in February, he returned to England, where he secured a job as an economist with a London bank. In the spring of 1937, Drucker was offered a position as a foreign correspondent for several British newspapers, and so, he and Doris left for the United States. The two married, and Drucker augmented his career, selling articles to *Harper's Magazine* and writing for the *Washington Post*. Drucker credits America's climate of "mutual help" in his ability to obtain employment so easily. He sold his first articles by cold calling publishers: "...the friendliness and the commitment to mutual help were genuine. So was the willingness to take a chance on a person" (Drucker, 1978, p. 298).

Yet, Drucker was also blessed with the resources and ability to emigrate, not to mention the connections inherent in his father's government position. Émigrés to the United States were required to file an affidavit illustrating financial solvency as a condition of entry, effectively screening out "undesirable" immigrants. Then, too, intellectuals such as Drucker had an advantage in the job market in terms of their training and experience, particularly those whose skills and backgrounds had a pragmatic application, such as Drucker's journalistic abilities. The American audience of the 1930s and 1940s was particularly receptive to the observations of European émigré intellectuals, as European education and heritage conveyed legitimacy and validity to those individuals' comments on American society (Heilbut, 1983). Finally, intellectuals benefited from a loophole in the National Origin Act, legislation that sought to curb immigration into the United States. Specific provisions included tests for mental competency and, most importantly, literacy, in order to cull "undesirable" immigrants from the pool of newcomers. Under a clause in section 4 of the act, non-quota immigrant visas could be granted to professors and their families, as long as those teachers served in higher education in the United States. Similarly, if artists, musicians, or other intellectuals could provide evidence of employment through some American institution, they, too, would be granted entry into the country as an exception to the quota system (Fermi, 1968). The American "willingness to help" was extended more generously to those immigrants who could prove their ability to contribute to the country's economic and cultural fabric, and Drucker was one of those fortunate enough to have both the training and resources to facilitate his emigration.

Drucker in America

Drucker arrived in the United States just as the country once again sank into recession following a very brief period of economic hope in 1936. Although he won re-election handily, Roosevelt faced questioning of his policies once it became clear that the New Deal programs of the earlier 1930s had not solved the nation's problems. Factions within the Roosevelt administration argued for either a balanced budget or a more Keynesian approach of increased government spending. Like Europe, America was stuck in a financial quagmire.

But in 1930s America, Drucker saw a very different society than what he had left behind in Europe and England. In the United States, "nobody looked backward—they looked forward. That was the excitement" (Drucker, 2003). In the Old Country, the Depression brought out the worst in people, according to Drucker. In America, however, the trials of unemployment and economic uncertainty resulted in a different response:

> The commitment to mutual help was a response to the Depression. Indeed it was the specifically American response to the Depression. There was nothing like it on the other side, where the Depression evoked only suspicion, surliness, fear, and envy.
>
> *(Drucker, 1978, p. 302)*

Drucker goes even further to say that the Depression sounded the death knell for Marxism in the United States. Instead of solidifying a class identity, the Depression "celebrated community...greatly strengthened the local, the parochial, the tribal in American life. It emphasized religious and ethnic and cultural diversities and turned them into boundaries" (Drucker, 1978, p. 302). Drucker focused on the social response to the Depression in America; indeed, the psychological impact of long-term unemployment would become a major cornerstone of his later management writing. But he also interpreted the American commitment to "mutual help" as a distinctly American response, one he had not seen in Europe. As an outsider, a European observer, his focus on the contrasts between the old world and the new is perfectly understandable.

Europe vs. America

This vision of America in contrast to Europe in terms of its response to the Depression was undoubtedly part of the inspiration behind the second of Drucker's first two books published in this country, *The Future of Industrial Man* (1942). The first, *The End of Economic Man* (1939a), is Drucker's scathing analysis of Nazi Germany and Stalinist Russia. Taken together, these books outline the core philosophical lynchpins of Drucker's management and social theories (see Chapter 2). In *The Future of Industrial Man,* Drucker outlines his idea that, in the United States, employment within the modern corporation could offer people status and meaning that was not based simply on economic worth but rather would offer a sense of community and citizenship while still providing dignity and respect for the individual.

While publishing these two books, Drucker pursued a career as a freelance writer. He wrote his earliest articles for British papers, describing the American experimentation in higher education which was "in the 1930s the most exciting thing" and unknown in Europe. Drucker also wrote about industry but rarely about the more common Depression-era topic of finance. While working as a journalist, he was asked by one of Franklin Roosevelt's assistants to join a small "hush-hush" group whose mission was to analyze America's potential for war production. Drucker says he has no idea why he was approached, brushing it off as he did so much of his career: "I cannot explain to you how any of the things I did happened. They all came in over the transom. I never planned anything" (Drucker, 1999). In actuality, many of Drucker's European émigré counterparts were enlisted to aid in the war effort. Franz Neumann and Herbert Marcuse, two leftists, worked in the Office of Strategic Services, and European refugees also served in the Office of War Information (Heilbut, 1983; Jones, 1999).

During the same period, Drucker actively sought out an academic position, helping to ensure that something would come over the transom. He solicited Dr. Robert Hutchins, President of the University of Chicago, for a position once *End of Economic Man* was published, using that as an in for a post. Hutchins received scores of letters from German professors during the early 1930s, according to historian Laura Fermi, who reviewed his files for her book, *Illustrious Immigrants*. As she points out, Hutchins and the University of Chicago were likely not alone in their desire to secure some of these prime scholars, but given the Depression in America, funds for new hires were limited, and there were a significant number of unemployed PhDs here as well (Fermi, pp. 72–73). Drucker's scrawled notes in the margin of his letters indicate that the response he received from Hutchins had to do with limited resources and positions (Drucker, 1939b, 1940). Drucker had better luck with the small liberal arts colleges. He landed a post at Sarah Lawrence College, first as an adjunct and then a professor, and was a full-time member of the faculty of Bennington College by 1942. The President of Bennington, Lewis Webster Jones, an economist, had read Drucker's book, *The End of Economic Man,* and asked Drucker to lecture on the work. Drucker's writing also caused a stir among the faculty at Bennington. Following his appointment, according to Drucker, several faculty members attempted to persuade Jones to rescind his decision, claiming that Drucker was a "reactionary" or "fascist" for implicating a Hitler-Stalin alliance (Tarrant, p. 23). Drucker also notes that *The End of Economic Man* got him into trouble with leftist sympathizers:

> I immediately became an enemy for the Communists and the fellow travelers. The *Daily Worker* ran a long piece on me in which it 'proved' that no such person as Peter Drucker existed and that this was the pen name of a sinister duo comprised of a high Nazi official and a high Washington State Department official. And Larry Todd, head of the Washington Bureau of Tass, the official Soviet news agency, personally organized and orchestrated a campaign against me, aimed at shutting my articles out of magazines and denying me any employment in newspapers or academia—and Todd, as everyone knows, never did anything except on orders from the Kremlin. Many years later [publisher Henry] Luce himself

told me that this overreaction to a book by a totally unknown author was the result of its strong endorsement by Winston Churchill.

(Drucker, 1978, p. 226)

President Jones won out, and Drucker received his position.

Bennington was also actively involved in developing a new, innovative curriculum, and Drucker was in part hired to synthesize and integrate the social sciences and humanities into courses that reached across traditional disciplinary boundaries. Drucker looks back on these years as some of the happiest in his life; although he was away in Washington on war business much of the time (providing intelligence on German industry), Vermont was a haven:

The moment you were off that hilltop you were in a world at war, but at that hilltop, you were in a world of its own, an oasis, which made it probably more meaningful than it would have been otherwise.

(Drucker, 1999, Tarrant, p. 7)

Bennington was Drucker's "own education. I was not an educated person. I had degrees. There's a difference." Doris, too, was happy, "fulfilling a longtime dream" of studying mathematics and physics while they began a family (Drucker, 2005b). It is not the story of an outdated family with rigid gender roles and expectations. The Drucker marriage was one of equality in every sense of the word. These years are a window into Peter as a person: a husband, a father, and a growing human being in the essence that he sought to foster through his work.

In terms of his work, he was "at my peak," writing numerous articles as well as one of his most important books, *Concept of the Corporation*, Drucker's study of General Motors as a prominent institution in American society (see Photo 1.3).

The Voice of Business

With corporations becoming more prominent in American society as well as its economy, *Concept of the Corporation* not only secured the organization as a topic of study, but it also more importantly established Drucker as the expert in the field of industrial organizations. A few years after the book's publication, he was asked to join the faculty of New York University's graduate management school in the summer of 1949. During the following two decades, Drucker produced an enormous body of written work. Published work during this period included the 1954 book *The Practice of Management*, which is still considered to be the most thorough analysis of the subject, as well as his more general books of social commentary, such as *The New Society* (1950). Drucker continued to write for popular and business magazines as well, contributing to *Harper's*, *Harvard Business Review*, *Fortune*, and the *Saturday Evening Post*. Most of his articles were on management-related topics, but Drucker also wrote as an observer and pundit of American culture and government.

Management's Larger Role

By the 1970s, as the post-World War II American economy began to sputter, Drucker began to turn away from the corporate sector as his area of interest. Bob Buford of The Leadership Network, a friend and client of Drucker's, believed that, in *Management: Tasks, Responsibilities, Practices*, Drucker was summing up and completing his years of work with large corporate organizations and had essentially begun to make a transition away from that sector toward the larger social realm. According to Buford, around the same time the book was published, Drucker told him he believed that the economy and business were basically healthy, but that society was sick. Drucker used the fact that he had never once felt that he had to lock the door of his house in Bennington, but now would not even think of doing such a thing (Buford, 2002). This anecdote is similar to one Drucker used in his memoirs, in which he describes feeling the need to bolt his front door in Germany for the first time ever (Drucker, 1978, p. 165).

Such an interpretation appears to have some evidentiary support. One reviewer commented that, in *Management: Tasks, Responsibilities, Practices*, "Now he has distilled 'Drucker'—a vast body of knowledge and opinions..." (*BusinessWeek*, 1974, p. 49). Following the book's publication in 1973, Drucker engaged in very different writing endeavors and with less of the exuberance he exhibited in his earlier years. The change in sheer volume of production is worth noting. During the 1950s, Drucker published 20 major articles and five books. The figures for the following decade are 28 major articles and four books. In the 1970s, however, Drucker published a mere 11 articles, and three of his seven books were either compilations or minor rewrites of earlier material (*People and Performance: The Best of Peter Drucker on Management*, Management Cases, and *An Introductory View of Management*, all published in 1977). One important book, *The Unseen Revolution: How Pension Fund Socialism Came to America* (1976), illuminated the growing role of employee stock (and, thus company) ownership in America and is one of Drucker's more scholarly endeavors in terms of its depth of research and conciseness of argument; as such, it represents something of a turn away from his typical writing technique and style. Drucker also spent a portion of the 1970s working on his memoirs, *Adventures of a Bystander*, which was published in 1978; it, too, is completely different from his other books. Although he continued to teach (at Claremont Graduate School, not NYU) and consult, it appears that his interest was indeed turning away from the large corporation in American society.

What would replace that emphasis was not at all clear initially. After the publication of *Management*, Drucker indicated his interest in three possible projects, none of which materialized: a book on American history and its reflection in current society; one titled *Can Government be Saved?*; and a work on money management for business (*Business Week*, 1974, p. 56). Following *Adventures of a Bystander*, Drucker continued to write, teach, and consult, but in new areas and genres. During the early 1980s, he experimented with writing fiction and turned out two novels, *The Last of All Possible Worlds* (1982) and *The Temptation to do Good* (1984). His articles took on an acrid tone at times, as he became increasingly critical of the turn corporate management had taken away from key values and results toward hype and accounting gamesmanship (Drucker, 1981, 1982, 1988).

The Social Sector

But the real rebirth of Drucker occurred during the 1990s when he found the new direction for his work: the non-profit organization, or what Drucker refers to as the social sector. The volume of his work indicates a renewed passion and interest; he wrote 73 articles in the 1990s, which nearly equaled the total number of articles published during the prior 30-year period. He published *Managing the Non-Profit Organization: Principles and Practices* (1990), which essentially provided the social sector with its own *Management: Tasks, Responsibilities, Practices*. As he himself notes, this did not involve any real change in his ideas or material but rather on his own target audience. Like many of his business and other clients, the evangelical churches he worked with said the same things:

> They don't hear us. They still say, "We are totally different." And not only are "We different – we Baptists are totally different from the Methodists," but also, "In Selma, Alabama, we are totally different from Birmingham, Alabama." Well, that was true of hospitals when I began to work with hospitals forty years ago. It is still true of universities very much. And that was true of businesses too, until after World War II, or even later. In Europe, it's still true.
>
> *(Drucker, 1999)*

Drucker continued to write for the business community, but the urgency, the call for change, is strikingly absent. There is almost a resignation that business will never heed his advice: "I still strongly maintain that the employee has to be given the maximum responsibility and self-control...But individuals...

need an additional sphere of social life" (Drucker, 1993b, p. 174). In 1993, Drucker told T. George Harris, former editor of the *Harvard Business Review*, that

> It's time to give up thinking of jobs or career paths as we once did and think in terms of taking on assignments one after the other. The stepladder is gone, and there is not even the implied structure of an industry's rope ladder. It's more like vines and you bring your own machete.
>
> *(Drucker, 1993c)*

Drucker's imagery is telling: business has, in his opinion, regressed, degenerated, to a lower state of existence.

Although the corporation failed to fulfill Drucker's dream of American community, the social sector would step in to fill the void. This was a fitting focus for Drucker's hope; after all, it was American's willingness to help each other during the Depression that so moved him when he first landed in this country. America was everything Europe was not: forward-looking, charitable, optimistic, and active. Drucker had turned his back on the miasma of pre-war nostalgia and European mass movements but not to fully immerse himself in the American society that blended individualism with community so well. As a bystander, Peter Drucker could never fit as a full participant in the American community, especially as a citizen of the organizations he saw as key to bridging the gap between individual and group identity. Drucker remained in part a European bystander even as he sought to fashion an identity that marks him as an American pundit.

Conclusion

Peter Paschek, a longtime friend of Drucker's, said that Drucker "always saw himself as an outsider, and, accordingly was perceived as an outsider...he saw himself as a steward of 'the moral sciences'" (Paschek, 2008). Born at the beginning of the twentieth century and passing in 2005 at the beginning of the twenty-first century, just shy of his 96th birthday, Drucker was a witness to a tumultuous period in history. Paschek recounts a meeting he had with Drucker in 1995, at the Botanical Gardens in Claremont. Drucker was in a bad mood and pondering the end of the twentieth century, what he dubbed as a "wasted century." Following the United States' invasion of Iraq in 2001, Paschek and Drucker corresponded weekly by fax. Drucker had told him he was thinking about writing a book titled "Incorrect Reflections on a Wasted Century." Paschek asked, "May I conclude that finally the 20th century wasn't a wasted century?" Drucker responded:

> NO. The only conclusion is that I wasted much of my time not writing the truly important books I should have written. My non written books

PHOTO 1.1   Caroline Bondi, undated, by Hans Makart.

greatly outnumber my written ones.—And some such as "The wasted century" or "Organizing Ignorance" might have been a great deal more important than the—easier ones- I wrote instead.—We are just now in a very depressing mood—I don't have to explain it, do I?

(Paschek, 2008)

PHOTO 1.2 Doris Drucker, undated.

These are the words of a man looking back but also looking forward. Drucker was never prone to nostalgia, yearning for some glory day of yesteryear; he learned that from observing his Austrian elders pining for life before the war. Yet, although forward thinking and optimistic, hopeful for humankind's ability to manage change and instability, he was also keenly aware of the limits of human institutions to survive and maintain a functioning society. As Paschek has written, Drucker was skeptical but not a pessimist (Paschek,

PHOTO 1.3   Peter Drucker with glasses, undated.

2008). This encapsulates the essence of Drucker's European roots and status as a bystander; his experience as a European in the early twentieth century could not help but create a skeptic. Yet, his observations of America as the model for a functioning society of institutions gave him optimism that well-managed organizations could prevent another societal breakdown.

Bibliography

Arnn, L., Masugi, K., and Schramm, P. (1984) 'Reviewing the moral sciences', *Claremont Review of Books*, III (1). https://claremontreviewofbooks.com/reviv ing-the-moral-sciences-a-conversation-with-peter-f-drucker/

Beatty, J. (1998) *The world according to Peter Drucker*. New York: The Free Press.

Bennis, W. (1985) 'A personal reflection', *New Management*, 2 (3), pp. 24–27.

Bonaparte, T. and Flaherty, J. (1970) *Peter Drucker: Contributions to business enterprise*. New York: New York University Press.

Brem, R. (1999) 'Interview with Peter F. Drucker', conducted September 1999.

Brinkmann, R. and Wolff, C. eds. (1991) *Driven into paradise: The musical migration from Nazi Germany to the United States*. Berkeley: University of California Press.

Buford, R. (1991) 'Interview with Peter F. Drucker', conducted 15 June 1991, transcript of audiotape 1, Dallas, TX: Leadership Network.

Buford, R. (2002) 'Interview with the author', conducted 20 November. Dallas, TX.

Drucker, D. (1999) Part of interview of Peter F. Drucker. Interview by author, tape recording, Claremont, California, 20 December 1999.

Drucker, D. (2004) *Invent radium or I'll pull your hair*. Chicago: The University of Chicago Press.

Drucker, D. (2009) Speech at First Global Peter Drucker Forum, Vienna, Austria, 19 November.

Drucker, P.F. (1939a) *The end of economic man*. New Brunswick, NJ: Transaction, 1993.

Drucker, P.F. (1939b) Letter from Peter F. Drucker to Dr. Robert Hutchins, President of University of Chicago dated 12 April, Peter F. Drucker Archives, Claremont, CA.

Drucker, P.F. (1940) Letter from Peter F. Drucker to Dr. Robert Hutchins, President of University of Chicago dated 2 April, Peter F. Drucker Archives, Claremont, CA.

Drucker, P.F. (1946) 'Keynes: Economics as a magical system', in Drucker, P.F. (ed.) *The ecological vision*. New Brunswick, NJ: Transaction, 1993, pp. 119–131.

Drucker, P.F. (1978) *Adventures of a bystander*. New York: John Wiley & Sons.

Drucker, P.F. (1981) 'Ethical chic', *Forbes*, 14 September.

Drucker, P.F. (1982) 'Why some mergers work and many more don't', *Forbes*, 18 January.

Drucker, P.F. (1988) 'Leadership: More doing than dash', *Wall Street Journal*, 6 January, p. 14. Reprinted in Drucker, P.F. (1992) *Managing for the future: The 1990s and beyond*. New York: Truman Talley Books/Dutton, pp. 119–123.

Drucker, P.F. (1993a) 'Reflections of a social ecologist', in Drucker, P.F. (ed.) *The ecological vision*. New Brunswick, NJ: Transaction, 1993, pp. 441–157.

Drucker, P.F. (1993b) *Post-capitalist society*. New York: Harper Collins.

Drucker, P.F. (1993c) Interview with Harris, T.G. 'The post-capitalist executive: An interview with Peter F. Drucker', *Harvard Business Review*, 71 (3), pp. 114–122.

Drucker, P.F. (1995) 'Peter Drucker talks about himself', interview by Broeck Wahl Blumberg, published in *Global Business Review*, July, pp. 1–5.

Drucker, P.F. (1999) Interview with Peter F. Drucker by the author, tape recording, Claremont, California, 20 December 1999.

Drucker, P.F. (2003) Interview with Witty, K., *Peter F. Drucker: An Intellectual Journey*. Videorecording. Wiley Europe: Leader to Leader Institute.

Drucker, P.F. (2005a) Personal conversation with author, Claremont, CA, 5 July.

Drucker, P.F. (2005b) *My personal history*. Tokyo: Nihon Keizai Shimbun. English translation of interviews by Makino, Y. (2009), Drucker Archives, Claremont, CA.

Fermi, L. (1968) *Illustrious immigrants: The intellectual migration from Europe, 1930-1941*. Chicago: University of Chicago Press.

Fernandez, S. (2009) 'Peter Drucker's leap to faith: Examining the origin of his purpose-driven life and its impact on his views of management', *Journal of Management History*, 15 (4), pp. 404–419.

Fleming, D. and Bailyn, B. (1969) *The intellectual migration: Europe and America, 1930-1960*. Cambridge, MA: Harvard University Press.

Gabor, A. (2000) *The capitalist philosophers: The geniuses of modern business— Their lives, times, and ideas*. New York, NY: Times Books.

Gay, P. (1991) ' "We Miss Our Jews:" The Musical Migration from Nazi Germany', in Brinkmann, R. and Wolff, C. (eds.), *Driven into paradise: The musical migration from Nazi Germany to the United States*. Berkeley: University of California Press, pp. 21–32.

Gilbert, F. and Large, D. (1991) *The end of the European era, 1890 to the present*. New York: W.W. Norton & Company.

Gleason, A. (1995) *Totalitarianism: The inner history of the cold war.* New York: Oxford University Press.

Graf, M. (1945) *Legend of a musical city.* New York: Philosophical Library.

Heilbut, A. (1983) *Exiled in paradise: German refugee artists and intellectuals in America from the 1930s to the present.* New York: Viking Press.

Janik, A. and Toulmin, S. (1973) *Wittgenstein's Vienna.* New York: Simon and Schuster.

Jelavich, B. (1987). *Modern Austria: Empire & Republic, 1800–1980.* New York: Cambridge University Press.

Johnston, W. (1972) *The Austrian mind: An intellectual and social history, 1848–1938.* Berkeley: University of California Press.

Jones, W. (1999) *The lost debate.* Urbana, IL: The University of Illinois Press.

Kent, D.P. (1953) *The refugee intellectual: The Americanization of the immigrants of 1933-1941.* New York: Columbia University Press.

Large, D. (1990) *Between two fires: Europe's path in the 1930s.* New York: W. W. Norton.

Lenzer, R. and Johnson, S. (1997) 'Seeing things as they really are', *Forbes ASAP,* 10 March, 127.

Lieblich, E. (2015) 'Assimilation through law: Hans Kelsen and the Jewish experience', in Loeffler, J. and Paz, M. (eds.), (2019), *The law of strangers: Jewish lawyers and international law in the twentieth century.* Cambridge: Cambridge University Press.

Linkletter, K. and Maciariello, J. (2009) 'Genealogy of a social ecologist', *Journal of Management History,* 15 (4), pp. 334–356.

McRobbie, K. (1999) ' "Old, badly peeled, half-raw potatoes" and Peter F. Drucker's other myths about Karl Polanyi', in McRobbie, K. and Polanyi Levitt, K., (eds.) (2006), *Karl Polanyi in Vienna: The contemporary significance of The Great Transformation.* Montreal: Black Rose Books, pp. 359–377.

Meynhardt, T. (2010) 'The practical wisdom of Peter Drucker: Roots in the Christian tradition', *Journal of Management Development,* 27 (7/8), pp. 616–625.

Paschek, P. (2008) 'Management as a social task: The relevance of Peter F. Drucker's work for our time', Global Drucker Symposium, June.

Paschek, P. (2020) *Peter F. Drucker: Erinnerungen an einen konservativ-christlichen anarchisten.* Baden Baden: Tectum Verlag.

Paschek, P. (2023a) Personal conversation with author, 15 March. Zoom call.

Paschek, P. (2023b) Personal conversation with author, 28 July. Zoom call.

"Peter Drucker: A New Compendium for Management," *Business Week,* 9 February 1974, 49.

Peukert, D. (1987) *The Weimar Republic.* New York: Hill and Wang.

Prag, J. (2010) 'Peter Drucker: The humanist economist', in Pearce, C., Maciariello, J., and Yamawaki, H. (eds.), *The Drucker difference: What the world's greatest management thinker means to today's business leaders.* New York: McGraw Hill, pp. 207–220.

Simon, H. (2002) "Peter F. Drucker: Man of the past, man of the future," essay submitted in response to solicitation from the Peter F. Drucker Archives Oral History Project. Translated by Burns, T. from German. Peter F. Drucker Research Library and Archives, Claremont, CA.

Stafford, T. (1999) 'The business of the kingdom', *Christianity Today,* 43 (13), pp. 42–50.

Starbuck, P. (2012) *Peter F. Drucker: The landmarks of his ideas.* Lulu.com

Steinfels, P. (2005) 'A man's spiritual journey from Kierkegaard to General Motors', *New York Times*, Section B, Page 5.

Tarrant, J. (1976) *Drucker: The man who invented the corporate society.* Boston, MA: Cahners Books.

Toubiana, M. and Yair, G. (2012) 'The salvation of meaning in Peter Drucker's *oeuvre*', *Journal of Management History*, 18 (2), pp. 178–199.

2

DRUCKER THE SOCIAL THEORIST

Introduction

At heart, Drucker was a social theorist; it was only an accident of timing and circumstances that he began to write on the subject of management. Management was merely one element of Drucker's larger theory of a functioning society of institutions, albeit a key element. Shaken by his personal experience in Europe of the 1920s and early 1930s, Drucker's life work was devoted to developing a theory of society that would help prevent the resurgence of fascism. Drawing on his readings in political theory, philosophy, the social sciences and history, over time, Drucker crafted a framework for a tolerable, bearable society, one that would provide the individual freedom bounded by responsibility for society as a whole. Drucker defined a free society that was grounded in legitimate authority and individual responsibility, one that would provide a place for the individual within society. The form of this functioning society, and its constitutive elements, changed over the course of Drucker's life as events unfolded. But at its core, Drucker's work ultimately sought to find a balance between individual existence and existence within society in such a way as to prevent the breakdown of the necessary institutions of such a free society.

Influences

Drucker's social theory was informed by many thinkers and figures whose work he studied early in his life. As a law student in Germany, Drucker had considerable free time, and spent it reading voraciously (see Chapter 1). In various interviews and writings, he discusses many of the individuals who influenced his life and work, and others have explored these connections

DOI: 10.4324/9781003410485-3

(Beatty, 1998; Flaherty, 1999; Maciariello and Linkletter, 2011). In terms of Drucker as a social theorist, several key figures stand out as particularly important influences.

Friedrich Julius Stahl (1802–1861)

Stahl was the subject of one of Drucker's graduate papers at the University of Frankfurt. Stahl was an ecclesiastical lawyer, politician, and philosopher; he was G.W.F. Hegel's successor as chair of the Philosophy Department at the University of Berlin. In an era of political instability, Stahl developed a framework of government that blended representative institutions with elements of monarchy. This system of government aimed at protecting individual rights and freedoms while still considering the needs of larger society. Stahl was also concerned with avoiding political extremes of radical revolution or reactionary resistance to change. For Drucker, Stahl sketched a path to a society where individual freedom was maximized through the exercise of responsibility and subordination to legitimate authority (see Chapter 7 for more detail).

Wilhelm von Humboldt (1767–1835)

Humboldt was a linguist and philosopher who, like Drucker, took issue with the ardent rationalism of the Enlightenment. He was an advocate of a broad, humanist education similar to the liberal arts tradition. Based on the German concept of *Bildung*, which is a process of individual development of personal character, wisdom, and virtue, Humboldt founded the University of Berlin with this vision. Concerned with the growing centralized power of the Prussian state, Humboldt hoped to fuse the bureaucratic government with the spirit of *Bildung* to allow for individual creative expression (Sheehan, 1970). Humboldt was one of a trio of German thinkers that Drucker pondered writing about while at the University of Frankfurt. He was attracted to Humboldt's aversion to central authority and advocacy for an education in the humanist tradition. Finally, Humboldt, like Stahl, sought to negotiate a way to unify various German interests around a middle-ground position between extremes, a hallmark of Drucker's approach to social theory.

Edmund Burke (1729–1797)

Out of the hundreds of books he read in the Hamburg public library, Drucker stated that Edmund Burke's 1790 work, *Reflections on the French Revolution* was one that changed his life:

> ...Burke's main thesis: that to find in such a period the balance between *continuity* and *change* is the first task of politics and politicians,

immediately resonated with this eighteen-year-old reader...It immediately became central to my own politics, to my own world view and to all my later work.

(Drucker, 2003, p. viii)

In his work, Burke compares the British constitutional tradition with the French revolution, arguing that France's utter rejection of the monarchy was an exercise in excess. Britain's more conservative, incremental change in political structure was preferable, as it avoided extremism (Burke, 1790/ 2005).

Ferdinand Toennies (1855–1936)

The other book that Drucker says "permanently changed my life" was the German sociologist Toennies' 1887 work, *Gemeinschaft und Gesellschaft* (*Community and Society*). In this book, Toennies explored the changing nature of human relations from an "organic" rural community of a pre-industrial era to an industrial society where interactions were based on commerce. Drucker took away from Toennies that there is both the need for individuals to have status within a community and to have function within society (Drucker, 2003, p. viii). This need to bridge individual identity with collective identity is a hallmark of Drucker's social theory, and Toennies' influence is quite clear.

Henri Bergson (1859–1941), Alfred Whitehead (1861–1947), and Jan Christiaan Smuts (1870–1950)

Bergson and Whitehead are representatives of process philosophy. Process philosophy was a late nineteenth-century effort to bridge two competing views: utilitarianism and German idealism. Utilitarian philosophers such as John Stuart Mill and Herbert Spencer favored material existence and measurable experience over the role of human emotions. On the other hand, German idealists such as Georg Wilhelm Friedrich Hegel prioritized the world of the human mind and imagination, which, they argued, could not be separated from the material realm in determining reality. Process philosophers sought a middle ground between these two worldviews, where human beings are seen as part of their larger experiences or processes in and of themselves. Process philosophy prioritizes the role of change and time over discrete experiences or emotions. Jan Christiaan Smuts developed the philosophy of holism to address the dilemma of how one can pursue individual freedoms while still finding meaning within society or community. Holism involves the idea that entities are more than simply the sum of their parts; individual human consciousness is connected to the larger world in a spiritual way.

Drucker mentions Bergson, Whitehead, and Smuts in the opening chapter of his 1957 book, *Landmarks of Tomorrow*. In this book, Drucker argues the need for a new worldview, one that is no longer grounded in the philosophy of Rene Descartes, with its emphasis on measurability, stasis, cause and effect, and certainty. Instead, he calls for a new philosophy based on configurations and processes that acknowledges growth, change, and patterns:

> Anticipation of the new vision can be found in many great thinkers: Aristotle, Leonardo, Goethe, Bergson, Whitehead. The first to comprehend it, however, was probably that astounding South African, Jan Christiaan Smuts—the closest to the 'whole man' this century has produced—with his philosophy of Holism twenty-five or thirty years ago.
>
> *(Drucker, 1957, p. 11)*

This move from cause to configuration, explained by Drucker, will require the ability to see seeming chaos and disorder as part of a larger system or process:

> Today our task is to understand patterns of physical, biological, psychological and social order in which mind and matter become meaningful precisely because they are reflections of a greater unity...This may sound like a big order—and one we are as yet far from being able to fill. Yet we may well have the new synthesis more nearly within our grasp than we think. On it are based powers we already exercise: the power to innovate, and the power to harmonize individual and society in a new dynamic order.
>
> *(Drucker, 1957, pp. 14–15)*

Drucker's language is lofty, but it conveys the need to balance the individual and society, as well as the need to see the world in all its complexity and dynamism (Bonaparte, 1970; Cook and Chapman, 1970).

These key individuals served as crucial influences on Drucker's development as a social theorist. As we shall see in the remainder of this chapter, Drucker's model of a functioning society of well-managed institutions is the direct result of the lessons learned from theses influences. Specifically, the themes carried forward into Drucker's social theory are:

- Balancing change and continuity.
- Providing individual status and function.
- Maximization of responsible individual freedom.
- Legitimization of authority.
- Acceptance of uncertainty and randomness as part of larger processes and configurations.

Explaining Totalitarianism

Drucker's first step in developing his social theory was to explain the breakdown of society that opened the door for totalitarianism in Europe. His personal experience with witnessing the rise of National Socialism in Germany was the impetus behind everything Drucker did for the remainder of his life. How could Europe have disintegrated in the 1920s and 1930s to the point where Hitler could have taken hold? And what could explain the horrors of Stalin and later Mao Zedong in China?

The End of Economic Man

Like many intellectuals who were fortunate enough to escape Nazi Europe in the 1930s, Drucker attempted to reckon with why the world had narrowly escaped the utter destruction of the free institutions of society. In 1951, Hannah Arendt, a German historian and political philosopher, published *The Origins of Totalitarianism*. Like Drucker, Arendt escaped Germany in 1933; unlike Drucker, Arendt was born into a practicing religious Jewish family and was a target of Nazi anti-Semitism because of her work on the subject. Her 1951 study of totalitarianism is complex, delving into the history of racism and imperialism, but, like Drucker, she explores the social factors that create a fertile ground for totalitarian movements.

Drucker's study of the origins of totalitarianism, *The End of Economic Man* (1939), traces the rise of totalitarianism to the failure of the economic creeds of the nineteenth century to live up to their promises. Capitalism was successful as an economic system. But as a social order and creed, it held out the promise of economic progress as leading toward individual equality and freedom in a free and equal society. Drucker states that "this promise was an illusion we all know. Economic progress does not bring equality, not even the formal equality of 'equal opportunity' " (Drucker, 1939, p. 39). Marxism's failure was even more dramatic, as it promised a classless society:

> Capitalism has been proved a false god because it leads inevitably to class war among rigidly defined classes. Socialism has been proved false because it has been demonstrated that it cannot abolish these classes…Both creeds and order failed because their concept of the automatic consequences of the exercise of economic freedom by the individual was false.
>
> *(Drucker, 1939, pp. 44–45)*

Thus, a definition of social meaning and existence that derives purely through economic explanations (based on theories held as truth in the eighteenth and nineteenth centuries) completely fell apart. What was left was a void of despair, fueled by inflation and unemployment after World War I:

> The old orders have broken down, and no new order can be contrived from the old foundations. The alternative is chaos; and in despair the masses turn to the magician who promises to make the impossible possible: to make the workers free and simultaneously to make the industrialist "master in his own house"; to increase the price of wheat and at the same time to lower the price of bread; to bring peace, yet to bring victory in war; to be everything to everybody and all things to all men. So it is not in spite of but because of its contradictions and its impossibility that the masses turn to fascism. For if you are caught between the flood of a past, through which you cannot retrace your steps, and an apparently unscalable blank wall in front of you, it is only by magic and miracles that you can hope to escape. *Credo quia absurdum*, that cry of a master who had known all the bitterness of deepest and blackest despair, is heard again for the first time in many a century.
>
> *(Drucker, 1939, p. 22)*

Economic Man was dead; fascism offered Heroic Man in his place: a definition of existence that subsumed individual identity into the totalitarian state.

Economics as a "Moral Science"

The primary error that led directly to fascism was the attempt to fashion economics as a moral or social science—that is, as a means of explaining the behavior of people in society. By insisting on the primacy of economic explanations for events, economic theorists cannot explain events that are driven by non-economic, social forces. When society has been defined by orderly, rational processes, how does one respond when those definitions no longer make sense? If freedom and equality are defined purely in economic terms, how can society function when economic theory clearly does not result in a rational system of freedom and equality, as promised? This, Drucker says, was the key to the rise of totalitarianism:

> This disintegration of the rational character of society and of the rational relationship between individual and society is the most revolutionary trait of our times...The developments under capitalism and Marxism did nothing to prepare Europe for a period in which fundamental rationality would be endangered. On the contrary: in the order of Economic Man the rationalization of the world is driven to a point where everything becomes not only understandable as a part of a rational entity but calculable as part of a mechanical sequence...The destruction of the order in which the

individual has a rational place and a rational function necessarily invalidates also the old order of values, which was a rational order of rational values. Freedom and equality, the two cornerstones of this order, are values which are intelligible and endowed with meaning only as applied to a rational society. Can they have any meaning to the bewildered, isolated individual in a society that has itself lost all rational meaning?

(Drucker, 1939, pp. 57–58)

Economic Rationality

It is not surprising, then, to find Drucker as an opponent of economic rationality. His uncle, Hans Kelsen, was a noted proponent of economic rationality. Drucker's early work in *The End of Economic Man* represents a hammering out of not just historical events but also political, social, and economic theory. The insistence on economics as a moral or social science to explain human behavior from an entirely rational perspective motivated Drucker's analysis of totalitarianism. It also informed later work as he moved toward developing a theory of a society that was *not* based on economic rationality.

Drucker's relationship with Kelsen was part of his familiarity with the Vienna Circle of logical empiricism. The Vienna Circle was a group of philosophers and social scientists who advocated the idea of making philosophy scientific; they embraced the view that scientific knowledge is the only valid, factual knowledge. One of the founders of the group was Otto Neurath, an Austrian who joined the German Army during World War I and worked for the War Production Board as a statistician (Drucker in an interview states that Neurath worked for the United States government, but there is no evidence of this). After the war, Neurath returned to Vienna and founded the Vienna Circle. Drucker notes that his mother was very close to some members of the Circle, and that he knew all of them, and his exposure to their ideas led him to reject economic rationality:

> The exclusion of the basic concepts, that what you cannot organize with logical rigor or quantify is meaningless, that they are non-problems, that's madness. And that's modern American economics…Economics always tries to play Beethoven with one finger, and it doesn't really come off.
>
> *(Arnn, Masugi, and Schramm, 1984)*

A few years after publishing *The End of Economic Man*, Drucker published an article in *The Review of Politics*. In "The Meaning and Function of Economic Policy Today," Drucker argued for a political concept of economic policy, one that factored in non-economic, social considerations. He proposed this as an alternative to Hitler, who used a political concept of economics for evil. The mistake was not that Hitler used a political concept of economics (for Drucker, that was ingenious, as it filled the void of Economic Man's destruction). The lesson to be learned from Hitler's economic policies was to apply political concepts to economic policy for good:

> Now again politics is coming into its own as that realm of social existence in which Man tries to realize his basic beliefs, tries to express his inherent freedom, and tries to live up to his final ethical responsibility. Hitler has used this opportunity to decide for evil; and he made economic means the means for the attainment of evil. We have not only the opportunity but the responsibility to decide for the good and to use economic means for the attainment of the good. And if we shirk this ethical decision by adhering to the 'economic' concept of economic policy, we only lend strength to the forces of evil.
>
> *(Drucker, 1943, p. 223)*

The end of economic man created a void that needed to be filled by something moral. Only then could economics be the agent of morality rather than a "moral science" of pure rationality.

Drucker remained critical of economic rationality throughout his career. He argued with advocates of rational economic theory, acknowledging its theoretical existence but providing numerous examples of human behavior that defied rational economic explanation. For example, when evaluating American gasoline consumption during the 1970s, a time of high prices and high unemployment, Drucker noted that gasoline consumption remained relatively static. Economic theory would predict that higher gas prices and lower wages would reduce demand. But, Drucker posited, "people in this country discovered that wheels are more important than food. Freedom is more important than food. Now that is not an economic fact" (Arnn, Masugi, and Schramm, 1984).

In a piece he wrote in 2008, Drucker's friend, Peter Paschek, opens with a quote from a German Minister of Economics in the 1990s: "Economics takes place in the economy." Drucker could not have disagreed more; as Paschek notes, "Economics takes place in society, and global economics takes place in the global society...Drucker understood this better than anyone else" (Paschek, 2008, p. 1).

Kierkegaard and Despair

Many authors have delved into the influence of Kierkegaard on Drucker's social theory (Beatty, 1998; Flaherty, 1999; Maciariello and Linkletter, 2011). Drucker invited this investigation, as he proffered that Kierkegaard was an instrumental factor in his life and career (Drucker, 1999, 2005).

While Kierkegaard's message of the limits of physical and social existence certainly impacted Drucker, Drucker's experience with Kierkegaard was very personal; while it did influence his social theory, it did to a lesser degree than the previously mentioned theorists. Kierkegaard's primary influence on Drucker was to convey a way for him to come to terms with world events of the late 1930s and early 1940s.

Drucker states that he chanced upon Kierkegaard's essay, *Fear and Trembling*, while working as a shipping clerk in Hamburg in 1928. Kierkegaard's 1843 work is an exploration of the story of Abraham's sacrifice of his son, Isaac. Why would God have asked Abraham to murder his beloved child as a sacrifice to the Creator? Why would Abraham have been willing to do so? Kierkegaard analyzes this Biblical story from the perspective of individual faith; individual existence lies separate from that in society but allows the individual to bear the despair of societal existence. Human existence is the recognition of the tension between living in society and the knowledge of one's own mortality and ultimate aloneness. Faith is the only bridge between this tension (Drucker, 1949).

Drucker published "The Unfashionable Kierkegaard" in 1949 during a period of "deep despair." The details of the Holocaust were becoming public, and Stalin unleashed a reign of terror that would unfold into the Cold War of the next two decades. Atomic weapons were a reality. Finally,

> all this horror was aggravated by the infatuation of the intellectuals with Stalin and with communist tyranny, and by the prattle of the "Establishment" about our having attained "eternal peace" and "the new world order"—and I, by that time, had of course myself become a member (albeit a junior one) of this Establishment.
>
> *(Drucker, 1993a, pp. 425–426)*

Drucker's deep pessimism about the state of the world in the years after the end of World War II did not play a major role in shaping his social theory and his search for a functioning, bearable society that would prevent fascism from reoccurring. It did, however, drive him to revisit Kierkegaard as a path for hope: "The philosophy of the totalitarian creeds enables man to die... Kierkegaard's faith, too, enables man to die; but it also enables him to live" (Drucker, 1949/1993a, p. 439).

Defining a Functioning Society

In the early 1940s, while World War II was still being fought, Drucker began to develop his blueprint for a free functioning industrial society. He argued that Nazi Germany was not the result of the peculiar nature of Germany's national character, history, or heritage but rather an attempt to fill the void created by the end of Economic Man. Once Drucker had analyzed the origins of totalitarianism, he turned to understanding the mechanics of society under National Socialism. By the mid-twentieth century, the nineteenth-century explanations of economic rationality and order no longer made sense, as he posited in *The End of Economic Man*. The new industrial society of the twentieth century needed a new social model, and Nazism provided one; it was an attempt to create "a functioning industrial society on the basis of slavery and conquest" (Drucker, 1942, p. 23). The only way to combat totalitarianism, then, was to provide an alternative model of a functioning industrial society that was based on freedom.

Virtue, Freedom, and Responsibility

Key to understanding Drucker's concept of a free, functioning industrial society is grasping his definitions of virtue, freedom, and responsibility. His definitions are guided in large part by western traditions of philosophy and political theory absorbed over years of study.

The concept of virtue is built into Drucker's model for a bearable industrial society. Many have previously explored the influence of Judeo-Christian principles and the Aristotelian concept of virtue ethics in Drucker's work (Kurzynski, 2009; Malcolm and Hartley, 2009; Meynhardt, 2010; Maciariello and Linkletter, 2011). Drucker's idea of management as key to a functioning society of organizations involves an understanding of the historical tradition of the liberal arts. Originating in Greek and then Roman society, the concept of training people (at that time, elites only) in the liberal arts was driven by the idea of creating citizens capable of making informed decisions and leading society. Such training in rhetoric, grammar, logic, mathematics, and other subjects was intended to build character and instill societal values. This liberal arts ideal was transplanted to European, American, and British universities, where education (until the late nineteenth century) focused on inculcating culturally derived characteristics of virtue.

Drucker was very much a product of this liberal arts ideal history in Europe; he refers to management as a "liberal art" on more than one occasion. In this sense, ensuring a functioning society of institutions requires not just an understanding of finance and accounting, but the recognition that we are "deeply involved in spiritual concerns—the nature of man, good and evil" (Drucker, 1989, p. 231). This is why Drucker argued that there could be no separate rule of ethics for business. Either we agree that all individuals are guided by the same moral codes of conduct (the Western tradition), or we agree that ethics can be situational, based on the non-Western tradition of Confucius, where relationships guide right action. Drucker draws on Aristotle's idea of prudence as a virtue: individuals (especially leaders) should base their behavior on how it *might* be perceived, "and if there is any doubt, it is 'questionable' and to be avoided" (Drucker, 1981/1993a, p. 205). This "Ethics of Prudence" is countered with the "Ethics of Interdependence," where appropriate behavior is determined by one's relationships with others. Perception has nothing to do with virtue in this case; what drives behavior is the personal relationship between the individuals (not the public view). Interestingly, Drucker provides a highly individual and personal view of virtue (Confucian model) and a socially driven one as well (Aristotelian model). Once again, Drucker shows us he is thinking about the balance between life in society and life as an individual.

Drucker stated that "...I stressed all along that organization does not deal with power but with responsibility. This is the one keynote of my work that has remained constant over more than 40 years" (Drucker, 1985a, p. 8). Freedom and responsibility are interconnected for Drucker. Drawing on the work of Stahl, Drucker frames freedom not in terms of license but in terms of accountability. Stahl argued that freedom was "not unrestricted but from the start has a specific content, standard and boundaries" (Stahl, 1845/2002). For Stahl, accountability was to legitimate monarchical authority as guided by a Christian God. For Drucker, freedom requires accountability for one's choices and their larger impact on others:

> Freedom is not fun. It is not the same as individual happiness, nor is it security or peace and progress. It is not the state in which the arts and sciences flourish. It is also not good, clean government or the greatest welfare of the greatest number. This is not to say that freedom is inherently incompatible with all or any of these values—though it may be and sometimes will be. But the essence of freedom lies elsewhere. It is responsible choice. Freedom is not so much a right as a duty. Real freedom is not freedom from something; that would be license. It is freedom to choose between doing or not doing something, to act one way or another, to hold one belief or the opposite. It is never a release and always a responsibility. It is not "fun" but the heaviest burden laid on man: to decide his own individual conduct as well as the conduct of society, and to be responsible for both decisions.
>
> *(Drucker, 1942, pp. 109–110)*

Freedom also requires an understanding of human beings as imperfect, flawed creatures, particularly when it comes to matters related to the treatment of others. Drucker derives this model of human nature from a Judeo-Christian tradition of human nature as "imperfect, weak, a sinner, and dust destined unto dust, yet made in God's image and responsible for his actions" (Drucker, 1942, pp. 110–111). If humans were perfect, then the concept of free will would have no meaning, as freedom would involve no repercussions. But imperfect people will make imperfect decisions, resulting in consequences to themselves and others—sometimes grave and unforeseen consequences. The point Drucker makes is profound: the price of a free society is the recognition that a free and functioning society will, by definition, be imperfect.

A Functioning Industrial Society

By the early 1940s, Drucker recognized that "the corporation is the representative social institution and...management is the decisive social power [and] mass production in big units is the representative social form of our society" (Drucker, 1942, p. 78). Having defined a free society, he had to fashion a way for the new industrial society of the twentieth century to function without resorting to coercion and violence, as did the totalitarian state of Nazi Germany. The problem was that the industrial society did not provide economic stability or meaning; the Economic Man of the nineteenth century was lost. The new industrial society had to answer the challenges posed by the influencers of his social theory. Specifically:

• How could the new industrial organizations balance change and continuity, particularly with respect to economic disruptions that caused unemployment and inflation?
• How could the industrial worker of this new era, who replaced the rural farmer or local merchant of Toennies' vision, find status and function?
• How could industrial society maximize individual freedom with the understanding of its linkage to responsibility?
• How could managerial authority in the new industrial organizations be seen as legitimate?
• How could change, which was inevitable, be managed to minimize disruption and avoid chaos?

These elements, driven by Drucker's early influences and experiences, coalesced around his initial social theory of a functioning free industrial society that would present a challenge to the Nazi's attempt to forge a model of a functioning industrial society of unfreedom. Throughout his career, Drucker would take these questions and reform them to fit the society in which he found himself. As Derrick Chong notes, Drucker's social order involving business organizations as social institutions with moral imperatives made room for compassion for others within a capitalist system (Chong, 2013). Drucker had to fashion a way for business to not just focus on economic matters but to also consider disciplines that informed human relations.

Self-Governing Plant Community

Drucker's early solution to the problem of providing status and function to the industrial worker was the idea of the self-governing plant community.

Drucker developed this fully in his 1950 book, *The New Society: The Anatomy of Industrial Order*. True to its title, Drucker forges a plan for industrial society that answers all of the questions posed by his analyses of totalitarian systems. It is a work that focuses on the human element of work and society: how can the economic disruptions that created the end of Economic Man be managed to create a new definition of existence? As such, it is an optimistic attempt to craft a new "Man" that is not "Economic" or "Heroic" but rather something embodying the world envisioned by his earlier influencers.

Key to this world of legitimate authority, balance of change and continuity, freedom with responsibility, and status and function was the idea of the plant-based community. A free society requires citizenship and participation; Drucker argued that, in modern industrial society, the previous model of citizenship at the local level was no longer meaningful: "The decay of the traditional local governments, especially of town, city and country, is indeed primarily the result of the shift of focus to enterprise and plant community" (Drucker, 1950, p. 338). The influence of Toennies is clear, as Drucker attempted to find a replacement for the lost, older rural society with localized citizenship in the new industrial society.

Drucker's concept of a plant community was also designed to solve the inherent conflict between the business's purpose and the interests of its members. Of necessity, the primary responsibility of business "will always be to the economic performance of the enterprise and not to the welfare and interests of the enterprise's members." This inherent conflict cannot be overcome by hiring the best people, providing high-quality training, or instilling a sense of social responsibility. Even the most enlightened leadership "will still be managers, charged with an objective economic function and responsibility." The only way to resolve this inherent tension is to create a pluralist structure, where management discharges its economic responsibilities and a subordinate, yet autonomous self-governing plant community of workers that has jurisdiction over the social functions of life in the workplace (Drucker, 1950, pp. 281–282). Along with this plant community, the company would have a guaranteed annual wage to provide some sense of job security and protection from the kinds of economic disruption that characterized the Great Depression. This would also allow the worker to align their interests with those of the company. Drucker envisioned the plant community as having complete autonomy over those areas that have little to nothing to do with economic matters (shift scheduling, health and safety concerns, parking, and training, to name a few). Management and community have shared interest in some areas, such as profit sharing, benefits, job categorization, and the like. In essence, Drucker saw the self-governing plant community as a vehicle for providing workers with status and function within the organization and as an answer to the "split allegiance" between workers and management. It was a means to provide workers with the "managerial attitude" needed so that they could take ownership of and pride in their jobs. The self-governing plant community also demanded that management view labor as more than just an uneducated, easily replaceable worker (what Drucker termed "Slot Machine Man") (Drucker, 1950).

Although Drucker would continue his search for community, he soon realized that the self-governing plant community was not the vehicle for this. Looking back, he evaluated this concept: "Fifty years ago I believed the plant community would be the successor to the community of yesterday. I was totally wrong" (Stafford, 1999, p. 47). The failure of the self-governing plant community haunted Drucker for decades. In a letter to management writer Jim O'Toole, Drucker discusses the influence of the Welsh textile factory manufacturer and socialist utopian, Robert Owen (1771–1858). Owen founded the New Lanark textile mill in Scotland and the New Harmony plant in Indiana, based on the idea that communal living and shared responsibility and resources would uplift conditions for the working class. He believed that human character was formed under circumstances of education, exposure to morals and values, and expectations of performance and responsibility. Understandably, Owen's vision resonated with Drucker's idea of a self-governing plant community. As he told O'Toole:

> You discuss Robert Owen and, in effect, write him off as a failure. So did I in 1938—I was the first, to my knowledge, in this century to discuss him NOT as a footnote in history but as a living legacy. To be sure, Lanark did not have followers – and I never fully understood this. (By the way, Owen did live up to your advice and unceasingly preached, propagated, publicized Lanark—for a decade it was the most-visited and most-talked about "sensation" in Europe—even Balzac has a fashionable rich Princess go there (it's in <u>Eugenia Grandet</u>, I believe). But no one imitated him even though Lanark had a much bigger return on investment with its employee policies than any other textile plant in the world at that time- or since. WHY? I have never understood it. BUT to dismiss then—as I did fifty-five years ago and as you do now—Owen as a failure, is to miss the most important fact: FOR YOU AND FOR ME—HE still lives. And every movement towards creating the plant community since Owen—including all YOUR writing and mine—has been inspired by him. OWEN was the PROPHET—and without a prophet the people perish.
>
> *(Drucker, 1995, p. 4)*

A dream inspired by a prophet, still recognized by Drucker 45 years later. As Rosabeth Moss Kanter notes, "At root, Drucker is a management utopian, descended as much from Robert Owen as Max Weber" (Kanter, 1985, p. 10). Why had he misread the situation? As John Tarrant points out, Drucker's experience with the inner workings of industrial organizations was still relatively young in the late 1940s. As such, he tended to lend more credence to events and pronouncements that today would draw skepticism. Drucker also accepted as natural an industrial order based on a stratified society where one's position was accepted as fixed; he had yet to experience the fluidity of American class identity (Tarrant, 1976). Chong remarks that Drucker's philosophical and political background, along with his American experience, led him to embrace the American model of capitalism rather than considering others (Chong, 2013). This is true for Drucker's early work in the 1940s and 1950s, but, as commerce became more globally connected, he evaluated alternative models of social organization. Finally, the change from an industrial society to one based on knowledge forced a reassessment of assumptions. As society transformed to one dominated by knowledge rather than capital or labor, Drucker began to look to knowledge work as a possible source of community and belonging for working people.

Knowledge Society

As manufacturing jobs gave way to service sector and managerial jobs beginning in the late 1960s, Drucker began to dramatically rethink the nature of his functioning society. The industrial society that Drucker witnessed in 1940s and 1950s America was giving way to what he termed the Knowledge Society (see Chapter 5). The new industrial order that Drucker envisioned in 1950 no longer fit with his larger project. Yet, the tenets of his social theory remained. How could the new knowledge society, which was replacing industrial society, be a functioning society? Essentially, Drucker confronted the same questions posed earlier by an industrial society:

• How could the knowledge worker find status and function?
• How could knowledge society maximize individual freedom with the understanding of its linkage to responsibility?
• How could managerial authority in the knowledge society be seen as legitimate?
• How could change, which was inevitable, be managed to minimize disruption and avoid chaos?

Management became the key to this new functioning society of institutions (see Chapter 2). Ultimately, Drucker's many writings on management are designed to facilitate his larger theory of a functioning society of institutions. Establishing management as a legitimate discipline and field of study and practice, one that could be taught and professionalized, legitimized its authority (if properly practiced with a firm grounding in virtue, integrity, and responsibility). Drucker's insistence on performance and productivity aligned with organizational mission and vision allows a balance between the economic responsibilities of the institution and the individual's fulfillment of goals and personal development. Understanding the role of knowledge as a driver of economic production in a society effectively changes the nature of the relationship between management and workers. Whereas in 1950 Drucker was concerned with the imbalance of power between labor and management, he was writing about the role of teams and less hierarchical relationships some 20 years later (Drucker, 1973). Finally, encouraging innovation and entrepreneurship at all levels of organizations, along with continuous learning and self-development, built in individual responsibility for managing oneself and coping with inevitable change (see Chapters 5 and 6). Looking back on his career, Drucker considered this aspect of his work to be an important contribution. No earlier management writer had insisted on individuals taking the initiative for being able to perform; "…and most management books still center on managing others rather than on managing oneself" (Drucker, 1985a, p. 8).

Society of Organizations

Drucker early on realized that the business organization's primary responsibility was for economic performance. Yet, who would be responsible for the needs of larger society? Early on, Drucker argued that, in a society of industrial organizations, it was the public sector that must watch over the interests of the greater good. Later, however, he draws on the principle of pluralism to make a case for countervailing powers in society; without one dominant power, the interests of the larger community would be protected from overreach by any one sector (see Chapter 7). A pluralist society of organizations that represent a multitude of interests, not just for-profit, became crucial to the realization of a functioning society. Now, Drucker saw a functioning society as one of many different organizations, all single purpose, but none holding inordinate power or authority. Management was the glue that held such a diverse society together:

> We are beginning to realize that management itself is the central institution of our present society, and that there are very few, and mostly minor, differences between managing a business, managing a diocese, managing a hospital, managing a university, managing a research lab, managing a labor union, or managing a government agency.
>
> *(Drucker, 1985a, p. 9)*

Post-Capitalist Society

Beginning in the late 1980s and early 1990s, Drucker began to write about a "post-capitalist" society of organizations that represented opportunity for growth and citizenship. This new society of organizations was defined by single-purpose, specialized institutions designed to make knowledge productive. Increasingly, post-capitalist society was pluralist, as more and more organizations filled specialized functions (health care, research, education, religious activities, youth programs), many of which were unrelated to business. Yet, all of these organizations required effective management to be part of a functioning society (Drucker, 1950). In fact, organizations, by definition, impact society: "Results in an organization exist only on the outside. Society, community, family are self-contained and self-sufficient: they exist for their own sake. But all organizations exist to produce results on the outside" (Drucker, 1993b, p. 54). So, although organizations are themselves embedded in the culture in which they operate (in terms of geography and other factors), organizations are removed from that culture because of their single-purpose nature. The organization's internal culture is driven by the task at hand, yet the means of communication may be different. Drucker remarks that, while German, Japanese, English, and American physicians may communicate information differently to their patients, they readily share and understand the latest developments in their field (Drucker, 1993a). People in higher education understand this same culture of sharing new research but would be lost at a convention of automobile manufacturers.

Further complicating the nature of this new post-capitalist society of organizations is the fact that these organizations are destabilizing forces in society. Drucker had already published *Innovation and Entrepreneurship* (1985) in which he argued that organizations needed to build in systematic abandonment and the ability to innovate in order to respond to increasing change. Now, Drucker states that organized abandonment and continuous innovation and improvement must be built into every organization. As innovative agents, organizations in general—not just business organizations—are destabilizing forces in society: "Organizations in the post-capitalist society thus constantly upset, disorganize, and destabilize the community. They must change the demand for skills and knowledges" (Drucker, 1993b, p. 60). In addition to this, organizations must take into consideration their roles in society itself. Earlier in his career, Drucker had seen this as the role of government, to watch over the common good. But, by the 1990s, Drucker pointed out that there was no other entity "in the society of organizations to take care of society itself" save for the organizations themselves. Thus, organizations had to be socially responsible but within the limits of their legitimate use of power; part of being a responsibility-based organization was understanding the limit of that organization's power (Drucker, 1993b).

As we saw in Chapter 3, Drucker ultimately tasked management with serving two roles: fulfilling the single purpose of the institution while also balancing the needs of larger society. The idea of the social responsibility of business required businesses to consider the larger impacts of their activities on society and to also be conscious of ways in which they might draw on their strengths and unique purposes to help mitigate social problems (ideally by making a profit). This is not to say that businesses should attempt to solve social problems that are outside of their area of expertise, competence, and values. Drucker extended this concept to all organizations in a post-capitalist society (with the same caveats and restrictions): "...organizations do have a responsibility to find an approach to basic social problems that can match their competence and can, in fact, render social problems opportunity for the organization" (Drucker, 1993b, p. 102). Key to this idea of socially responsible organizations of all kinds is responsibility—both organizational and individual. "Entitlement" and "empowerment" are merely substitute terms for power and rank; better to talk of what one is responsible for rather than what one is entitled to (Drucker, 1993b, p. 109).

The Social Sector

In the new post-capitalist society, Drucker saw the non-business organizations as wielding the most social power. This is why he advanced such a passionate argument for instilling the same sense of managerial responsibility and accountability in these organizations that he did for business management (Drucker, 1993b). However, Drucker also saw these non-business entities as key to citizenship in the new society of organizations. By the early 1990s, Drucker had abandoned his earlier model of the industrial facility or even the for-profit sector as the locus for status and meaning and began to focus on non-profits (what he referred to as the "social sector") as the place for people to find status and function. Drucker's earlier focus on government and business as the two primary sectors of society gave way to his more pluralistic view of a society of diverse organizations—organizations that, with their own specialized interests and missions, could help balance the needs of the individual with that of the common good.

After looking to the self-governing plant community and the knowledge organization as possible sources of community, Drucker eventually turned to the non-profit sector as the locus of community and citizenship. Speaking of his idea of industrial citizenship, he stated in an interview:

> We proved totally incapable [of that] even in Japan. The reason is that everybody does the same job. What holds them together is what they do from nine to five, and not what they aspire for, what they live for, what they hope for, what they die for. That's a community.
>
> *(Stafford, 1999, p. 47)*

Gone is the belief that the stimulation and challenge of knowledge work will provide a sense of community; instead, the increasing specialization of knowledge work results in a siloing effect where workers are isolated and independent, removed from the larger mission of the organization (which remains primarily economic in nature).

Yet, workers, especially knowledge workers, "need an additional sphere of social life, of personal relationships, and of contribution outside and beyond the job, outside and beyond the organization, indeed, outside and beyond their own specialized knowledge area" (Drucker, 1993b, p. 174). Drucker saw the volunteer in non-profit organizations as the new citizen in the new society of organizations; the social sector could provide a sense of community, at least in the United States and, Drucker, argued at the time, in the former Soviet Union. In Japan, he predicted that the employee community would remain important for most workers. But elsewhere, the social sector would be pivotal in providing status and function in society (Drucker, 1993b).

Drucker's championing of the social sector eventually resulted in non-profits using market-based approaches to grow their organizations. This led to an explosion of social entrepreneurs, emerging funding opportunities, and new organizations filling social needs that had not been met by other institutions (Orr, 2010). Rick Warren of Saddleback Church relied on Drucker's management models and ideas to grow his organization to the successful entity it is. Frances Hesselbein, National Director of the Girl Scouts of the United States of America from 1976 until 1990, also was a close colleague of Drucker's and benefited from his consulting advice; she spearheaded the creation of the Peter F. Drucker Foundation for Non-Profit Management, which is now the Leader to Leader Institute. In 1990, Drucker published *Managing the Non-profit Organization*, which included not just his own ideas about management but interviews with leaders in the social sector discussing their challenges and successes with growing their organizations. Most of Drucker's consulting work late in his life was pro-bono work for these non-profit entities, as he saw them as the key to membership in a functioning society and "central to the quality of life in America, central to citizenship and indeed…[central to] the values of American society and of the American tradition" (Drucker, 1990, p. xiii).

It is the social sector that will provide the sense of community that Toennies sought to preserve and for which Drucker longed a substitute. Drucker did not turn his back on capitalism or the private sector, but he began to see its social limitations:

I am for free market even though it doesn't work too well. But I have serious reservations about capitalism as a system because it idealizes economics as the be-all and end-all of life. It is one dimensional. Today I believe it is socially and morally unforgiveable when managers reap huge profits for themselves but fire workers. As societies, we will pay a heavy price for the contempt this generates.

(Drucker, 1988/2002, p. 149)

With its overemphasis on "Economic Man" and one aspect of existence, the private sector could not provide, in the newly developing knowledge society, meaningful citizenship for most people. Only those organizations dedicated to changing and improving human beings in more than just an economic way could provide such meaning for existence.

Conclusion

Beginning with a social explanation for totalitarianism, Drucker's life work was to find a model for a functioning, tolerable society that would provide meaning to both individual and social existence. From an industrial free society that included the concept of a self-governing plant community to a post-capitalist society of pluralist organizations, including a vibrant social sector, Drucker revisited and revised this model many times over his lifetime. Each social vision sought to link freedom with responsibility, legitimate authority, minimize the negative impacts of inevitable change, and, most importantly, allow people to reconcile the tension between individual and societal existence in a realistic way.

Although a social theorist, Drucker presented his ideas in the form of his work on management and society not as philosophy but as a theoretical framework to guide practical matters of existence. Even so, he was, at heart, concerned with people's lives, not just theory: "...I've always been more interested in people than in ideas, but I've always been better as a writer with ideas than with people; that's why I've postponed writing a novel so very long" (Arnn, Masugi, and Schramm, 1984). Drucker's memoir and two novels, interestingly, are in fact works of social theory in disguise. *Adventures of a Bystander* (1978) is no ordinary memoir but rather a collection of vignettes about people who influenced Drucker. The stories are, indeed, entertaining, but they are assembled to convey Drucker's vision of Europe between the two world wars, as well as America immediately after the culmination of World War II. In this memoir, Drucker uses individual stories to portray a "paralyzed, brain-dead" European society, contrasted with an American society that reflected "depression and hope" as well as "nonconformity and diversity." Ultimately, "society is, after all, made up of individuals and their stories" (Drucker, 1978, p. viii). Drucker's two novels are also about individuals reflecting their societies and institutions. His first novel, *The Last of all Possible Worlds* (1982), comes on the heels of his memoir; it tells the story of nine people living in Europe in 1906, depicting the "pre-war" years that Drucker treats with utter disdain. His second novel, *The Temptation to do Good* (1984), addresses the role of institutions in society and the people inside those institutions; complex decisions related to ethics and performance face Father Heinz Zimmerman, president of a Catholic university. Gossip and intrigue reveal the challenges of managing a social institution in which human beings, susceptible to dark forces and impulses, behave like human beings. Unleashed from his work on management and society, Drucker used his fiction to provide us with living, breathing models of society—in some cases, a society that is tolerable at best.

Bibliography

Arendt, H. (1951) *The origins of totalitarianism*. New York: Harcourt, Brace, Jovanovich.

Arnn, L., Masugi, K., and Schramm, P. (1984) 'Reviewing the moral sciences', *Claremont Review of Books*, III (1). https://claremontreviewofbooks.com/reviving-the-moral-sciences-a-conversation-with-peter-f-drucker/

Beatty, J. (1998) *The world according to Peter Drucker*. New York: The Free Press.

Bonaparte, T.H. (1970) 'The philosophical framework of Peter F. Drucker', in Bonaparte, T.H. and Flaherty, J. (eds.), *Peter Drucker: Contributions to business enterprise*. New York: New York University Press, pp. 23–34.

Burke, E. (1790, 2005) *Reflections on the Revolution in France*. Stilwell, KS: Digireads. com Publishing.

Chong, D. (2013) 'The relevance of management to society: Peter Drucker's oeuvre from the 1940s and 1950s', *Journal of Management History*, 19 (1), pp. 55–72.

Cook, E.J. and Chapman, A.F. (1970) 'Drucker, Holism, and Smuts', in Bonaparte, T.H. and Flaherty, J. (eds.), *Peter Drucker: Contributions to business enterprise*. New York: New York University Press, pp. 56–64.

Drucker, P.F. (1939/1995) *The end of economic man*. New Brunswick, NJ: Transaction.

Drucker, P.F. (1942) *The future of industrial man*. New Brunswick, NJ: Transaction.

Drucker, P.F. (1943) 'The meaning and function of economic policy today', *The Review of Politics*, 5 (2), pp. 216–224.

Drucker, P.F. (1949) 'The unfashionable Kierkegaard', originally published in *Sewanee Review*, reprinted in Drucker, P.F. (1993) *The Ecological Vision*. New Brunswick, NJ: Transaction, pp. 427–439.

Drucker, P.F. (1950) *The new society: The anatomy of industrial order*. New Brunswick, NJ: Transaction.

Drucker, P.F. (1954) *The practice of management*. New York: Harper & Row.

Drucker, P.F. (1957) *Landmarks of tomorrow*. New York: Harper & Brothers.

Drucker, P.F. (1973) *Management: Tasks, responsibilities, practices*. New York: Harper & Row.

Drucker, P.F. (1978) *Adventures of a bystander*. New York: John Wiley & Sons.

Drucker, P.F. (1981) 'Can there be "business ethics"?', originally published in *The Public Interest*, reprinted in Drucker, P.F. (1993) *The ecological vision*. New Brunswick, NJ: Transaction, pp. 195–214.

Drucker, P.F. (1982) *The last of all possible worlds*. New York: Harper Collins.

Drucker, P.F. (1984) *The temptation to do good*. New York: Harper Collins.

Drucker, P.F. (1985a) 'Drucker on Drucker', *New Management*, 2 (3), pp. 7–9.

Drucker, P.F. (1985b) *Innovation and entrepreneurship*. New York: Harper & Row.

Drucker, P.F. (1988/2002) *Managing in the next society*. New York: St. Martin's Press.

Drucker, P.F. (1989) *The new realities*. New York: Harper & Row.

Drucker, P.F. (1990) *Managing the non-profit organization: Principles and practices*. New York: Harper Collins.

Drucker, P.F. (1993a) *The ecological vision.* New Brunswick, NJ: Transaction.

Drucker, P.F. (1993b) *Post-capitalist society.* New York: Harper Business.

Drucker, P.F. (1995) Letter from Peter F. Drucker to Dr. Jim O'Toole, Aspen Institute, dated 17 April 1995, Peter F. Drucker Research Library and Archives, Claremont, CA.

Drucker, P.F. (1999) Interview with the author, Claremont, CA, 20 December.

Drucker, P.F. (2003) *A functioning society.* New Brunswick, NJ: Transaction.

Drucker, P.F. (2005) *My personal history.* Tokyo: Nihon Keizai Shimbun. English translation of interviews by Makino, Y. (2009), Drucker Archives, Claremont, CA.

Flaherty, J. E. (1999) *Peter Drucker: Shaping the managerial mind.* San Francisco, CA: Jossey-Bass.

Kanter, R.M. (1985) 'Drucker: The unsolved puzzle', *New Management* (Winter), pp. 10–12.

Kurzynski, M. (2009) 'Peter Drucker: Modern day Aristotle for the business community', *Journal of Management History,* 15 (4), pp. 357–374.

Maciariello, J. and Linkletter, K. (2011) *Drucker's lost art of management: Peter Drucker's timeless vision for building effective organizations.* New York: McGraw Hill.

Malcolm, S.B and Hartley, N.T. (2009) 'Peter F. Drucker: Ethics scholar *par excellence*', *Journal of Management History,* 15 (4), pp. 375–387.

Meynhardt, T. (2010) 'The practical wisdom of Peter Drucker: Roots in the Christian tradition', *Journal of Management Development,* 27 (7/8), pp. 616–625.

Orr, S. (2010) 'The twenty-first century: The century of the social sector', in Pearce, C., Maciariello, J., and Yamawaki, H. (eds.), *The Drucker difference: What the world's greatest management thinker means to today's business leaders.* New York: McGraw Hill, pp. 119–134.

Paschek, P. (2008) 'Management as a social task: The relevance of Peter F. Drucker's work for our time', unpublished essay.

Sheehan, J. (1970) *German history: 1770–1866* (Oxford History of Modern Europe). New York: Oxford University Press.

Stafford, T. (1999) 'The business of the kingdom', *Christianity Today,* 43 (13), pp. 42–50.

Stahl, F.J. (1845/2002) *Rechts- und Staatslehre auf der Grundlage christlicher Weltanschauung* (*The Philosophy of Law and State on the Basis of the Christian Worldview*), translation by Alvarado, R., published as *Principles of Law* (2002), Aalten, NL: Woodbridge Publishing.

Tarrant, J. (1976) *Drucker: The man who invented the corporate society.* Boston, MA: Cahners Book.

3
DRUCKER AND THE PRACTICE OF MANAGEMENT

Introduction

Drucker states that he was likely born with an interest in organizations (Drucker, 1999). Yet, it is only by circumstances of history that he became known as the authority on modern management. His early work involved developing an explanation for the rise of the totalitarianism he witnessed in the 1930s in Europe, and a blueprint for a functioning society based on what he saw in America when he arrived there in the late 1930s (see Chapters 1 and 2). Drucker traced the rise of totalitarianism to the breakdown of traditional institutions and economic systems in Europe. The "demons" of unemployment and war broke any sense of rational order; neither capitalism, with its promise of economic advancement, nor socialism, with its promise of economic equality, made sense. As a result, the majority of people lost hope, and turned to irrational solutions. When economic definitions of existence no longer made sense, the idea of "heroic man," an existence based on sacrificing individual identity for the fascist cause, took hold (Drucker, 1939). Drucker's observations of industrial America gave him hope that a tolerable, imperfect society of industrial organizations could provide people with status and function in their lives—that is, a position of respect in the community and an individual purpose in life (Drucker, 1942a). As the industrial capacity of America increased, first for war production during that country's entry into World War II and later to meet surging demand in a post-war environment, the industrial corporation took on its own kind of heroic existence for many consumers and economists who marveled at the nation's economic expansion. Drucker's interest in the large business organization was from a societal perspective: how did this new, important entity fit with

DOI: 10.4324/9781003410485-4

larger society, and, more importantly, how could it help to serve as the key to his idea of a functioning society that would give people meaning, rationality, and belonging so that they would not turn to the promises of fascism again?

Concept of the Corporation

With the realization that the modern corporation was an entity worthy of study (and one that had received very little attention from those outside the corporate world), Drucker decided to turn his attention to analyzing the inner workings of the private business organization.

Although Drucker asked numerous companies if he could use them as a test case, most turned him down; some were downright suspicious of his motivations. Drucker had all but given up on the idea when he received a call from General Motors in 1943 asking him if he would be interested in studying their organization (Drucker had not solicited that company in his initial volley of letters). Although top management at GM, notably Alfred Sloan, was lukewarm about the idea, vice president of finance Donaldson Brown had read Drucker's two books and was impressed with what he had seen (Flaherty, 1999, pp. 52–53). The result of Drucker's inside view of General Motors was the 1946 work, *Concept of the Corporation*, which presented a not entirely flattering view of GM as the representative corporation in American society. Through this work, Drucker moved from a theoretical model established in *The Future of Industrial Man* to a more specific case study. Although the book describes the inner workings of one specific company, the title is true to the book's content: it is a very explicit discussion of how *conceptually* the modern corporation should function in American society as contrasted with how GM *actually* worked during the early 1940s.

In *Concept of the Corporation,* Drucker introduced several ideas that became key to his management writings throughout his career. He would develop these ideas over time, building some out, refining others to reflect the changing nature of society from an industrial manufacturing economy to a knowledge-driven economy (see Chapter 5).

Management as a Social Function

Drucker states in his introduction to the book that his analysis has three primary components: to look at the institution as autonomous; to study the corporation in terms of the beliefs and promises of the society it serves; and to evaluate the institution's functional relationship to larger society. Already, Drucker was thinking in terms of management as a social function, a concept he would flesh out in more detail in later works. But as early as 1946, he was pointing out that both our statesmen and our business leaders have to find solutions to the problems of the industrial society which serve at the same time equally the functional efficiency of the corporation, the functional efficiency of society and our basic political beliefs and promises.

(Drucker, 1946, p. 19)

The Single-Purpose Institution vs. The Common Good

In *Concept of the Corporation*, Drucker was already working through the tension between single-purpose institutions and the need to consider greater societal needs. The corporation is an economic engine, but it is also part of larger society. How do we resolve this tension between pursuing individual interests and reconciling those with the larger needs of society? This is a philosophical question that has been addressed by thinkers in many cultures through the ages. Drucker struggled with this question through his entire oeuvre. Which entity should watch over the needs of the whole? Or would the whole thing work out if each organization pursued its own self-interest under the guise of a moral framework? In large part, this question remained unanswered in Drucker's work. At this early point, Drucker argued that managers were responsible for solving this problem. There was no laissez-faire way out, nor a natural harmony between interests. Tensions were real, and part of management's role was to recognize this and deliver.

The Importance of Values

One way that organizations can do this is to reflect the larger values of the society in which they exist. The industrial society of 1940s America was segregated racially, and increasingly hostile to women working outside of the home. The nature of manual labor was changing, as the demand for skilled labor began to replace the need for unskilled labor, resulting in class divisions based on education and training. Technological advances that began during World War II would escalate, presenting a perceived existential threat to industrial workers (see Chapter 8). Yet, American society still prided itself on its founding ideals of equality, freedom, and "pursuit of happiness."

As Drucker points out in *Concept of the Corporation*, the important social institution of American society, the corporation, did not reflect American values. While the country's ideals have always been aspirational, the idea of justice of economic rewards for effort expended and equal opportunity for advancement are foundational to the fabric of the country. Drucker discusses the concept of "middle-class society," which, as is true today, "makes no sense if taken literally" (Drucker, 1946, p. 137). His description of America's "middle-class society" should be required reading for Americans of every era. He aptly points out that this phrase encapsulates the American obsession with equality, but also

> a chance for each member to have a meaningful, a useful, a full life. Indeed, the traditional argument in favor of a middle station is that it alone allows a man to lead a dignified and meaningful life—a life in which he has status and function as an individual.
>
> *(Drucker, 1946, p. 138)*

The corporation, at least General Motors, did not reflect these values. Equal opportunity for advancement means that promotions have a rational, logical basis: "This question of the criteria for advancement constitutes the real problem the modern corporation has to solve..." (Drucker, 1946, p. 142). If promotions are perceived as irrational, not organized in a comprehensible system of assessment, workers will view them as illegitimate. This will result in organizations that, in the eyes of their employees, wield power irrationally, and therefore are not worthy of support. A healthy society of organizations requires that institutions reflect the values of their society so that those who work within them will recognize management as legitimate authority, see themselves as a part of the organization, and see the organization as reflective of the larger values that they embrace.

Values, to Drucker, were not just societal. They were also personal. Throughout his work, he refers to the importance of ethics, character, values, morals, and integrity in management and leadership (see Chapter 4). Drucker's study of General Motors also involved a study of the people inside the organization, particularly Alfred Sloan. Sloan modeled the kind of personal integrity and character that Drucker believed would constitute effective, legitimate authority within an organization. When he later referred to management as a "liberal art," Drucker was primarily addressing matters of human character and an understanding of the human condition. When placed in positions of power, how do human beings behave? How should we think about such psychological, theological, and social matters when it comes to management? How can we best slow down the inevitable evils that will unfold in organizations? While engaged with very practical matters of day-to-day activities of managers, Drucker was always thinking about the larger social implications of the practice of management—particularly its role in influencing and shaping (as well as reflecting) the human condition.

Status and Function

Drucker also argues that corporations are, in fact, mini-social communities within themselves. The complexity of human interactions, particularly in larger organizations, results in the need to consider various dimensions of human relations. When Drucker was looking at General Motors, labor-management relations were strained. During the Great Depression in the late 1930s, the United Auto Workers union (UAW) actively organized and conducted strikes against General Motors as part of a campaign to bring about work reforms and union recognition. General Motors recognized the UAW in February 1937. As the United States entered the war, workers shifted from peacetime production to producing armaments, which involved retraining and work reassignments. With men off fighting the war, women were recruited to work in the factories, resulting in a gender shift in the labor force. Black men were promoted to positions once held by white men who were off fighting, creating racial tensions as well. Once the war was over, work duties, personnel, and responsibilities were shuffled again, creating more uncertainty. In short, it was a time of upheaval for what was at the time a major industry in society.

Drucker comments on the impact this had on the worker at the time in terms of his or her being part of a community:

> All of these disturbing factors are effective only because of the absence of an integration of the automobile worker into industrial society through equal opportunities and through status and function. The memory of the labor troubles of the thirties, the lack of homogeneity between management and labor, supply only the sparks; the dynamite lies in the fact that the automobile industry, as our youngest and most representative mass-production industry, exhibits the unsolved basic problem in its clearest form.
>
> *(Drucker, 1946, pp. 177–178)*

Because the plant community does not provide the worker opportunities to advance and find meaning (status and function), any upheaval is seen as a personal affront. By giving the worker the opportunity for real achievement, participation, and advancement, the discontinuities that are the result of production shifts, automation, and other disruptions will be less problematic, according to Drucker.

Part of the problem was the paternalistic attitude that management took toward labor. Earlier, Drucker wrote a piece addressing the growing Nazi threat, and the perception that suspension of private enterprise would be the way to defeat Hitler. Why was the American public so against private business? The problem was not in private business but in its practice, as American industry grew into an enterprise of mass production. Drucker called on American industry to free the worker as an individual:

> ...they [workers] did not feel that they had enough of a personal stake in free enterprise. They did not identify themselves with it. They did not have

enough pride in the business or in the plant in which they worked to fight for its independence...What is weakening free enterprise today is the lack of responsibility and initiative in the modern industrial plant. Baseball fields and model houses are not enough, nor are high wages and ideal working conditions. If we want free enterprise to become a community to which the individual belongs and for the independence of which he is willing to go to bat, we must give him the responsibility and range of an adult. Paternalism is all right for children, but grown men and women need the pride of achievement. Because they do not have enough of it in modern industry, they are not interested enough to fight for industry.

(Drucker, 1942b, p. 50)

The importance of status and function, of really having a "seat at the table," of being responsible for one's work and not just showing up to do tasks, was an early focus of Drucker's work on management. As he turned his attention toward knowledge workers, Drucker never resolved the problem that industrial workers faced in a changing society; in a sense, he turned his back on the very workers with whom he was initially concerned (see Chapter 5).

In the 1940s, Drucker also identified the challenge of the changing nature of work, something that still haunts us today. How do we address the realities of technological, social, and economic changes that lead to different demands for labor skill sets? World War II showed that manual workers were able to pivot in terms of their skills. They could apply the same abilities used to build cars to build tanks. More importantly,

Perhaps none of the lessons which the war has taught industrial management is more important than that of the extent to which talent and ability in the plants had been allowed to go to waste in the years before the war.

(Drucker, 1946, p. 149)

Workers, including "unskilled" workers, showed that they could contribute to a cause greater than themselves. How do we allow those workers who are less skilled to have status and function in society? In modern industrial society, economic rewards are supposed to be enough. But, as Drucker points out, they are never enough. It is the dignity of self-sufficiency, of independence, of "being someone" in society as well as having a purpose that gives meaning. But the large industrial organization in the 1940s did not provide this; it made the worker a dependent, a functionary who was subservient, without any autonomy or responsibility, much less any social position. Economic rewards were supposed to be sufficient. But the emphasis on economic rewards (the "Economic Man" of Drucker's 1939 book) only results in disappointment. Dignity, status, and function reside in the nature of work and the workplace as part of the social fabric. This is challenging when work itself becomes less fulfilling. Can that unskilled worker retrain to become the skilled worker of the future? Drucker challenges both management and the worker to think this through.

The Human Side of Management

In *Concept of the Corporation*, Drucker staked out his lifelong position that corporations (along with all organizations, as he would later argue) involved human effort. The entire basis of modern industry, particularly mass-production industry, was the organization of human effort toward an end. Drucker likened the corporation to an army in that what was most important was the social structure of the enterprise, particularly with respect to relations of command and responsibility among people. How do people interact with each other in order to organize effectively to achieve results? Drucker uses the metaphor of the institution as a tune: "it is not constituted by individual sounds but by the relations between them" (Drucker, 1946, p. 26).

One of the challenges presented by the large modern corporation is that it needs to find a way to identify and cultivate leadership. Large organizations will require more leaders than those seen as "natural" leaders; and there may be capable leaders in lower positions that do not get the opportunity to develop needed skills. Institutions need ways to find and develop talent, focusing on strengths, rather than weaknesses. As Drucker would develop later, he posited that the most important aspects of leadership were instilling trust and loyalty, a true esprit de corps among the organization's members (Drucker, 1946, pp. 26–27); he later referred to this as the "Spirit of the Organization" and the "Spirit of Performance" (see Chapter 4).

Drucker addresses the topic of power and its distribution in organizations, from a human perspective and also from a structural approach (see Federalism below). Power and responsibility need to be distributed in a balanced way such that there is a central authority, but also a "strong and autonomous local leadership" that is willing to take on responsibility (Drucker, 1946, p. 29). The distribution of power and authority must also be rational but avoid a reliance on bureaucracy (so as to allow flexibility and adaptability as needed). Succession decisions involving people have to be justifiable by recognized merit, not by "genius" or "brilliance." Early on, we can see Drucker focusing on the issues of power, people, and performance that would come to play such a prominent role in much of his work (Linkletter and Tabesh, 2022).

Decentralization/Federalism

Drucker based his analysis of General Motors' decentralized structure on his earlier political assessment of the debates on the American Constitution and *The Federalist Papers* (see Chapter 7). When the former colonies were debating whether or not to have a federal government that would better unify the loose confederation of states, questions of power loomed over the conversation. How much authority should a federal government have? How would sovereign rights at the state level be protected? The essays written by John Jay, Alexander Hamilton, and James Madison, collectively referred to as *The Federalist Papers*, presented arguments in favor of a federal system, and answered criticism lodged by the Anti-Federalists (Maciariello and Linkletter, 2010).

When Drucker analyzed decentralization in General Motors, he realized it was more than just dividing labor into smaller units. It was, Drucker realized, a philosophy, "*an essay in federalism*" that successfully combined "the greatest corporate unity with the greatest divisional autonomy and responsibility; and like every true federation, it aims at realizing unity through local self-government and vice versa" (Drucker, 1946, p. 46). At the corporate level, at least as embodied by General Motors, Drucker found several benefits of decentralization as a philosophy of management. It sped up decision-making, because of the clarity of who held what degrees of authority and responsibility. It helped avoid conflict of interest between divisions and kept factionalism at bay (meaning corporate intrigues would be minimized). Because lines of authority were clear, the organization's structure reflected democratic values of freedom, allowing open discussion of decisions (transparency, in today's language) and buy-in when a decision was ultimately made. Finally, because of this transparency, weaknesses were exposed; weak managers and divisions cannot hide, carried by the success of others (Drucker, 1946, pp. 47–48).

The Role of Profit

One last idea that Drucker introduces in *Concept of the Corporation* that would be a key component of later management writing is his definition of profit and its function. In the text, Drucker includes a chapter titled "Production for 'Use' or for 'Profit'?" (Drucker, 1946, pp. 230–263). This chapter is a structured response to a debate taking place in America and Europe during the late 1930s and 1940s over which system, capitalism or socialism, was most beneficial to society. The paroxysms of the Great Depression led many political economists and philosophers to question the benefit of capitalism to society. How could a system that had caused such widespread hardship and disarray possibly be a positive force in society? Socialists argued that production for profit resulted in a system that left people's needs unmet. When the exchange value of production was prioritized, some goods may not be produced in sufficient quantities, leaving people without what they need. Emphasizing the utility value (meeting actual needs), argued socialist philosophers, would be a better way of meeting societal needs and avoiding poverty, disruption in the capital markets, and other sources of upheaval.

Drucker had already established himself as a critic of socialism in *The End of Economic Man*, but he was also critical of capitalism in that text. Now, as he studied the industrial corporation as a social institution, Drucker had to address the role of profit in society. Well-steeped in the economic theories of Marx, Hayek, and others engaged in the debate since the 1800s, Drucker turned to the more pragmatic aspects of profit in terms of its function for an institution's existence in society (Smith, 2010). Drucker states that the debate over the justification for profits "rests on a misunderstanding of the nature of the economic process. Every economic transaction is by definition a gamble on the future. In every economic transaction there is thus a considerable element of risk…The more complex the economy becomes, the more complex become the risks incurred in any economic activity." Profit, then, is a risk premium, "and the basis of all economic activity, whether capitalistic, socialist or cave man. An economy which does not make due provision for risks must eat up its substance and must become poorer and less productive" (Drucker, 1946, p. 231). In an elegant argument, Drucker establishes profit as a moral obligation of business to cover its future expenses—known and unknown. It has nothing to do with human motivation and desire; it has to do with the obligation of an organization to exist—and, therefore, to remain part of a functioning society of institutions that gives people status and function. An unprofitable automobile manufacturer will go out of business and cause enormous disruption in society. This realization led to the 2009 joint bailout of General Motors by Canada and the United States government; the perils of unprofitability became real in the global financial crisis of 2008. While the decision to rescue General Motors was highly controversial, it illustrates Drucker's argument regarding the enormous social cost of ignoring profit as a risk premium (Jackson, 2010).

Drucker the Consultant

Concept of the Corporation established Drucker as the voice of American business management. While the book was not well received within General Motors, its publication made Drucker a highly-desired consultant in the growing field of management consulting. His list of clients included many large U.S. companies, including Sears, General Electric, Coca-Cola, Citicorp and IBM. By the 1970s, John Tarrant would write that Drucker was the most well-known individual management consultant in the business, bucking the trend of management consulting firms employing groups of people in prestigious organizations such as McKinsey. Drucker remarked that this was a matter of temperament; he was more effective working alone, and functioned better performing all tasks himself, including administration (he notoriously answered his own phone, to the surprise of many callers) (Gibbons). As Tarrant points out, this is not surprising, given that Drucker's development of management into a distinct discipline allowed him to show people how little they actually knew about management, and how much they needed his consulting services. His approach was to ask the questions that constitute his theory of the business (in Drucker's words, "stupid questions"). For some, this probing was earth-shattering. For others, it represented a marginally effective approach (Tarrant, 1976). Drucker referred to consulting as "an unlicensed practice of psychiatry" because he developed personal relationships with many of his clients, who often revealed information about their private lives and personal concerns (Gibbons, 1970, p. 319).

As the nature of management changed, Drucker's consulting work changed as well. He consulted for non-profit and governmental entities, not just corporations, providing pro-bono work for the American Red Cross, the Salvation Army, and other groups he saw as essential to a functioning society. He also served as an international consultant to several governments, private entities, and public corporations.

Drucker the Teacher

Drucker began his teaching career not in business, but in economics at Sarah Lawrence College, a small liberal arts school in New York. He joined the faculty two years after he emigrated to the United States, in 1939. In 1942, he moved to Bennington College in Vermont, another small liberal arts college, where he taught political philosophy until he joined the management faculty of New York University in 1949, buoyed by his work on General Motors. In 1971, Drucker moved to Claremont, California to teach at the Claremont Graduate School of Management (see Photo 3.1).

Drucker's teaching style was a blend of case methods and Socratic discussions. He firmly believed that management students should be working or have had some work experience before they enter graduate school. Similarly, he advocated that management faculty should not be purely academic, but also have practiced the discipline in order to teach it effectively. Always skeptical of the reliance on academic credentials, Drucker believed that there needed to be a balance between experience in the practice of management and the study of management (Cohen, 2008).

Government–Business Cooperation

Drucker has said that the *Concept of the Corporation* established the study of organization as a major subject (Drucker, 1946, p. x). This is likely true, but the increased role of American corporations in the American war effort during World War II also may have turned the spotlight onto large organizations as entities worth noticing. As was the case during World War I and the New Deal, government and business adopted a corporatist model

PHOTO 3.1   Drucker in the classroom, undated.

of cooperation after Pearl Harbor drew the United States into the war. Roosevelt established the War Production Board under the command of Don Nelson, Sears' top executive. The War Department was filled with "dollar-a-year" men like Nelson, who agreed to work for the war effort for no salary. William Knudsen, President of General Motors, oversaw production for the War Department. The influence of corporate executives' experience on the conduct of war was unmistakable. These men brought not only statistical and analytical skills, but also experience in mass marketing. Marketing drove public campaigns to conserve raw materials and work at maximum capacity. Corporate executives working in the public sector used marketing techniques to establish brand loyalty among the troops, incorporating Coca-Cola's and other products' logos into materials distributed to the armed forces. Government and business had cooperated before, but, with corporations now an integral part of society, the relationship was different (Zunz, 1990).

This difference was not lost on the public. Big business was an increasingly important economic force; by 1948, corporations held almost 60 percent of the nation's income-producing wealth (Zunz, 1990, p. 1). But working people felt the impact on their daily lives as well. During the 1940s, large corporations became the employers of more and more Americans. By 1944, some 30 percent of the nation's total labor force worked in businesses employing ten thousand or more people, as opposed to only 13 percent in 1939. The rise of corporate plant communities, such as General Motors' company town in Muncie, Indiana, as well as a host of public relations campaigns placed the American corporation in the forefront of the public eye. Thus, although Drucker's book was one of the first to analyze a large business, his interest in the modern corporate organization was reinforced by the "miracle" of American war production and the increasingly visible role of business in the public sector (Blackford, 1991; Marchand, 1998).

Drucker's prolific writing reflects the growing market for his type of books and articles, as corporations continued to expand their influence on the American public as well as the government sector. Following the war, much of the country's industrial capacity that had been used for war production had to be put to peacetime use or lie idle. In many cases, firms pursued a strategy of diversification in order to effectively use this capacity. Companies such as General Electric and Westinghouse expanded into consumer appliances and, as their product lines broadened, restructured around divisional lines in order to market to a new type of customer. Other companies diversified into new technologies and alternative products to put their production equipment to peacetime use. As companies restructured their operations, they also became more complicated in terms of their management structure, which in turn resulted in an increased number of corporate managerial positions (Chandler, 1962, 1977). Even those who did not hold management jobs knew that they might aspire to such positions and reading books and articles about how to be a good employee, or how to manage one's time effectively undoubtedly appealed to a wide audience during the post-war period.

Then, too, the tensions of the Cold War enhanced the reputation of the business world in the years after World War II. As Marchand notes in his analysis of wartime advertising, American capitalism was often equated with patriotism and freedom (Marchand, 1998, pp. 316–317). The very nature of the polarization of communism and capitalism revolved around the invocation of "free markets," "free trade," and economic competition associated with business. The existence of American businesses reinforced the beauty of free enterprise.

The Man in the Gray Flannel Suit

But there were also concerns beginning to surface with respect to the large corporations, particularly with the influence they were having on human individuality and expression. The 1951 publication of C. Wright Mills' work, *White Collar: The American Middle Class* helped to foster the image of the company man as conformist bureaucrat, a model that was further enhanced by William Whyte's sociological study, *The Organization Man* (1956). Thanks in part to Whyte and Mills, the standard image of the organization man became that of the faceless man in a suit. Whyte in particular emphasized the dangerous loss of the individual propagated within the American corporation, yet placed the blame not on business itself, but rather on society's image of it:

> The fault is not in organization, in short: it is in our worship of it. It is in our vain quest for a utopian equilibrium, which would be horrible if it ever did come to pass; it is in the soft-minded denial that there is a conflict between the individual and society.
>
> *(Whyte, 1956, p. 13)*

Echoed in these words is the oft-voiced Cold War concern with communist societies: the loss of the individual voice to a mass, totalitarian system of total equality. This construct of communist countries during the Cold War was a fiction; those societies were not models of total equality, but rather based on rigid hierarchies of authority. But the changing nature of work in a newly corporate America fueled concerns that were heightened in a politically charged environment.

Paired with this concern about conformity and loss of individuality was the related worry that corporate life would exact a toll on the human psyche. The emotional and psychological impacts of corporate life permeated not just management writings but also popular culture and scientific and sociological publications written for the general public.

Popular culture of the fifties explored the ways in which managers and businessmen experienced alienation, emasculation, and stress in their home lives as well as at work. Novels such as *Executive Suite* (Hawley, 1952) and *The Man in the Gray Flannel Suit* (Wilson, 1955), both made into major motion pictures, were representative of how popular culture attempted to come to terms with the growing presence of the knowledge worker in American society. In print media, sociologists and other management writers were also interested in issues of motivation and psychology. Abraham Maslow wrote his *Motivation and Personality*, published in 1954, which laid out his famous hierarchy of needs. Douglas McGregor discussed the need for business to address *The Human Side of Enterprise* (1960), and Frederick Herzberg published his book, *The Motivation to Work* in 1959. Increasingly, American society was interested in reading about management as a profession, not only because more and more people worked in management jobs, but also because these new types of workers were facing new kinds of problems in a changing society. Something had happened to the American businessman: he was no longer the entrepreneurial voice, but rather the tool of the soulless corporation. Likely fueled by cold war fears of totalitarianism, such representations were, of course, stereotypical, but nevertheless reflected an undercurrent of wariness on the part of the public that the new management culture was somehow eliminating the individual, the pioneer spirit, from American society.

Finance Capitalism

The new business organizations, too, were different from the enterprises launched by early corporate pioneers such as Carnegie and Ford. The rise of the large conglomerates during the late fifties and sixties created organizations that defied conventional management wisdom, and that could only be rationalized on the basis of quantification. Seeking new investments in a post-war boom environment, many companies began to look outside of their specific areas of expertise to identify acquisition possibilities. Textron, the first of such conglomerates, was comprised of defense manufacturers, a golf cart company, a financial services wing, and a consumer products division. Whereas the acquisitions of the merger wave of the late nineteenth century had focused on developing supply networks, distribution systems, or fewer competitors, the new merger wave created companies with unrelated businesses in different markets with different customers.

Such investment decisions were based on financial projections, for the most part; this was an era of matrix-based management theories, and companies were looking for new opportunities to invest funds thrown off from their "cash cows." Other firms, such as Philip Morris, diversified in order to manage the risks associated with producing and distributing one specific product type. Accountants and finance people ran companies from the top instead of manufacturing managers or marketing minds. The domination of financial efficiency and "bottom-line management" led to anxieties about job security, heightened by the increasing role of technology and automation in the workplace, a growing theme during the sixties and into the seventies. Again, popular culture reflected these trends in the corporate world. Movies such as *The Pajama Game* (1957) featured efficiency experts hired to speed up production lines at the expense of employee relations, and *How to Succeed in Business Without Really Trying* (1967) mourned the loss of the value of craftsmanship embodied in the advent of the "bean counters" and the profit ethic in American business.

The Practice of Management

Thus, although these were years of heady economic progress, they were also decades of status anxiety for managers. Peter Drucker, NYU professor and renowned management consultant, redeemed the businessman, legitimizing him as a professional and raising the status of management to a practice. By 1962 his book *The Practice of Management* was deemed "a classic and...required reading at the Harvard Business School" ('Top advisor to top brass', 1962, p. 34). But it was Drucker's emphasis on management's need to take risk, to avoid the stale bureaucracy and gray flannel suit rigidity that stereotyped management and business in much of popular culture, that much of his readership lauded. His description of managers as creative, bold, courageous actors came as a breath of fresh air to corporate executives and management functionaries in a climate of Cold War fears of totalitarianism.

Drucker defines a manager by their function and contribution, not their position in the hierarchy or bureaucracy. This primary contribution is, ultimately, one of allowing others to also have a function and contribute: "The one contribution he [the manager] is uniquely expected to make is to give others vision and ability to perform. It is vision and moral responsibility that, in the last, analysis, define the manager" (Drucker, 1954, p. 350). Managers are a moral force in society that enable others to have status and function; this is an enormously powerful picture of what, at the time, many saw as a functionary role, a person who shuffled paper in an office. For Drucker, "The manager is the dynamic, life-giving element in every business. Without his leadership the 'resources of production' remain resources and never become production" (Drucker, 1954, p. 3). Managers not only are the key to the survival of free enterprise, but they are also leaders in society that others look to and are key to the survival of the free world: "Truly, the entire free world has an immense stake in the competence, skill and responsibility of management" (Drucker, 1954, p. 5). Quite a resounding rejoinder to the image of the man in the gray flannel suit, albeit an aspirational one.

Management by Objectives and Self-Control

Drucker introduces the concept of management by objectives and self-control in *The Practice of Management*, and it is in this text where he most fully presents the idea.[1] Drucker refers to management by objectives and self-control as "a 'philosophy' of management. It rests on an analysis of the specific needs of the management group and the obstacles it faces. It rests on a concept of business action, human behavior, and human motivation. Finally, it applies to every manager, whatever his level and function, and to any business enterprise whether large or small. It insured performance by converting objective needs into personal goals. And this is genuine freedom, freedom under the law" (Drucker, 1954, p. 136). Essentially, management by objectives and self-control provides Drucker with a way of reconciling the tension between individual existence and existence in society. Within an organization, people contribute their own individual strengths, but these must be built into a team and directed toward a common effort and mission. This "true team" allows for individual action, free will, and contribution, but makes sure that efforts "pull in the same direction" to produce a whole "without gaps, without friction, without unnecessary duplication of effort" (Drucker, 1954, p. 121). Because management is responsible for their contributions to their area of influence, and ultimately to the larger organization, they must set their own objectives. It is not enough to give a person "a sense of participation"; rather, he or she must have genuine responsibility (and commensurate authority) for their performance objectives and subsequent measurements.

Drucker's concept is often shortened using the acronym "MBO"; unfortunately, this eliminates the important element of self-control that Drucker emphasizes. Self-control directly impacts motivation, "a desire to do the best rather than just enough to get by" (Drucker, 1954, p. 130). If management by objectives and self-control becomes only about the objectives and not about an understanding of human motivation and behavior, then it simply becomes a tool rather than a philosophy. Perhaps this is why the implementation of Drucker's concept has not always been successful, as organizations tended to view management by objectives and self-control as more driven by objectives set by top management rather than participation of a "true team" that allows for the realization of personal goals; MBO has been referred to as "a fad that will remain in the graveyard" (Micklethwait and Wooldridge, 1996, p. 153). As Tarrant notes, Drucker realized as early as the 1950s that management by objectives and self-control was susceptible to mistranslation, often resulting in "management by results," an emphasis on the "bottom line" that creates leaders who are insecure if they don't deliver, and then punish subordinates for failing to meet concrete results rather than larger objectives (Tarrant, 1976).

Drucker himself has contributed to the misunderstandings of his philosophy of management by objectives and self-control. In his 1973 book, *Management: Tasks, Responsibilities, Practices*, Drucker treats the topic considerably differently. Gone is the language of the "true team." Instead, he focuses much more on matters of compensation and structure in terms of implementation. Performance is paramount, and the idea's ability to reduce misdirected and wasted efforts plays a prominent role. Drucker defends management by objectives and self-control from critics, arguing that it asks people to make high demands on themselves (and that people will, in fact, do so if expected to). In attempting to forge a philosophy that allows for individual freedom while maintaining allegiance to a community's larger goals and objectives, Drucker sets himself up for misinterpretation, particularly when his language turns more toward performance and measurements, compensation and structures rather than team and individual fulfillment (Drucker, 1973).

Theory of the Business

Finally, in *The Practice of Management*, Drucker established what came to be known as his "Theory of the Business": the basic questions that every organization (not just businesses) must answer to understand why they exist. Although these questions seem common sense today, they were actually groundbreaking at the time. In the 1950s, it was firmly held that corporations existed to earn a profit; in fact, Drucker recognized this in his redefinition of profit as not a motive but a practical matter of covering the costs of risk (see previous section). Famously, Drucker argued that the purpose of business was to "create a customer." After all, the customer (or client) determines what the business or organization will be and do, how it will best be structured, what products or services it will offer, how much it should charge, and, ultimately, whether it will survive (Drucker, 1954).

Drucker's focus on the customer drove his belief that marketing and innovation were the two key functions of entrepreneurship in organizations. All other functions were subsidiary to these that produce wealth and expand opportunity. Therefore, in order to constantly innovate and stay in touch with customer desires, Drucker developed a set of questions that businesses must revisit regularly to evaluate their purpose and mission. What is our business? Who is our customer? What does the customer consider value? What will our business be in the future? What should it be? (Drucker, 1954). His Theory of the Business, driven by a focus on innovation and marketing, was novel at the time, and contributed to Drucker's fame as a management consultant to many top companies (Darroch, 2010). Yet, the concept of business as a life-giving force, a source of not just economic growth but expansion of opportunity and societal wealth, came under fire as cultural, political, and social conditions changed dramatically on a global basis.

The Legitimacy of Management

As the 1960s turned into "the sixties," managers came under attack as part of the "Establishment" as tensions rose over the Vietnam War, race conflict, and feminism. Books such as *Managing for Results* (1964), *The Effective Executive* (1966), and, especially, *Management: Tasks, Responsibilities, Practices* (1973), told executives and managers that they were society's heroes, the ones who should be entrusted with guiding and shaping the country's agenda. Even technology, which threatened job security, could actually be harnessed for productive good, as Drucker argued in several articles and in *The Age of Discontinuity* (1968). Amidst a culture of pessimism, Drucker's was a voice that told the organization man he was no automaton, but rather an agent of powerful change and progress.

Drucker also served as a voice for the conservative counterpoint to the liberal trend of Johnson's Great Society and the expansion of social welfare programs. A sharp critic of large government, Drucker was an early advocate for privatization and the curtailment of government power during the sixties and seventies (see Chapter 7). Neo-conservative editor and author Irving Kristol compared *The Age of Discontinuity* to John Kenneth Galbraith's *The Affluent Society* and Michael Harrington's *The Other America*, two important and widely read liberal critiques of American social policies. In Kristol's view, Drucker's conservative book was "a major work of great brilliance, and [made Galbraith's and Harrington's work] look like ephemeral pamphlets by comparison" (Kristol, 1969, p. 189). Not only did Drucker provide legitimacy to the businessman, but to his conservative political and social views as well. In the face of perceived attacks by academia, the business community had its own champion for its social conservatism and status within American society and culture.

The American production miracle was already showing signs of stress by 1973, when the Yom Kippur war and subsequent OPEC oil embargo helped stagflation become a household word. As Wall Street losses mounted daily, Main Street lost confidence in business. To make matters worse, the Watergate scandal, followed by the inability of the Carter administration to combat the nation's energy woes, led to a crisis of confidence in government as well. Taxpayers in California and elsewhere revolted against what seemed to be the failed policies of a decade of social welfare and other government spending programs.

The recession of the 1970s, coupled with the reality check of social fragmentation and an expensive and losing war overseas, shook American culture as well as business. Alvin Toffler's *Future Shock* was published in 1970, while the economy was actually still quite rosy. Toffler's book was a bestseller, waking the public to the fact that reality was not a tidy teleological progression, but rather disorderly and unpredictable, and predicted that America was in for a massive restructuring in the private sector. Canadian Henry Mintzberg's 1973 study of managers (*The Nature of Managerial Work*) revealed that Whyte and David Riesman were correct: managerial work was dehumanizing and monotonous. Reminiscent of the early critiques of Taylorism, Mintzberg illustrated that managers, just like Taylor's shovelers, were slaves to the moment, alienated from their work, and governed by imposed tasks.

Not only were managers no better than automatons, they were perceived as ineffective as well. American manufacturers, especially automobile makers, were in a state of crisis as they lost ground to overseas competitors. Japanese cars sold for fractions of the cost of American cars and were much more reliable. By the mid-1970s, it seemed that something had gone terribly wrong with American business and the businessman.

Where was the champion of the businessman during this crisis? Drucker continued to defend the organization man in the face of the backlash of the seventies. In the Preface to a later edition of Management: *Tasks, Responsibilities, Practices*, he admonishes the anti-establishment critics of business:

Our society has become, within an incredibly short fifty years, a society of institutions...It is understandable that the sudden realization of this change in the crystal structure of society has evoked an angry response, "Down with organization!" But it is the wrong response. The alternative to autonomous institutions that function and perform is not freedom. It is totalitarian tyranny...To make our institutions perform responsibly, autonomously, and on a high level of achievement is thus the only safeguard of freedom and dignity in the pluralist society of institutions. But it is managers and management that make institutions perform. Performing, responsible management is the alternative to tyranny and our only protection against it.

(Drucker, 1973/1974, pp. ix–x)

Yet, Drucker wields a two-edged sword in this paragraph. He calls on society not to give up on its established organizations and their managers. But he also makes it very clear that those managers must perform and perform responsibly. And, given the financial manipulations that were involved in the merger activities of the late 1960s and 1970s, it seems that Drucker was not convinced that management was behaving in a responsible manner; by the 1980s, it was clear that he was convinced many were not.

Drucker began to sound warnings about excessive executive pay in the late 1970s. His concern was the gap between CEO compensation and median compensation for workers. In 1977, Drucker called for this ratio of executive to worker pay to be no higher than 20 to 1, save for exceptional cases of outstanding performance (Drucker, 1977, p. 20). His argument was that wide disparity between executive and worker pay would strain the social bonds within an organization. Perceived inequalities in compensation would lead to resentment and, as a result, poor performance. In addition, as social figures, executives needed to be aware of how they were viewed by the public; increasing disparity between executive and worker pay fueled cries against corporate greed and stock price manipulation through merger and acquisition activities.

By the 1980s, Drucker was concerned that management, at least business management, was no longer a legitimate authority in society. This was troubling. In order to have a functioning society, the sources of power had to be legitimate; otherwise, power is only force. Going back to his roots in European political philosophy, Drucker reminds his audience in the 1980s that

To be legitimate, power has to be grounded outside of it in something transcending it that is accepted as a genuine value, if not as a true absolute by those subject to the power—whether descent from the gods or apostolic succession, divine institution or its modern, totalitarian counterpart the scientific laws of history; the consent of the governed, popular election or, as in so much of modern society, the magic of the advanced degree. If power is an end in itself, it becomes despotism and both illegitimate and tyrannical.

(Drucker, 1986/1993, p. 165)

So what happened to make business management suspect in the eyes of the public? Why was it no longer perceived as legitimate?

Social Responsibility of Management

The primary reason for business management's fall from grace was its failure to live up to its promises to actually consider the interests of all stakeholders. In the 1950s, Ralph Cordiner, CEO of the General Electric Company (one of Drucker's consulting clients), attempted to institute a version of stakeholder theory, where top management is the "trustee for the balanced best interest of stockholders, employees, customers, suppliers and plant communities." As Drucker notes, the statement was pablum for an annual report, signaling good intentions that went unrealized. After all, "good intentions are not enough to make power legitimate. In fact, good intentions as the grounds for power characterize the 'enlightened despot'" (Drucker, 1986/1993, p. 167). What, in fact, happened was that stockholders became the sole focus of corporate managers; finance capitalism ruled the day, and stock prices were the yardstick used to make decisions from everything from capital expenditures to personnel development to marketing, innovation, and growth. Milton Friedman famously argued in 1970 that the only social responsibility of business was to return wealth to its shareholders (Friedman, 1970).

This emphasis on stock prices ultimately drove executive compensation (often delivered in the form of stock options) and exacerbated the problem of pay inequality within organizations. Professionals should be paid well, but Drucker chastised management for putting pay before responsibility and standards, and called on limitations on executive income (Drucker, 1986/1993). Finally, management had to recognize its role as a social function: "for management of the big business to attain full legitimacy, it will have to accept that to remain 'private' it has to accept that it discharges a social, and that means a 'public,' function" (Drucker, 1986/1993, p. 172). As Wallace has argued, this tension between value-based management and stockholder theory was, in many ways resolved by Drucker's model of maximization of the organization's wealth-producing capacity, which did not necessarily mean emphasis on short-term stock price increases to the sole benefit of shareholders at the expense of the longer-term viability of the firm (Wallace, 2010).

Drucker's increasing dissatisfaction with the turn of events in corporate America led him to rethink and repackage his own ideas for the new climate of the 1980s. He turned his attention away from the large organizations, which he had not so long ago hoped would be the locus of citizenship and non-economic status in society, toward small, entrepreneurial ventures and the social sector. His book, *Innovation and Entrepreneurship* (1985) solidified his earlier ideas about the key role of innovation in organizations and the need to make innovation part of the routine practice of management (see Chapter 6). He also articulated that management was not simply a function of business, but rather a discipline practiced by all organizations (Drucker, 1986/1993). The primary problem posed by the developments of financial capitalism in the 1980s, however, was who would oversee the needs of the community? In Drucker's earlier models of a functioning society, the government would be the overseer of the common good (see Chapter 7) and industrial capitalism would provide mechanisms to allow for the community's concerns to balance those of the individual (Chapter 2). By the 1980s, Drucker realized this model no longer worked in practice. Single-purpose institutions needed to maintain their focus in order to be successful. A hospital cannot possibly do more than serve patients in the community. A data surveillance firm has to focus on helping clients prevent security breaches. For institutions to work, they need to have mission and vision, and it needs to be focused. So, the question remains: who will watch out for the concerns of the larger society?

Drucker returned to his rather lukewarm answer that he began with in *Concept of the Corporation*. The only solution is that management of all of the institutions of society "see it as their job to reconcile concern for the common good with the pursuit of the special mission for the sake of which their institution exists" (Drucker, 1986/1993, pp. 164–165). Ultimately, Drucker tasked managers of all institutions in every sector with two responsibilities: the performance of their institution and the well-being of the community as a whole. Likening the situation to that of a symphony orchestra, Drucker notes that each instrumentalist is responsible for her own part. But the score is the community, and without the commitment to the score "there is only noise" (Drucker and Maciariello, 2008, p. 230).

Ahead of his time, Drucker discussed the social responsibility of business. While managers' primary responsibility was to ensure that their institutions perform the functions for which they exist, they are also concerned with the well-being of society; a healthy institution "cannot exist in a sick society" (Drucker and Maciariello, 2008, p. 213). Drucker called on all institutions (not just business) to assume what he referred to as "leadership beyond the walls": leadership that not only is responsible for the performance of the organization, but also takes community responsibility outside of the organization (Drucker and Maciariello, 2008, p. 229). As Chong notes, Drucker was calling for good stakeholder relationships as early as the 1950s (Chong, 2013).

Drucker on Japanese Management

Drucker points to the Japanese of the 1980s as an example of how management can, in fact, balance responsibility for institutional performance with a concern for society. In a keynote address delivered to the Academy of Management Congress in Chicago in 1986, Drucker chastised American businesses for only paying lip service to the idea of stakeholders. In Japan, management "brings together in a common interest a number of constituencies: employees first, then customers, then creditors, and finally suppliers. Stockholders are only a special group of creditors, rather than 'the owners' for whose sake the enterprise exists" (Drucker, 1986/1993, p. 167). For Drucker, Japanese management represented some of the best features of balancing the needs of the institution with those of society, and, beginning in the late 1970s and early 1980s, he began to write extensively on the topic.

Drucker first traveled to Japan in the 1950s, beginning a long-term interest in that country's management as a reflection of its society and culture. Although he had been exposed to Japanese art during his years in London, his work on management helped connect him to Japanese industry and government as they used many of his ideas to help rebuild Japan's economy after the devastation of World War II. Drucker was awarded the Third Order of Merit by the Japanese government in 1966 based on the contributions of his management seminars held at Tokyo and Osaka in July 1959 and subsequent visits. Drucker's books were translated into Japanese, and he enjoyed a wide following of readers from the business and government sectors. According to Susumu Takamiya, Drucker's book *The Practice of Management* was widely influential, as were his social books from that era (*Landmarks of Tomorrow* and *The Age of Discontinuity*). Drucker's focus on innovation and opportunity, on working with change and capitalizing on disruption, was the right message for Japanese society just as they were rebuilding and recovering (Takamiya, 1970).

Most of Drucker's writing on Japanese management was published in the 1970s and 1980s, as the manufacturing economy in the United States floundered and Japanese competitors posed a threat. He observed that Japanese managers approach decision-making very differently from western managers. Drucker pointed out that decision-making in Japan is based on building consensus, by carefully defining the question, not the answer. Only when consensus is reached as to the nature of the actual problem is the decision made, at which point there is buy-in from the group. This practice, Drucker notes, removes the need to "sell" a decision to dissenters in an organization. While time consuming, once consensus is reached, the actual decision and subsequent action are quite rapid. The advantages of this approach are that it allows for more effective decisions, as everyone in the organization has been presold and therefore there is little to no problem in actually implementing decisions. Because the process is so slow, it also forces management to focus on larger decisions and not waste time on smaller issues. As was observed by many, Japanese management focused on "bottom up" rather than "top down" relationships, emphasizing the group rather than the individual (Drucker, 1971, 1973).

Globalization

Japan was not the only country whose management Drucker scrutinized. Very early on, he was considering the global nature of management. In *The Age of Discontinuity* (1969), Drucker studied the changing nature of currency exchange, as well as the growing influence of the multinational corporation. Multinationals, he argued, were the creators of economic and social development, providing avenues for new leaders to emerge and different cultures to transcend boundaries yet still respect one another.

The key to an effective global economy, Drucker posited, was not technological innovation, but effective management. Earlier nations had become economic powers through technology (Great Britain through textiles and steam engines, Germany through chemistry, steel and the modern bank, the United States through telecommunications, automobiles, and aviation). But Japan became an economic superpower in the late twentieth century through learning the management lessons of World War II, especially about managing people as a resource, not a cost. The mechanical model of technology that dominated the early twentieth century had ended; now, management and technology involved processes and information that required knowledge workers, not manual workers. As a result, Drucker stated that the key to economic development was creating a solid managerial knowledge base (Drucker, 1988).

In the 1990s, as the world became more interconnected in large part due to the advent of the internet, the nature of organizational communication and operations changed dramatically. Leadership authority Jean Lipman-Blumen, a colleague of Drucker's, refers to this development as the end of the Geopolitical Era and the emergence of the Connective Era. The Geopolitical era was characterized by clear geographical boundaries and political ideologies and was dominated by authoritarian leaders using a model of "command and control." In contrast, the Connective Era, which began at the end of the twentieth century, emphasized more collaborative models of leadership, with alliances and shifting coalitions focusing on narrower, specific short-term objectives (Lipman-Blumen, 2010).

Geopolitical events also drove what Drucker referred to as a decline in sovereign powers' ability to dictate terms of trade. With the fall of the Soviet Union, a superpower was broken into individual nation states, each with a separate identity and economic interest. Even before this event,

Drucker was referring to changes in the global economy, noting that the era of "superpowers" was over, and that there would only be competitors. Decision making and economic relations would therefore be characterized by alliances based on region, such as the European Economic Union, the North American Free Trade Agreement (which was still in its infancy), and as Drucker correctly predicted, an Asian alliance of some kind (what would become the Asian-Pacific Economic Cooperation). He foresaw the need for some kind of transnational environmental policy, given development programs' impact on natural resources, particularly in developing nations. In keeping with his desire to balance the freedom of the organization to pursue its special interests with the needs of the common good, Drucker began to call for some kind of legal guardrails for the increasingly global community that he saw (Drucker, 1989). Drucker's concern for social responsibility of business, and the potential impacts of development programs on developing nations, in some ways foreshadowed the arguments of globalization's critics, who point to the ways in which globalization has favored developed nations and skilled workers over developing nations and unskilled workers. Critics highlight data that show exacerbated inequalities and problems associated with climate change, tax policies, trade balances, and technology (Rodrik, 1997; Stiglitz, 2002).

Conclusion

Drucker's work on management was purely an accident of the circumstances of his time and place in history. In search of a model for a functioning society that would stave off fascism by providing individuals with status and function, he happened upon the industrial society of post-World War II America, with its rapid expansion of manufacturing as it converted wartime to peacetime production. The transformation of western society into a society of organizations dominated by knowledge rather than industry catapulted Drucker's life work in management. His early study of General Motors may have positioned Drucker as a management consultant and teacher, but he was never really a business figure. In reality, his work on management, beginning with *The Concept of the Corporation*, was about how to ensure that organizations of all kinds would function effectively, responsibly, and with an understanding of people as a resource.

Drucker's contributions to the study and practice of management seem common sense today, but they were in fact revolutionary for his time. The consideration of values runs deep throughout his management writings, driven by his view of management as ultimately about the human condition and the need for individual and social meaning. His early explorations of manufacturing organizations, as well as his later writing on knowledge workers, demand that all workers are accorded dignity and respect; while

Drucker may not always have the answer for how to address structural unemployment, or the inevitable disruptions presented by technological change, he is clear in his call for a consideration of the human impacts of economic and technological disruptions. Regardless of social status, all people deserve to be seen as human beings.

Similarly, Drucker constantly demands that authority and responsibility be disseminated to the lowest possible level in organizations. Giving people the maximum appropriate autonomy, along with the tools and resources for self-development and growth, is the only way to organize for performance and accountability. The concepts of decentralization and management by objectives and self-control are ultimately about these matters of power, autonomy, and responsibility.

Finally, Drucker was thinking about corporate social responsibility before the term existed. His view of institutions as reflective of larger values in society, and their need to think through the impact of individual organizational decisions on the greater whole, reflect the concern with stakeholder theory. For-profit institutions are not run merely to earn a profit; profit is a risk premium, a moral responsibility for that organization to think through its larger obligations, not just its short-term financial objectives. As the definition of society becomes increasingly global, and organizations are even more interconnected, Drucker's ideas take on new relevancy. As we will see in the next chapter, his concept of a society of institutions involves thinking about the constant need to maintain some stability in times of great change, as well as the need to balance the interests of the individual with those of the whole.

Note

1   I am indebted to my friend and colleague, Rick Johnson, for bringing Drucker's changing descriptions of MBO to my attention.

Bibliography

Blackford, M.G. (1991) *A history of small business in America*. New York: Twayne.
Chandler, A. (1962) *Strategy and structure: Chapters in the history of industrial enterprise*. Cambridge, MA: MIT Press.
Chandler, A. (1977) *The visible hand: The managerial revolution in American business*. Cambridge, MA: Belknap Press.
Chong, D. (2013) 'The relevance of management to society: Peter Drucker's oeuvre from the 1940s and 1950s', *Journal of Management History*, 19 (1), pp. 55–72.
Cohen, W.A. (2008) *A class with Drucker: The lost lessons of the world's greatest management teacher*. AMACOM.
Darroch, J. (2010) 'Drucker on marketing: Remember, customers are the reason you are in business', in Pearce, C., Maciariello, J., and Yamawaki, H. (eds.), *The*

Drucker difference: What the world's greatest management thinker means to today's business leaders. New York: McGraw Hill, pp. 255–267.

Drucker, P.F. (1939) *The end of economic man.* New Brunswick, NJ: Transaction.

Drucker, P.F. (1942a) *The future of industrial man.* New Brunswick, NH: Transaction.

Drucker, P.F. (1942b) 'Total war requires free enterprise', *The Saturday Evening Post,* 3 October, pp. 14–50.

Drucker, P.F. (1946) *Concept of the corporation.* New York: John Day.

Drucker, P.F. (1954) *The practice of management.* New York: Harper & Row.

Drucker, P.F. (1964) *Managing for results: Economic tasks and risk-taking decisions.* New York: Harper & Row.

Drucker, P.F. (1966) *The effective executive.* New York: Harper & Row.

Drucker, P.F. (1968) *The age of discontinuity: Guidelines to our changing society.* New York: Harper & Row.

Drucker, P.F. (1971) 'What we can learn from Japanese management,' *Harvard Business Review,* 49, pp. 110–112.

Drucker, P.F. (1973) *Management: Tasks, responsibilities, practices.* New York: Harper & Row.

Drucker, P.F. (1973/1974) *Management: Tasks, responsibilities, practices.* New York: Harper & Row.

Drucker, P.F. (1977) 'Is executive pay excessive?' *Wall Street Journal,* 23 May 23, p. 20.

Drucker, P.F. (1986) 'Management: The problems of success', Keynote address, Academy of Management Congress, Chicago, reprinted in Drucker, P.F. (1993) *The ecological vision: Reflections on the American condition.* New Brunswick, NJ: Transaction, pp. 153–175.

Drucker, P.F. (1988) 'Management and the world's work', *Harvard Business Review,* September.

Drucker, P.F. (1989) *The new realities.* New York: Harper & Row.

Drucker, P.F. (1995) *The end of economic man.* London: Transaction.

Drucker, P.F. (1999) Interview with the author, Claremont, CA, 20 December.

Drucker, P.F. and Maciariello, J.A. (2008) *Management: Revised edition.* New York: Harper Collins.

Flaherty, J. E. (1999) *Peter Drucker: Shaping the managerial mind.* San Francisco, CA: Jossey-Bass.

Friedman, M. (1970) 'The social responsibility of business is to increase its profits', *New York Times Magazine,* 13 September, pp. 122–126.

Galbraith, J.K. (1958) *The affluent society.* Boston: Houghton Mifflin Company.

Gibbons, J.F. (1970) 'An interview with Drucker in the role of a consultant', in Bonaparte, T.H. and Flaherty, J. (eds.), *Peter Drucker: Contributions to business enterprise.* New York: New York University Press, pp. 315–336.

Harrington, M. (1962) *The other America.* New York: Macmillan Publishing Company.

Hawley, C. (1952) *Executive suite.* New York: Ballantine Books.

Herzberg, F. (1959) *The motivation to work.* New York: Wiley.

Jackson, I.A. (2010) 'Drucker on government, business, and civil society: Roles, relationships, responsibilities', in Pearce, C., Maciariello, J., and Yamawaki, H. (eds.), *The Drucker difference: What the world's greatest management thinker means to today's business leaders.* New York: McGraw Hill, pp. 17–34.

Kristol, I. (1969) 'The new era of innovation', *Forbes,* February 1969, p. 189.

Linkletter, K. and Tabesh, P. (2022) ' "When asked what I do, I say, 'I write' ": A systematic text analysis of Peter Drucker's writings', *Journal of Management History*, 29 (3), pp. 344–368.

Lipman-Blumen, J. (2010) 'A pox on charisma: Why connective leadership and character count', in Pearce, C., Maciariello, J., and Yamawaki, H. (eds.), *The Drucker difference: What the world's greatest management thinker means to today's business leaders*. New York: McGraw Hill, pp. 149–174.

Maciariello, J. and Linkletter, K. (2010) 'The next book Peter Drucker would have written: Federalism and management as a liberal art', *Management Decision*, 48 (4), pp. 628–655.

Marchand, R. (1998) *Creating the corporate soul: The rise of public relations and corporate imagery in American big business*. Berkeley: University of California Press,

Maslow, A. (1954) *Motivation and personality*. New York: Harper and Brothers.

McGregor, D. (1960) *The human side of enterprise*. New York: McGraw Hill Companies.

Micklethwait, J. and Wooldridge, A. (1996) 'Peter Drucker: The guru's guru', *The McKinsey Quarterly*, 3, pp. 145–159.

Mintzberg, H. (1973) *The nature of managerial work*. New York: Harper & Row.

Rodrik, D. (1997) *Has globalization gone too far?* New York: Columbia University Press.

Smith, R. (2010) 'The Drucker vision and its foundations: Corporations, managers, markets, and innovation', in Pearce, C., Maciariello, J., and Yamawaki, H. (eds.), *The Drucker difference: What the world's greatest management thinker means to today's business leaders*. New York: McGraw Hill, pp. 221–254.

Stiglitz, J. (2002) *Globalization and its discontents*. New York: W. W. Norton & Company.

Takamiya, S. (1970) 'Peter Drucker and Japanese management', in Bonaparte, T.H. and Flaherty, J. (eds.), *Peter Drucker: Contributions to business enterprise*. New York: New York University Press, pp. 250–263.

Tarrant, J. (1976) *Drucker: The man who invented the corporate society*. Boston, MA: Cahners Books.

Toffler, A. (1970) *Future shock*. New York: Random House.

'Top adviser to top brass' (1962), *Forbes*, 89 (4), p. 4.

Wallace, J.S. (2010) 'Value(s)-based management: Corporate social responsibility meets value-based management', in Pearce, C., Maciariello, J., and Yamawaki, H. (eds.), *The Drucker difference: What the world's greatest management thinker means to today's business leaders*. New York: McGraw Hill, pp. 47–59.

Whyte, W.H. (1956) *The organization man*. New York: Simon & Schuster.

Wilson, S. (1955) *The man in the gray flannel suit*. New York: Simon & Schuster.

Zunz, O. (1990) *Making America corporate, 1870–1920*. Chicago: University of Chicago.

4

DRUCKER AND EFFECTIVE LEADERSHIP

Introduction

Leadership as a subject is well-worn territory. A cursory review of the literature on the subject yields a wealth of topics: toxic leadership, empathetic leadership, transformational leadership, compassionate leadership—the list goes on. Entire journals are devoted to the subject. Until late in his career, Drucker felt that leadership was an overused term that was poorly defined. What, in fact, is leadership? How do we identify leaders? Can anyone be a leader? Can leadership be learned? Are there specific traits associated with good leaders? Just as Drucker was professionalizing management as a practice and a profession in the mid-twentieth century, the leadership debate was just getting underway. Drucker was suspicious of the sudden fascination with leaders for many reasons. First of all, he had experienced "effective leadership" in Nazi Germany under the charismatic rule of Adolf Hitler, whose ability to sway crowds with dynamic if wildly illogical speeches was breathtaking. Secondly, Drucker had spent considerable effort to show that good management was not about charisma or personality but rather effective, consistent practices; in his words, leadership was "more doing than dash" (Drucker, 1988/1992). Drucker believed that there were very few "natural" leaders in organizations—far too few to meet the needs of effective management for functioning institutions. But he always recognized that leadership was a component of the work of management. For Drucker, leadership was not about personality traits or characteristics but rather abilities and practices and—ultimately—character:

DOI: 10.4324/9781003410485-5

For it is through character that leadership is exercised; it is character that sets the example and is imitated. Character is not something managers can acquire; if they do not bring it to the job, they will never have it.

(Drucker and Maciariello, 2008, p. 286)

Ultimately, Drucker folded leadership into his larger project of a functioning society that balanced change with continuity. Leadership was not just about the individual but about the organization as a part of society. It was the responsibility of all organizations (and their members) to be change leaders in order to cope with the realities of increasing uncertainty. This is a timely message for leaders of all kinds today.

The Dangers of Charisma

Sociologist Max Weber first discussed the role of charismatic leadership and authority in his treatise, "Politics as a Vocation." Weber defines charisma as

the authority of the extraordinary and personal gift of grace (charisma), the absolutely personal devotion and personal confidence in revelation, heroism, or other qualities of individual leadership. This is 'charismatic' domination, as exercised by the prophet or in the field of politics by the elected war lord, the plebiscitarian ruler, the great demagogue, or the political party leader.

(Weber, 1918/1946)

Weber expresses concern that the emotional nature of the political message will result in a dangerous trend in politics.

Drucker's concern with charismatic leadership stemmed from his experience with witnessing the rise of Hitler in 1930s Germany. In 1931, Drucker was promoted to senior editor of the *Frankfurter General-Anzeiger*, one of Germany's leading daily papers. As part of his work, he covered political speeches, including those of Nazi party officials. Drucker recalls the nonsensical propaganda of one agitator's speech, shouting "We don't want lower bread prices, we don't want higher bread prices, we don't want unchanged bread prices—we want National Socialist bread prices" to a cheering throng of supporters (Drucker, 2005). In the 1990s, Drucker reminisced about how German society had been so blind to Hitler's charisma:

Looking back, it is simply unimaginable how deaf and blind people were. I had read Hitler's *Mein Kampf* and I had heard him speak. And there was no doubt that he meant every single thing that he said. But everyone was saying, "He couldn't have meant that seriously, such ridiculous things." First of all, the arrogance. Here was this lance corporal who hadn't even finished upper secondary school. There was no way he could become anybody. "And if he does, we can control him." I remember a long discussion I had with a leading conservative politician…That must have been in the middle of 1932. And he was completely convinced that such a vulgar proletarian, that anyone of noble birth could wrap him around their finger. And I asked, "Have you actually listened to him?" He nearly threw me out. He said "What! I should listen to such riff raff? How dare you!" That's very hard to imagine in retrospect.

(Brem, 1999)

Drucker recognized the appeal of Hitler's form of propaganda (and his peculiar ability to persuade people through his charisma) to a people desperate for miracles.

In an era when people thought that charisma was an important quality of leaders, Drucker argued that leadership was not about personal magnetism, but about how one used one's abilities. What was the goal of leading people? To what end was leadership being used? Drucker often referred to the trio of charismatic leaders in his era—Hitler, Stalin, and Mao—as "misleaders" who, while effective at leading masses of people, caused enormous damage to human beings: "History knows no more charismatic leaders than this century's triad of Stalin, Hitler, and Mao—the misleaders who inflicted as much evil and suffering on humanity as have ever been recorded" (Drucker, 1988/1992, p. 119). Drucker points out that charisma can lead people to be inflexible, unwilling to acknowledge and recognize their mistakes, and incapable of change. Such leaders can develop blind spots that eventually become their undoing, as they are convinced of their own invincibility (Drucker and Maciariello, 2008).

Some of most effective leaders were not charismatic, argued Drucker. He uses examples from history to make his case, stating that Dwight Eisenhower, George Marshall, and Harry Truman were effective leaders, but had less charisma than a "dead mackerel." Drucker also points to Abraham Lincoln as an uncharismatic leader who nevertheless accomplished much. Finally, Winston Churchill before World War II was "bitter, defeated, almost broken" yet saved Britain and Europe from Hitler (Drucker and Maciariello, 2008, p. 289).

Over and over, Drucker cautions against looking for specific leadership "traits" or "qualities," stating that none of history's effective leaders shared a given set of attributes. Rather, they were effective because of their adherence to mission and objective, and their ability to implement and execute.

Avoid the Demagogue or the Organizational Dictator

Clearly, Drucker's concern with charismatic leadership was based on his experience with fascism in Europe. Yet, this concern carried over to leadership and authority in organizations as he began to study these topics in new institutions—first corporations and then the pluralistic institutions of society. Drucker did address leadership early in his career. He works through an idea of leadership as he applies his social theory to his analysis of General Motors in the book that launched his management consulting career, *Concept of the Corporation* (1946). He lays out the case that managerial authority must needs be reliant on more than a single, capable authoritarian. When inevitably that dictator weakens, if there is no succession plan of capable individuals ready to step in, intrigue ensues, as those waiting in the wings calculate their best chances to "seize the throne." If the organization adopts the philosophy that only a "genius" is capable of leading, then, when no other brilliant individual surfaces, there will be a fight to replace the "indispensable" leader (Drucker, 1946, pp. 26–27). In politics, the charismatic leader becomes the demagogue who wreaks havoc on society, believing that they are the only ones who can offer solutions. In organizations, the lack of a group of well-trained, if not necessarily "brilliant," successors ensures a version of *Game of Thrones*.

Drucker insightfully predicted the shortage of leadership and management talent that would be needed by organizations. If corporations continued to rely on the "brilliant man" theory of executive leadership, there simply would not be enough people to lead. What was needed was a way to train and produce effective leaders (Drucker would turn to calling them "managers" or "executives" for the next several decades). His project of professionalizing management, of making it a practice that could be taught and learned by average human beings, was driven by this belief in the need for competent leadership by ordinary people—not just gifted, brilliant charismatic orators.

"A Pox on Charisma"

Leadership scholar Jean Lipman-Blumen, a colleague of Drucker's at Claremont Graduate University, notes that not only was Drucker concerned about the misuse of charisma in leadership, he denied the concept of leadership for years. She states that, for most of her tenure at the Drucker/ Ito Graduate School of Management, Drucker said that he didn't believe in leadership, as he viewed it as a fad that cast a "long shadow" on field of management as worthy of respect (Lipman-Blumen, 2010, p. 150). Bill Cohen, Franco Gandolfi, and others have postulated that Drucker's fear of the term "leadership" derives from the German use of the term "fuhrer" under Hitler's reign; Hitler's insistence on being called "the leader" (Der Fuhrer) may possibly have influenced Drucker's attitude about that term

(Cohen, 2009; Gandolfi, 2022). At any rate, as Lipman-Blumen points out, Drucker began to acknowledge the growing literature on leadership.

Theories of Charismatic Leadership

In 1978, John MacGregor Burns published *Leadership*, in which he contrasted two styles of management: transactional and transformational. In many ways, Burns' description of transformational leadership echoed what Drucker referred to as "the spirit of performance" (discussed later in this chapter). Transactional leadership envisions a leader-follower relationship as involving discrete exchanges based on the self-interest of the two parties in a *quid pro quo* arrangement. Transformational leadership involves alignment with higher motivations and goals rather than mere exchanges that are mutually beneficial. Transformational leadership recognizes that people can be motivated by purposes larger than their own self-interest. In his description of what leadership is not, Burns captures the negative aspects of so-called charismatic leaders:

> Many acts heralded or bemoaned as instances of leadership—acts of oratory, manipulation, sheer self advancement, brute coercion—are not such. Much of what commonly passes as leadership—conspicuous position-taking without followers or follow through, posturing on various public stages, manipulation without general purpose, authoritarianism— is no more leadership than the behavior of small boys marching in front of a parade, who continue to strut along Main Street after the procession has turned down a side street toward the fairgrounds...The test of their leadership function is their contribution to change, measured by purpose, drawn from collective motives and values.
>
> *(Burns, 1978, p. 427)*

Bernard Bass analyzed the ways in which transformational leaders function. He argued that charisma was a component of transformational leadership, but that it did not always lead to positive results. Without an alignment with a larger moral purpose, charisma could be a negative trait (Bass and Riggio, 2006). This was part of a larger discussion developing around the idea of whether leadership was based on a set of traits that needed to be identified (character traits) or whether leaders could be developed through training (Bennis and Nanus, 1985; Collins, 2001). More recently, a veritable cottage industry of leadership assessment programs has sprung up, including the Leader Character Insight Assessment (LCIA) tool (Crossan, Furlong, and Austin, 2023). At any rate, the question of leadership charisma remains: is it effective in some organizations or situations? What exactly constitutes effective leadership? The conversation that began long before Drucker, when Aristotle, Plato, and Machiavelli evaluated the nature of power and governance, has continued well into the modern era. The matter of charisma remains a concern.

Leadership vs. Management

Historically, there has been a back-and-forth discussion/debate as to whether or not there is a difference between leadership and management. In 1977, Harvard Business School professor Abraham Zaleznik argued that traditional definitions of management did not embrace needed qualities of leadership, which included inspiration, vision, and passion. Managers respected stability and control, order and predictability, while leaders welcomed chaos and flexibility toward schedules in order to take into account creativity (Zaleznik, 1977). John Kotter published his book, *A Force for Change: How Leadership Differs from Management,* in 1990. While Kotter eschews the model of the charismatic leader, he, like Zaleznik, perpetuates the idea that management is a conserving function, focusing on maintaining the status quo and avoiding risk in order to prevent surprises in the day-to-day operations of an organization. Leadership, in contrast, is all about embracing change and risk as normal parts of the life of an organization. Leaders are forward-oriented and inspire people to align with a mission. Kotter, however, makes the case that both leaders and managers are crucial to an institution's success (Kotter, 1990). Warren Bennis focused on the activities of managers vs. leaders rather than their mindsets. In his pioneering work, *On Becoming a Leader*, Bennis differentiates leadership and management as follows:

- The manager administers; the leader innovates.
- The manager maintains; the leader develops.
- The manager focuses on systems and structure; the leader focuses on people (Bennis, 1989).

Drucker's Evolution on Leadership

As discussed above, Drucker wrote about leadership as early as his study of General Motors, *Concept of the Corporation*. In his early work, we can see the tension between the idea of management as a professional, administrative function, and leadership as a motivational force. Before the leadership vs. management controversy began brewing in the 1980s, Drucker was trying to reconcile these two aspects of organizational governance. As the literature evolved, his language began to change, and Drucker, for a while, wavered between using "manager," "executive," and "leader" in his writings.

The leaders in Drucker's *Concept of the Corporation* come from the ranks of ordinary men; they are not "geniuses" or "indispensable" individuals, but rather people who need to be developed through exposure to leading others and learning from mistakes. By the 1950s, however, Drucker was rethinking the idea of leadership; he still referred to the process of making common people into uncommon ones, but managers began to take precedence over leaders as he codified his work on the subject. Leadership was important, but it could not be created, promoted, taught or learned. Leadership requires attitudes and aptitudes; aptitudes either exist or they don't, and attitudes are very difficult to change (not to mention the ethical question of whether it is right to manipulate someone else's personality). Management, however, can "create the conditions under which potential leadership qualities become effective" (Drucker, 1954, p. 159). The practice of management, carried out properly, allows for leadership to emerge. And practices can be replicated by anyone regardless of their aptitudes or attitudes.

In this sense, Drucker began to move away from "leadership" toward "management" as the key to keeping organizations functioning and providing the proper motivational spirit.

As the knowledge society replaced the post-World War II industrial manufacturing economy (see Chapter 5), Drucker began to use the term "executive" rather than manager to reflect the changing nature of work and reporting relationships. Increasingly, people engaged in knowledge work are self-directed and self-managed; they may have authority over others, and someone has authority over them and their decisions/activities, but the concept of a "supervisor" or "manager" began to be less clear. Drucker began to explore the idea of self leadership in *The Effective Executive* (1966). In the old manufacturing society, few leaders were needed; they may have been wrong and ineffective in many cases, but they delivered orders that were followed. The same was true for the military and other command-and-control models of leadership. In the knowledge society, such models of leadership were ineffective, as "supervisors" often had no training in their subordinates' areas of expertise. In a society where individuals were increasingly executives (even if they managed only themselves or a handful of people), models of management and leadership were changing (see Chapters 3 and 5). It is not surprising to see Drucker's language change as well.

Management and leadership for Drucker were interchangeable by the late 1980s and early 1990s. Leadership was work, focusing on and communicating the organization's goals and mission: "The leader's first task is to be the trumpet that sounds a clear sound" (Drucker, 1988/1992, p. 121). Leaders also focus on responsibility rather than rank and privilege and seek strength in subordinates and associates. Most important is the role of trust: "whether he holds fast to a few basic standards (exemplifying them in his own conduct), or whether 'standards' for him are what he can get away with, determines whether the leader has followers or only hypocritical time-servers" (Drucker, 1988/1992, p. 121). For Drucker, there is nothing to effective leadership that involves cleverness, personality, charm or persuasion. It is based on consistency and mundane, yet ethical and reliable, practices. As Drucker relates a conversation he had with a human resources executive about the key to effective leadership, her response was: " 'But that's no different at all from what we have known for years are the requirements for being an effective manager.' " Drucker's retort? "Precisely" (Drucker, 1988/1992, p. 123).

Social Leadership

Yet, Drucker did acknowledge that, like it or not, managers were perceived by the public as society's leaders. He began to recognize the class divisions created by the new knowledge society, where educational status marked a divide between the "ruling elite" of the knowledge workers and the waning status and power of the manual worker (see Chapter 5). In this sense, leadership became increasingly important to Drucker; while the activities of leaders within organizations may not necessarily change from organization to organization, their societal position represented a seismic shift.

In the late 1980s, Drucker noted that prior to this era, businesspeople in Western Europe, Japan, and the United States were treated as second-class members of society, tainted by their association with commerce and capitalism. Leaders came from the learned elite, primarily the political elite. By the 1980s, executives were revered as society's leadership. Yet, Drucker points out, the capitalists of the late twentieth century had neither the wealth nor the power of the titans of industry of 1900. J.P. Morgan and Alfred Krupp were instantly recognizable; the CEOs of the late twentieth century were faceless, nameless individuals. Yet, they were perceived as the leadership of society: "however short-lived, illogical, irrational, even undesirable it may be, it is a fact that business and business people are perceived as the leadership group in today's developed countries" (Drucker, 1987/1992, p. 116). One can sense Drucker's amazement and dismay at the fact that corporate executives had become the role models for leadership in modern society. Because this change had already happened, he called for an increased emphasis on not just the functions of management, but the attributes of the manager. We see increasing concern with executive behavior and how it mirrors values. Not only does this impact the public's perception of leadership and integrity, but it also influences the role of leaders in organizations. Drucker often used the old saying, "The higher up the monkey goes, the more of his behind he shows" to refer to the need for executive integrity at the top of any organization: "nothing is noticed more quickly—and considered more significant—than a discrepancy between what executives preach and what they expect their associates to practice" (Drucker, 1987/1992, p. 116).

Morality, Virtue, and Ethics

The more Drucker viewed business as one of many representative organizations in a society of pluralist institutions, the more he emphasized the importance of morality, virtue, and ethics in management leadership. Virtue was a component of his social philosophy from the beginning (see Chapter 2), but its application to the practice of management became increasingly visible in his work as he recognized the fact that businesspeople were perceived as leaders in society. Writing in 1981, Drucker confronted the growing interest in teaching "business ethics" in management programs. He argued that there was no such thing as a separate set of ethics or values for businesspeople; rather, they were guided by the same set of principles that governed behavior in any organization in society. These include a clear definition of relationships, rules for conduct according to those relationships, and a focus on right behavior rather than behavior to be avoided. Most of all, managers and professionals must practice behavior that would make them the kind of person they "would want to see in the mirror in the morning" (Drucker, 1981/1993, p. 214). Beginning with his earliest books on management, Drucker emphasized the importance of integrity in management (Drucker, 1954). He would eventually refer to integrity as "the touchstone" of management, something inherent in a person's character that one either has or doesn't have. Ultimately, a lack of integrity disqualified a person from being a manager, much less a leader (Drucker, 1973/1974).

The Spirit of Performance

Drucker's notion of "spirit of performance" was part of his vision of what true leadership involved. Early on, he wrote that institutions that were successful and durable were capable of spurning "an intellectual and moral growth beyond a man's original capacities." Pointing to the Catholic Church and the Prussian Army, Drucker remarks that effective leadership in organizations of any kind involves motivating and organizing people for common effort, but also providing the environment for people to achieve "moral victory" over themselves (Drucker, 1942, p. 28). In other words, leaders instill in others the ability to be more than they would otherwise be on their own. This can appear to be a patronizing attitude, but Drucker's point is that ordinary human beings can, in fact, achieve extraordinary things if given the opportunity and led effectively.

By the 1950s, Drucker still heralded the leader as an important source of spirit in organizations, but not the sole driving factor. As we have seen, managers had replaced leaders as the primary force behind organizational energy. Leaders were too few and far between to be relied upon solely to create the spirit of an organization. Rather, "Management must work on creating the spirit by other means. These means may be less effective and more pedestrian. But at least they are available and within management's control" (Drucker, 1954, p. 159). This is a much more pragmatic view of creating an environment for individual and organizational growth and success; rather than relying on a small group of trained and talented leaders, average people without particular aptitude or affinity for leadership can also help to create an environment where individuals can achieve "moral victory" over themselves and work together to achieve communal goals. One wonders perhaps if Drucker's experience as a management consultant led him to temper his earlier belief that ordinary people could learn to be leaders. Eventually, the "spirit of the organization" gave way to the "spirit of performance." True leadership, based on the practice of management on a day-to-day basis, was grounded in performance. Ultimately, leadership involved doing, not inspiring. While this fits with Drucker's' consistent mantra that leadership is not about personality, wit, or charm, there is a much more pragmatic tone in his discussions of "spirit" in his later writing (Drucker, 1973/1974).

Acceptance

Jean Lipman-Blumen, an authority on the subject of leadership, worked closely with Drucker, and had the opportunity to observe his transformation over time. She remarks that, while he denied the concept for years, "in the last decade of his life, Peter Drucker began—perhaps somewhat ruefully—to acknowledge books on leadership. Even then, however, he remained lukewarm to charisma and focused, instead, on the foundational issues of character, performance, results, and responsibility" (Lipman-Blumen, 2010, pp. 150–151). Lipman-Blumen is spot on in her description of Drucker's acceptance of leadership as a concept. Drucker had recognized the fact that societal leadership was changing but had to come to grips with the fact that this meant that organizations needed to train managers as leaders, not just managers. True to form, Drucker stuck to his guns and continued his emphasis on "character, performance, results, and responsibility" rather than on identifying and developing specific leadership traits or qualities.

Leadership is a Foul-Weather Job

In *Managing the Non-Profit Organization*, Drucker devotes an entire chapter to the topic of leadership, calling it a "foul-weather job." By this point in his career, he turned his attention to the social sector as the source of status and function for individuals. Drucker had published *Innovation and Entrepreneurship* a few years earlier and had developed the viewpoint that all organizations needed to innovate and adapt to change (see Chapter 6). In "Leadership is a Foul-Weather Job," Drucker describes the importance of crisis leadership; leaders must anticipate a crisis and have a battle-tested team built on mutual trust. Importantly, he takes the position that leaders are neither born nor made—they are self-made (Drucker, 1990, p. 21). Again, the role of integrity and character are crucial; the crisis leader should be someone on whom others can model themselves, and someone who is "we" focused rather than "I" centered: "The task matters, and you are a servant" (Drucker, 1990, p, 27). Here, Drucker echoes the work of former AT&T executive Robert Greenleaf, who published *Servant Leadership* in 1977. Greenleaf advocated that effective leaders should take the position as servants to their followers rather than function as authoritarian order-givers. As Drucker stated, the concept was driven by the belief that the task or mission at hand was more important than the leader themselves. Drucker and Greenleaf were friends for many years before Greenleaf wrote his book, and Drucker penned the foreword to a publication of Greenleaf's writings after his passing in 1990 (*On becoming a servant leader: The private writings of Robert K. Greenleaf*).

The Change Leader

In one of his last publications, Drucker devotes a chapter to the topic of change leadership. In this work, he presents change leadership as an organizational challenge, not just the job of an individual. Here, Drucker takes the tension between the individual and the collective to a new level. Mirroring servant leadership, Drucker's leader is not focused on "me," but on "we": the task or the organizational needs (the mission). Now, organizations themselves must elevate beyond a mission-only focus and think about looking ahead: "One cannot *manage* change. One can only be ahead of it…It is therefore a central twenty-first century challenge for management that its organization become a change leader" (Drucker, 1999, p. 73). In other words, leadership is not merely embodied in an individual manager or executive; the entire institution must be infused with a new kind of spirit: the spirit of leading change. In spite of this, the organization has to have a "personality" that shows some level of predictability, comprehension, and fixed values in spite of change (Drucker, 1999, p. 90). The theme of a balance between continuity and change, which is integral to all of Drucker's work, is now part of organizational leadership in society; "we" as an organization are part of a larger "we" of society. Drucker has moved from leadership being exhibited through the daily practices of management professionals to the way an entire organization responds to the realities of change—and the need for some degree of continuity and consistency.

Conclusion

We seem to have made little progress in understanding leadership since Drucker was alive and writing on management (and, later, leadership). There is a plethora of scholarship on the subject, but do we really understand what makes a leader? Or what constitutes good leadership? Practitioners and scholars continue to debate whether leadership is a matter of traits or characteristics that can be assessed, quantified, and developed, whether leadership is a set of practices, or whether leadership is a mindset. In fact, the definition of leadership itself is up for debate. Is it culturally defined? Is there a gender component? How do we identify toxic leaders? Do certain situations call for different leadership abilities? There is, frankly, too much speculation on the subject and little substance.

In the vast array of work on leadership, Drucker's contribution is simple and can be boiled down to a few takeaways:

- Leadership is about behavior and actions, not personality.
- Historically, effective leaders have not shared any common personality traits, viewpoints, backgrounds, or other recognizable commonalities.
- Leadership is a component of competent management; not everyone can be a leader, but managers need to be part of the leadership group.
- Character, primarily integrity, is crucial to leadership; people will forgive almost any other omission from a leader, but not the lack of integrity (nor will they forgive an organization for promoting or retaining a person without integrity).
- Trust is the key to leaders having followers.
- Organizations as a whole have to exhibit change leadership in the 21st society; leadership is not on the individual level but on the organizational level.

Bibliography

Bass, B. and Riggio, R.E. (2006) *Transformational leadership*. Mahwah, NJ: Lawrence Erlbaum Associates.

Bennis, W. (1989) *On becoming a leader*. Reading, MA: Addison-Wesley.

Bennis, W. and Nanus, B. (1985) *Leaders: Strategies for taking charge*. New York: Harper & Row.

Brem, R. (1999) 'Interview with Peter F. Drucker', conducted September 1999.

Burns, J.M. (1978) *Leadership*. New York: Harper & Row.

Cohen, W.A. (2009) *Drucker on leadership*. New York: John Wiley & Sons.

Collins, J. (2001) 'Level 5 leadership: The triumph of humility and fierce resolve', *Harvard Business Review*, 79, pp. 67–76.

Crossan, M., Furlong, W., and Austin, R.D. (2023) 'Make leader character your competitive edge', *MIT Sloan Management Review*, 64 (2). https://sloanreview.mit.edu/article/make-leader-character-your-competitive-edge/

Drucker, P.F. (1942) *The future of industrial man*. New Brunswick, NJ: Transaction.

Drucker, P.F. (1946) *Concept of the corporation*. New York: John Day.

Drucker, P.F. (1954) *The practice of management*. New York: Harper & Row.

Drucker, P.F. (1966) *The effective executive*. New York: Harper & Row.

Drucker, P.F. (1973/1974) *Management: Tasks, responsibilities, practices.* New York: Harper & Row.

Drucker, P.F. (1981) 'Can there be "business ethics"?', originally published in *The Public Interest*, reprinted in Drucker, P.F. (1993) *The Ecological Vision.* New Brunswick, NJ: Transaction, pp. 195–214.

Drucker, P.F. (1987) 'The mystique of the business leader', *Wall Street Journal.* Reprinted in Drucker, P.F. (1992) *Managing for the future: The 1990s and beyond.* New York: Truman Talley Books/Dutton, pp. 113–117.

Drucker, P.F. (1988) 'Leadership: More doing than dash', *Wall Street Journal*, 6 January, p. 14. Reprinted in Drucker, P.F. (1992) *Managing for the future: The 1990s and beyond.* New York: Truman Talley Books/Dutton, pp. 119–123.

Drucker, P.F. (1990) *Managing the non-profit organization: Principles and practices.* New York: Harper Collins.

Drucker, P.F. (1992) *Managing for the future: The 1990s and beyond.* New York: Truman Talley Books/Dutton, pp. 113–117.

Drucker, P.F. (1999) *Management challenges for the 21st century.* New York: Harper Collins.

Drucker, P.F. (2005) *My personal history.* Tokyo: Nihon Keizai Shimbun. English translation of interviews by Makino, Y. (2009), Drucker Archives, Claremont, CA.

Drucker, P.F. and Maciariello, J.A. (2008) *Management: Revised edition.* New York: Harper Collins Publishers.

Frick, D. and Spears, L., eds. (1996) *On becoming a servant leader: The private writings of Robert K. Greenleaf.* San Francisco, CA: Jossey-Bass.

Gandolfi, F. (2022) Personal conversation with author, 27 September.

Kotter, J. (1990) *A force for change: How leadership differs from management.* New York: Free Press.

Lipman-Blumen, J. (2010) 'A pox on charisma: Why connective leadership and character count', in Pearce, C., Maciariello, J., and Yamawaki, H. (eds.), *The Drucker difference: What the world's greatest management thinker means to today's business leaders.* New York: McGraw Hill, pp. 149–174.

Maciariello, J.A. (2006) 'Peter F. Drucker on executive leadership and effectiveness', in Hesselbein, F. and Goldsmith, M. (eds.), *The leader of the future 2: Visions, strategies and practices for the new era.* San Francisco, CA: Jossey-Bass/Wiley, pp. 3–27.

Weber, M. (1918) 'Politics as a vocation', in Gerth, H.H. (trans.) and Mills, C.W. (ed.) (1946) *From Max Weber: Essays in sociology.* New York: Oxford University Press, pp. 77–128.

Zaleznik, A. (1977) 'Managers and leaders: Are they different?', *Harvard Business Review*, 55 (1), pp. 74–81.

5
DRUCKER AND THE KNOWLEDGE SOCIETY

Introduction

Drucker's work on knowledge is probably some of his most profound and prescient. He approached the topic from many different directions, looking at the changing nature of knowledge itself and its ability to change society for better or worse. He also closely analyzed the changing role of knowledge in society and its impact on work, workers, and social problems. While Drucker is well-known for coining the term "knowledge work," his own writing and thinking on the subject of knowledge is much more broad and far-ranging.

Defining Knowledge

Drucker's writing on knowledge spanned from the 1950s to the late 1990s. In those six decades, the nature of knowledge changed exponentially. Developments in science and technology accelerated, as did the ability to share knowledge, breaking barriers based on geography, space, and time. Whereas radio broadcasts had been the primary source of information in the early years of the twentieth century, in the 1950s, television began to be widely adopted in western countries, followed by other nations in the late 1950s and 1960s. In the early 1990s, internet access became available to more affluent nations, and by the end of the decade was widely accessible, although with varying degrees of quality. By 1999, BlackBerry and other smart phones were available, allowing even more rapid and free exchange of information. Drucker died in 2005, just as the explosion of smart phones was beginning, so his definition of "knowledge" and humanity's access to it is rooted firmly in his twentieth-century life. Even so, the definitions of

DOI: 10.4324/9781003410485-6

knowledge that Drucker provides in a dated context allow us to contemplate the ethical and moral dilemmas posed by the rapid nature of change in our society with respect to data, information, and, ultimately, knowledge.

New World View

Drucker began to consider the definition of knowledge in the late 1950s Cold War Era. In his social writing, he began to ponder the concept of a "post-modern" world requiring a new perspective. In *Landmarks of Tomorrow* (1957), Drucker begins the book with a discussion of the shift from a Cartesian view of the world to one that is distinctly different. Until this new, post-modern era, Drucker states that the prevailing view of the world was driven by reliance on observation, evidence, and the belief in certainty. Events could be understood directly by their causes, quantitative logic, and measurements of observed reality. The post-modern world of the mid-twentieth century required a new world view, one that valued integration, culture, forms, processes, and patterns, and understood that not everything was predictable, measurable, identifiable, or knowable—at least not in the moment. Drucker referred to this shift as a movement "from cause to configuration" (Drucker, 1957, p. 4). The mechanistic world of stasis, of unchanging cause and effect, gave way to one of random events, where growth and change are constant. In this world, knowledge was not a static body of information that could be collected into a complete and finished work, but rather a constantly changing, seemingly disjointed collection of informational shards that required continuous effort to process into a cohesive whole (see discussion of Drucker's holism and influences in Chapter 2). Drucker's use of the term "post-modern" in 1957 predates what is known as "postmodernism." Postmodernism was a sentiment expressed in art, literature, music, criticism, and other aspects of culture, primarily in the West. It was, as the term implies, a direct reaction to modernism, a critique of any attempt to form a coherent narrative or any expression of faith in progress. Post-modern literature, for example, shunned the possibility of a single narrative of any event, taking the position that truth could be perceived differently by different agents. Drucker's characterization of this new post-World War II world as embodied by configuration rather than cause foreshadows this cultural approach.

Knowledge and Power

Drucker finishes *Landmarks of Tomorrow* with a discussion of the nature of knowledge and its relationship to power. The book is concerned with topics that might seem relevant to an audience today: economic inequality, the impact of technology on society, the role of education in the work force, government dysfunction. Much of what Drucker has to say is powerful. But his final chapter on "The Human Situation Today" is a Cold War plea to understand that the post-modern world of his era is a very dangerous one. It is a dated plea, but it nevertheless contains a timeless message.

Drucker asserts that the definitions of knowledge and power have changed with respect to human beings:

> Twentieth-century man has achieved the knowledge to destroy himself both physically and morally. This new absolute has added a new dimension to human existence. There is no danger that man will ever run out of ignorance; on the contrary, the more we know, the more we realize how little we know—in all areas of knowledge, in all sciences and all arts. Yet the knowledge we have acquired is absolute knowledge giving absolute power. There may well be even more "absolute" weapons of destruction than those we already possess. But there is no going beyond total, final extinction; and that we can already inflict on ourselves...Now we can, in a few seconds of mania, make the whole earth unlivable for all of us...At the same time we are acquiring what is perhaps even more potent—and certainly even less controlled—knowledge: the knowledge to destroy man psychologically and morally by destroying his personality.
>
> *(Drucker, 1957, p. 258)*

The language is powerful, and redefines knowledge in a negative, perhaps evil way.

Drucker's world of the late 1950s was one that experienced the real threat of nuclear war. The Pacific front of World War II ended when the United States dropped two atomic bombs on Japan; whether that action ultimately saved lives on both sides by ending the war is a subject of debate, but there is no question that United States' decision unleashed the reality of nuclear weapons into the world. By the time of the Eisenhower administration in 1953, the Korean War was over, but the United States was concerned about containing Soviet influence in the world after Stalin's era. Eisenhower's administration pursued a strategy of nuclear arms build up to project American military strength and serve as a deterrent. The weapons were costly but perceived as less expensive than a long ground war involving troops on foreign soil.

Another area of weaponry considered was psychological manipulation or propaganda. The Nazis, under Joseph Goebbels, had mastered the art of propaganda, using antisemitic images and slogans to solidify public support. In the United States, the psychological community was involved in a heated debate about the nature of human behavior. Carl Rogers, of the University of Chicago, and B.F. Skinner of Harvard, engaged in a conversation about the control of human behavior, captured in a 1956 article in *Science* Magazine. Rogers advocated that human beings are capable of controlling their own behavior through free will and are motivated intrinsically; his humanistic approach emphasized people's ability to change and control their own destinies. In contrast, Skinner's behavioral model viewed human beings as entities that respond to environmental stimuli; behavior can be explained by external, not internal factors. As a result, people could be motivated to feel certain emotions and change behavior through operant conditioning—rewards and punishments (Rogers and Skinner, 1956). This new area of psychological research was of interest to the U.S. military because of its implications for control; the lessons of Nazi propaganda could potentially be used for more positive goals.

Drucker translates this reality into a discussion of the relationship between knowledge and power. His previous experience with witnessing the rise of fascism in Europe made him particularly sensitive to abuses of knowledge in the service of power. At his essence, Drucker sought to preserve a tolerable society where people could find meaning as individuals and also have a sense of belonging to something greater than themselves. In his new world of the late 1950s, knowledge was a bludgeon used against the individual both in terms of individual existence (psychological manipulation) and social existence (nuclear threat). It is no wonder that Drucker called for guard rails on governmental powers that had such destructive potential:

> We need law to deny all government the use of the new powers. Such law must be based on the commitment of large and strong political bodies which, in turn, requires a multiplicity of large nations, each strong enough to have a policy, each united enough to be free at home, each big enough to count. But the task also requires true international institutions embodying the common belief that no government can be allowed to exercise the powers of physical and moral destruction of man.
>
> *(Drucker, 1957, pp. 262–263)*

How enlightening to read Drucker as the champion of institutional checks on governmental power but as an advocate for "large and strong political bodies." Drucker was highly suspicious of governmental power (see Chapter 7), but it is interesting to see him recognize the need for international regulation of knowledge and its impact on humanity. His observations are eerily relevant to modern concerns with Artificial Intelligence and related technologies and their ethical, psychological, and cultural effects on society (see Chapter 8).

Knowledge as Work

Some ten years later, Drucker began to think about knowledge in a more pragmatic context. Rather than in geopolitical terms, how did knowledge work in society? How could the societal disruptions of the late 1960s, which threatened his idea of a functioning society of institutions, benefit from a rethinking of the concept of knowledge? In *The Age of Discontinuity* (1968), Drucker asserts that the developed world has moved from a society of industry to a society of knowledge. And, therefore, knowledge must be redefined in this new world. Knowledge is no longer the domain of the intellectual:

> For the intellectual, knowledge is what is in a book. But as long as it is in the book, it is only "information" if not mere "data." Only when a man applies the information to doing something does it become knowledge. Knowledge, like electricity or money, is a form of energy that exists only when doing work.
>
> *(Drucker, 1968, p. 269)*

It is not surprising that Drucker defines knowledge in terms of "work." He had framed management as "work" in his texts on that subject, and had, by the 1960s, begun to focus on the nuts and bolts of how knowledge was changing the nature of his functioning society of organizations.

As knowledge had increasing impact on society, Drucker commented that the value of knowledge might come into question. Historically, all knowledge was considered valuable; in the modern era, where knowledge became associated with power, different types of knowledge were viewed with value judgments. Were some kinds of knowledge more valuable? More useful? More dangerous? Because knowledge plays such a central role in society, the economy, and culture, it conveys enormous responsibility. Those with knowledge are no longer relegated to the ivory towers of academia; they are society's leaders. Knowledge provides access to opportunity; thus, those who possess knowledge must be held to a "high code of morality" (Drucker, 1968, p. 373).

Additionally, the nature of knowledge needed to be broad and multidisciplinary. While knowledge professionals may be highly specialized in their own disciplines and fields, they still need to be able to speak to one another, to understand the values of knowledge that lies outside their areas of expertise. Non-engineers and scientists need to understand technology, and those in the technical professions also need to value the humanities, political theory, economics, and the behavioral sciences, among other disciplines. The increasing silo mentality of knowledge presented a barrier to problem solving and managing organizations, activities that required an appreciation of multiple fields and disciplines without having to become a specialist in every area (Drucker, 1968, 1989). Drucker would later refer to the shift from "knowledge" to "knowledges" (Drucker, 1993); as knowledge necessarily becomes more and more specialized, it must also convert into meaningful action. Individual disciplinary specialists still needed to connect individual knowledges to the needs of the larger society.

Drucker would continually return to this theme of the need for a multidisciplinary approach to problem solving in a functioning society. An appreciation of knowledge of different kinds allows for an understanding of the complex nature of situations facing organizations and their constituencies, their stakeholders, and the concerns of society as a whole. Drucker was an early proponent of cross-disciplinary and interdisciplinary research, arguing that continuing specialized research within each discipline created not knowledge but merely "erudition" or "data" (Drucker, 1989, pp. 251–252). For Drucker, knowledge, ultimately, is "information that changes something or somebody—either by becoming grounds for action, or by making an individual (or an institution) capable of different and more effective action" (Drucker, 1989, p. 251).

Manual Work to Knowledge Work

Drucker's early work on institutions focused on industrial organizations. In *The Future of Industrial Man* (1942), he established the framework for a functioning industrial society in which manufacturing organizations would provide not just economic but social and individual meaning (see Chapter 2). By 1950, Drucker envisioned a new society of self-governing plant communities that would provide citizenship for workers and a framework for more effective management-labor relations (Drucker, 1950). Technological changes, such as automation, presented challenges to skilled workers, but retraining programs and changed attitudes about the nature of work would allow industrial workers to advance and retain their positions in society (Drucker, 1955). But just as Drucker was thinking about the changing nature of knowledge in society, he was also thinking about its dramatic impact on the nature of work. Because his earlier model of a functioning society of institutions was based on a society of industrial organizations, this shift from manual work to knowledge work represented a massive disruption in his social theory (see Chapter 2). As a result, Drucker spent a considerable amount of his career discussing the impact of the transition from skilled labor to knowledge work.

Behind Drucker's concern with this topic is the looming shadow of the Depression-era America he landed in when he came to the United States in 1939. While the nation had recovered somewhat from economic shock that began in 1929, the country had sunk back into another period of high unemployment and low economic output. Drucker wrote of "Depression shock," the psychological impact of unemployment in the 1930s that plagued industrial workers even 20 years later. His consideration of the lurking fear of losing one's source of income is quite poignant: "The 'depression shock' is by no means confined to those workers who actually were unemployed for any length of time during the Depression—by and large a minority...

Insecurity—not economic but psychological insecurity—permeates the entire industrial situation" (Drucker, 1950, p. 200). Therefore, when he began to see the shift from skilled, manual work to knowledge work, Drucker's concern was not just with societal and structural changes, but also with the human toll that such a large-scale shift would take.

The Plight of the Manual Worker

Drucker's discussions of manual workers range from sensitive to maddeningly patronizing. He views industrial workers from the perspective of history. Celebrating the advances of scientific management, Drucker claims that Frederick Taylor's ideas gave labor "productivity for the first time. It made him 'semiskilled'—but whatever skill there was, was in the design of his job; he himself needed none" (Drucker, 1968, p. 298). The manual laborer of the early twentieth century benefited from higher wages (even though, in Drucker's telling, the worker was not responsible for his increased productivity). In spite of this rather negative view of semiskilled labor, Drucker notes that socially, the industrial worker gained status, particularly during World War II, as "Rosie the Riveter" and other assembly-line workers turned out planes and other armament needed to prosecute the war effort. The manual worker became a symbol of American social cohesion and national pride (Drucker, 1968).

Early on, Drucker discusses manual workers in the context of their social position as well as managerial assumptions about their attitudes about work. Following World War II, there was much interest in how to motivate manual workers. In the 1950s, Drucker discussed the interest in measuring "job satisfaction" that was becoming the new way to try to motivate workers. Formerly, supervisors used fear (docked pay, loss of job, etc.) as motivation. But, in the new industrial society, there must be a replacement for fear. Drucker argues that job satisfaction is an inadequate measurement because it does not involve performance—it merely involves acquiescence. The proper means of motivation is responsibility (Drucker, 1954, p. 303). In this text, Drucker broaches a subject that remains a topic of debate even in contemporary literature: manual worker attitudes about work. Do workers want to take responsibility for their jobs, or do they prefer to be passive recipients of instruction? The stereotype of the blue-collar worker is that he shuns responsibility at work, and merely "works to live." Drucker says that this question is meaningless; workers must be forced to take responsibility whether they want it or not. He calls for labor to have a managerial vision (Drucker, 1954, p. 307). This places a burden on management, who must provide opportunities for leadership (Drucker, p. 309). Drawing on Taylor and scientific management, Drucker also states that manual work needs to be designed for humans, not machines (Drucker, 1954, pp. 292–293). The classic American silent movie, *Modern Times* (1936), depicts assembly-line workers as physically impacted by the repetitive work that they are required to perform at high speed. Drucker's call for worker responsibility is also a demand that management treat workers as human beings rather than cogs in a machine or sheep looking to be led (Chaplin, 1936).

As knowledge work began to replace unskilled labor, the social position of the manual worker began to return to its earlier, lower place. Drucker argued that the economic gains of the industrial worker would stick, and that union strength would likely save his job. However, the social status of blue-collar workers would continue to decline, and this is the trend that most worried Drucker:

> They can only become naysayers, timid obstacles to any change, reactionaries pining back to a "yesterday" that never was but that once looked as if it could and would be "tomorrow..." There is nothing government can do to cure the deep feeling of insecurity of the unskilled machine operator. Neither government nor management can eliminate the causes of the psychological malaise that haunts him. Participation of worker and union in management, or in profits, whatever else it might do, is irrelevant as a remedy for the real problem. Public policy can make sure, however, that the worker knows that government and management will take action to make him cope with change.
>
> *(Drucker, 1968, p. 300)*

Drucker's primary solution is a national program of continuous training, using Japan as a model, as well as Germany's commitment to industry and the Swedish concern with guaranteeing employment. While the transition from a manual economy to a knowledge economy was a global phenomenon, Drucker argued that the United States faced the greatest challenge (Drucker, 1968),

Beginning in the late 1970s, the United States began to lose manufacturing jobs at a steady pace. Between 1939 (the year Drucker came to the United States) and 1979, manufacturing employment rose steadily, with some fluctuations related to economic and business cycles. Manufacturing employment peaked in June of 1979 at 19.6 million. Following that period, jobs in manufacturing declined, overshadowed by growth in professional and business services, education, health, leisure, and hospitality. By June of 2019, manufacturers of both durable and non-durable goods lost more than one third of the jobs that existed in June of 1979 (Harris, 2020). Factors cited for the decline in manufacturing jobs include increased productivity (need for fewer workers), foreign competition, outsourcing, and increasing fixed costs (Brauer, 2008).

By the 1990s, Drucker was commenting on the shift to a knowledge society as a global phenomenon. While nearly complete in the United States, it was beginning in Japan and Europe. Thus, nearly 30 years after first broaching the topic, Drucker has adopted an even more pessimistic view of the blue-collar worker. He argues that inherent cultural attitudes and aptitudes will prevent most industrial workers from adapting to the new knowledge economy. According to Drucker, the new knowledge jobs require formal education and the ability to acquire and "apply theoretical and analytical knowledge." But perhaps more importantly, these new positions require a different mindset and a willingness to constantly learn and improve oneself. Whereas displaced farmers were able to transition to industrial jobs in the nineteenth century, this would not be possible for industrial workers in the twentieth century (Drucker, 1994, p. 62).

How has this played out? Some would argue that the rise in populist politics in many nations, including Turkey, Brazil, Germany, Britain, and the United States is a reflection of the disaffected working class in those countries. Following Drucker's earlier concern, the loss of social status, perhaps more than a loss of economic clout (or perceived loss), may have driven these workers to support authoritarian leaders who promise a return to cultural and social significance for those "ignored" or "left behind" in a global economy seemingly ruled by knowledge worker elites. The appeal of Donald Trump to rural Americans and those in the former industrial regions of the country may indicate that the social stratification Drucker feared has, in fact manifested in the United States and elsewhere.

A Knowledge Society

The changing nature of work from manual, industrial labor to knowledge work characterized the transformation to a knowledge society, a process begun in the United States in the late 1960s and, according to Drucker, complete by the 1990s, when the process would begin in Japan and Europe. The new knowledge worker posed several challenges for management, and for the workers themselves. The shift from an economic theory based on labor and capital to one based on knowledge presented the opportunity to rethink the role of human resources in organizations from both an economic and humanist perspective. The growth of knowledge work also presented several social disruptions not solely related to the nature of work. Thus, the new knowledge society of the twentieth century posed economic, management, social, philosophical, and intellectual challenges.

Post-Capitalist Society

For Drucker, the advent of a knowledge society signaled the end of the relevance of traditional economic thinking. He invoked the history of economic theory, beginning with mercantilism, which viewed the world's economy in terms of a zero-sum game of profitable trading balances; each power sought to maximize its exports through the use of government intervention, including tariffs and other barriers to imports. The classical economists in the vein of Adam Smith, emphasized the importance of free markets and trade, arguing that a lack of government intervention would benefit society through the maximization of profit. Karl Marx's economic theory contrasted to classical views, arguing that free markets were chaotic and favored capital, not labor. Labor became undervalued as a result, and increasingly was commoditized. By the mid-twentieth century, Marx's labor theory of value as well as capitalism's view of labor and capital as inputs or factors of production, were no longer valid, says Drucker:

> The old debate as to who is entitled to the fruits of increased productivity, capital or labor, can be answered simply: neither is "entitled" to anything. Neither can take credit for producing the fruits...The new industries and the technologies on which they are based are all founded on knowledge... At the same time, knowledge has become the central expenditure and investment of a modern economy. Knowledge has become the economy's central resource.
>
> *(Drucker, 1968, pp. 151–152)*

In this new, post-capitalist society, the means of production are no longer labor and capital, but knowledge.

Thus, in the post-capitalist knowledge society of the late twentieth century, labor had decreasing value (with the decline of manufacturing) and the primary capital rested in the form of pension fund assets, not wealthy individuals; Drucker would advance and develop the argument that knowledge workers had become the new owners of production in his relatively unheralded book, *The Unseen Revolution: How Pension Fund Socialism Came to America* (1976). And, as knowledge workers, educated people owned their own knowledge, which they could take from employer to employer. In this sense, they owned their own resource. The question was: how does one make such a resource productive?

Productivity

In one of the last books he wrote, Drucker devoted an entire chapter to the subject of knowledge worker productivity. In the early part of the chapter, he champions the triumph of scientific management. Taylor demystified the labor process, which had previously been seen as a craft or skill; in Drucker's words, Taylor "destroyed the romance of work" (Drucker, 1999, p. 138). By turning work into a series of routine motions, it could be replicated and taught. After World War II, scientific management led to the development of training programs that allowed for productivity advances in the United States to spread to other countries, including non-Western nations, many of whom enjoyed increased productivity with lower labor costs (and thus a manufacturing advantage in a globalizing economy). The challenge of manual worker productivity was no longer a mystery. The challenge for the twenty-first century, according to Drucker, was how to make knowledge work productive (Drucker, 1999).

Drucker argues that the reason knowledge worker productivity was such a challenge was that the factors contributing to productivity of this type of work were so different from those that led to productive manual labor. Knowledge workers are autonomous, managing themselves. While Drucker in the 1950s had made the case that labor needed to have a managerial attitude and take more responsibility, they still required supervision; knowledge workers often work with very minimal oversight. Knowledge work requires continuous innovation and learning. One might argue that, in an increasingly technological environment, this is true for manufacturing workers as well. But Drucker's point is that knowledge itself changes rapidly; while techniques and processes of manufacturing certainly change, the changing nature of knowledge by definition makes knowledge work more prone to the need for constant learning. Measuring the productivity of knowledge work involves quality, not quantity. Faculty are not evaluated in terms of how many students they teach, but how much they learn (and, perhaps, retain). Finally, Drucker makes the plea that knowledge be valued as an asset, not a cost. Whereas capital and labor were once the only factors of production, knowledge has become the primary input (Drucker, 1999, p. 142).

As Drucker considered the nature of knowledge worker productivity in a global society, he evaluated the ways in which different cultures leveraged knowledge into productive output. By the early 1990s, America was losing ground to Japan in terms of leveraging its knowledge into productive capacity; American technology was being deployed in Japan, where products American knowledge were actually made. Thus, while Japan may have lagged in terms of developing its own new knowledges, it was able to adeptly use American knowledge in a productive manner. Similar to America, Great Britain did not turn their knowledge achievement into products, services, or jobs. Germany was remarkably productive using old knowledge, but unable to turn new knowledge into wealth-generating capacity (Drucker, 1993). While Drucker's observations are dated, they do bring to mind the supply chain problems experienced during and shortly after the COVID-19 pandemic that was not only a global health threat, but wreaked enormous financial havoc and exposed the kinds of gaps in knowledge productivity that Drucker pointed out over 25 years earlier. Products are increasingly complicated and require many different kinds of knowledges and workers to produce (automobiles, smart phones, pharmaceuticals to name a few). Entire sectors and industries may rely on a handful of suppliers for key components, simply because specialization in knowledge work is required to make complex products. As a result, key components for products became scarce when border closures, plant shutdowns, and lockdowns created enormous problems with the global supply of such items as vaccine reagents, computer chips, and sensors. Relying on a few, select producers of specialty technology items has made sense from a productivity perspective, but the pandemic revealed the weaknesses in outsourcing knowledge productivity when those sources become unavailable (Shih, 2020). The topic of knowledge worker productivity has taken on a whole new meaning in the post-COVID environment. Drucker's claim that productivity is a survival requirement in a functioning society has certainly been proven true (Drucker, 1993, p. 177).

Managing Knowledge Workers

In addition to knowledge worker productivity, Drucker discusses the challenges associated with managing knowledge workers. As discussed above, the two topics are interrelated; knowledge workers' autonomy and need for continuous learning/self-development create difficulties with respect to measuring performance but also in terms of supervision. The relationship between knowledge worker and manager is that of a colleague rather than a superior and subordinate, so the traditional methods of management associated with labor no longer make sense (Drucker, 1989, p. 180). Yet, Drucker argues, knowledge workers are both dependent and independent. They need an organization in order to make their knowledge useful, and to have tools with which to do so, but they own their own means of production (the knowledge they possess (Drucker, 1993, pp. 64–65). In the late twentieth century, this was certainly true. But increasingly, knowledge workers own their own tools (portable computers, smart phones) that allow them to produce as long as they have access to the internet. Information sharing is easier than ever, and global collaboration is possible using a host of relatively inexpensive tools that can be used for and tailored to many specific needs. The portability of work and information was made even more apparent during the global pandemic, where entire sectors moved to a virtual environment (including real estate, entertainment, mental health treatment, and legal and accounting services). One global impact of the pandemic was a sharp increase in entrepreneurial activity; from 2019 to 2022, many countries saw record-breaking levels of new venture starts ('The resilient boom in entrepreneurship', 2023). With organizations shedding jobs during the pandemic, or ordering people to work from home, knowledge workers learned that they could, in fact, perhaps survive without an organization. One wonders how this newly found freedom of the knowledge worker will impact society in the long term.

Burn Out and Quiet Quitting

In Drucker's mid-twentieth-century world, knowledge workers were still employees (the world had yet to experience the wave of downsizing and 'rightsizing' of white-collar workers that began in the mid-1990s, where workers suddenly became "independent contractors"). Even so, Drucker recognized the psychological gap that existed for knowledge workers who expected personal satisfaction from their work beyond monetary compensation and social status within the organization. Knowledge workers wanted to be seen as professionals with status *outside of the organization.* As discussed below, this presents a potential divide between the educated and uneducated in a society who view work very differently. Drucker recognized this very early on. He saw the disconnect between the realities of being "an employee" in an organization with what knowledge workers expected in terms of professional and personal satisfaction. Because studies on motivation had focused on manual workers, organizations—and by extension society— was unprepared for the psychological needs of the new knowledge worker:

> Knowledge workers cannot be satisfied with work that is only a livelihood. Their aspirations and their view of themselves are those of the 'professional' or the 'intellectual.' If they respect knowledge at all, they demand that it become the base for accomplishment.
>
> *(Drucker, 1968, p. 289)*

Concerns with "quiet quitting," or the tendency for workers to disengage when they feel that they are not valued on the job, reflect Drucker's concerns about motivation and knowledge workers. According to a 2023 Gallup poll, approximately 50 percent of the U.S. workforce are not engaged at work, meaning they do the minimum amount required and are psychologically detached from their work. Younger workers are particularly susceptible, as they express feeling a lack of support and direction from management (Harter, 2023). This is not just an American phenomenon; according to Gallup, quiet quitting costs the global economy almost $9 trillion per year (Clifton, 2023). While the term is new, quiet quitting is not; Drucker clearly identified its symptoms, and it has been practiced throughout history (Johnson, 2023).

In contemplating the fate of the knowledge worker, Drucker presents a remarkably prescient awareness of what would become a commonplace concern of affluent society: burn out. Unfortunately, Drucker contrasts the knowledge worker's plight with the limited capacity of the manual worker to highlight this important issue. To some degree, he is correct in that the working life span of the manual laborer is shorter by virtue of the work being done. A roofer cannot physically maintain the stamina needed to do such demanding work beyond a certain age. A manager can continue working well beyond her seventies, assuming she remains in good mental health, because the physical demands of the work are much less. The challenge for knowledge workers, then, is to extend the interest in the work into advanced years. Drucker's era did not yet have the term "burn out," but he certainly described it to a tee:

> Yet no matter how satisfying the individual task, a good many knowledge workers tend to tire of their jobs in early middle age. Long before they reach retirement age, let alone long before they become physically and mentally disabled, the sparkle, the challenge, the excitement have gone out of their work. There is ample evidence that despite the extension of schooling, working lifespan is still too long for all but a limited number. For manual workers early retirement seems to offer a solution, as witness the eagerness with which it has been accepted in the American automobile, steel, and rubber industries despite heavy financial penalties. The manual worker does not, it seems, suffer from a 'problem of leisure.' Time does not hang heavy on his hands, even though he shows little desire for the 'cultural pursuits' that are pressed on him by the educated. He can sit in a cottage or trailer in Florida, apparently happy and busy with a small garden, occupied with fishing, hunting, and gossiping, without much desire to go back to the mill.
>
> *(Drucker, 1968, pp. 290–291)*

Drucker's contrast between the knowledge and manual worker in retirement is painful to read in its patronizing treatment of American labor. But his point is important: the nature of work, which increasingly centered around education, began to create a class division where the less educated saw work as a means to live, and the educated saw work as an integral part of their identity. As discussed below, this class divide has only increased, reinforcing Drucker's observations of the difference between manual and knowledge workers.

If knowledge workers are destined to suffer some form of burn out, they are responsible for managing themselves and taking control of their careers. As early as 1968, Drucker was calling on knowledge workers to understand that they may have to reconfigure their lives midstream, arguing for a second career phase: A second career at middle age

> is a great deal more satisfying—and fun—than the bottle, a torrid affair with a chit of a girl, the psychoanalyst's couch, or any of the other customary attempts to mask one's frustration and boredom with work that, only a few short years ago, had been exciting, challenging, and satisfying.
>
> *(Drucker, 1968, p. 296)*

The stereotypical middle-age male references to affairs, alcoholism, and stigmatized therapy date Drucker's remarks. But his point is clear: many a person (at this point in time, women are just as likely to succumb to career frustration and boredom) seeks another outlet for status and function in life and society when work ceases to provide those roles. This is a social problem that exists today just as much as it existed in Drucker's time: how do knowledge workers deal with the reality of career burn out? The answer is that "We must make it possible for the middle-aged knowledge worker to start a second knowledge career" (Drucker, 1968, p. 292). Considering that Drucker would, 20 years later, be working with non-profit organizations on how to recruit middle-aged knowledge workers as volunteers, this insight is remarkable. It also mirrors his own trajectory from a consultant to major corporations to one who favored pro-bono consultation with the social sector as more meaningful work. Drucker himself experienced his own second knowledge career of sorts as he sought to solve a problem he identified early on.

The Educated Person

As Drucker addressed the challenges of managing oneself and lifelong learning for knowledge workers, he also redefined the role of an educated person and knowledge in the new, post-industrial society. Essentially, the definition of an educated person in Drucker's early twentieth-century Europe and the definition of an educated person in industrial American society would somehow need to converge to create a new idea of learning and knowledge.

In the European tradition (and what would become the American liberal arts tradition), a learned person was one who was removed from the world of commerce and trade. The educated elite were to learn an inherited set of cultural values based on key texts (the "canon") so that they could become citizens of virtue and cultural leaders. The German university system (as designed by Humboldt) embraced the concept of *Bildung*, which is difficult to translate but generally means character formation through education. This idea of self-development and self-actualization was adopted into the British and American ideal of the "gentleman," the man of letters who cultivates a life of virtue and sound judgment elevated above the mundane world of physical labor or business. This model of an educated person represents a social "archetype...[embodying] society's values, beliefs, commitments" (Drucker, 1993, pp. 210–211). In the new knowledge society, the educated person will need to be represented by individuals who make learning and knowledge relevant. Rather than residing in the proverbial ivory tower, educated people must live and work in society, using knowledge to make a difference and to work toward a functioning society of institutions. This

is, in fact, what Drucker means by management as a liberal art: there must
be a fusion between the practical skills and tools of day-to-day work and
the cultural values learned through the humanities, arts, social sciences,
and other disciplines that have historically been the realm of the "liberal
arts." Educated people will face the challenge of living and working in two
cultures: that of the intellectual and the manager (Drucker, 1993, pp. 8–9).

This requires a new view of education and knowledge. Education must
have a social purpose, not just be for learning's sake. Drucker advocates
the widespread adoption of Germany's dual track of trade and academic
education, recognizing the value of both pragmatic skill acquisition and
academic learning. Lifelong learning needs to take place not just in schools,
but in all institutions (business organizations, hospitals, public institutions)
where ongoing knowledge acquisition is part of being a knowledge worker.
Lest a meritocracy become a plutocracy, this learning must be available
to all. Finally, the humanities need to be made relevant through practical
application (such as management as a liberal art), and technology training
has to be accessible to even those who are not technically educated (Drucker,
1989). It is only through the accessibility of knowledge, and the redefinition
of the educated person, that all can hope to find status and function in the
new knowledge society.

Social Challenges: Race

Drucker came to America when that country still practiced racial and
ethnic segregation. The United States Supreme Court ruled in 1896 that
state segregation laws did not violate the equal protection clause of the
14th amendment. The so-called "separate but equal" ruling in the Plessy
vs. Ferguson case opened the door for the proliferation of Jim Crow laws
allowing separation of black and white life (as well as segregation of Mexican
Americans and other non-whites). It was not until 1964, with the passage of
the Civil Rights Act, that discrimination on the basis of race, ethnicity, sex
and religion was prohibited by federal law.

Drucker was concerned about the effects of segregation on larger society
and its ability to function in a way that reflected the dominant cultural values
of America. Following the Civil Rights Act and the gains of the American
Civil Rights movement, Drucker was aware of the disproportionate impact of
the transition to a knowledge society on African American workers, although
his telling of history is rather skewed.

As Drucker points out, African American men benefited from the surge
in industrial employment in the post-World War II era. However, it is not
true that "The Negro...found little resistance when he moved in" to work in
industrial centers in the north (Drucker, 1968, p. 306). Beginning in the early
twentieth century, Black Americans migrated out of the rural south to escape
not just poverty but also the proliferation of Jim Crow laws. This Great

Black Migration, which continued until the decline of manufacturing jobs began in the 1970s, was one of the largest internal migrations of people in the nation's history. As industrial centers developed in the northeast, Midwest and West, Blacks migrated into these urban areas in large numbers. While most of the violent resistance to these new residents took place in the early years of the Great Black Migration, Black workers faced obstacles in the plants, often hired only for the lowest-paying jobs with the most difficult work conditions. Many labor unions sought to bar African Americans from active participation and, in some cases, from membership. Through the work of Black labor activists including A. Philip Randolph, who was one of the principal organizers of the 1963 March on Washington for Jobs and Freedom, labor activism was joined with the cause of racial injustice by the late 1960s; Martin Luther King was assassinated in Memphis, where he had given a speech to striking sanitation workers.

Therefore, the shift to the knowledge economy that Drucker notes beginning in the late 1960s is particularly relevant to the racial history of the United States. The significant social and economic gains provided to African Americans by industrial jobs began to reverse with the decline in manufacturing and, as Drucker comments, this demographic faced enormous obstacles in adapting to a knowledge economy. Because of generations of structural racism and lack of opportunities in education, African Americans could not possibly be expected to retrain and retool in a matter of a decade or two. As Drucker remarked with respect to industrial workers in general, the real damage was not economic, but social, with an associated loss of "self-respect... hope, and promise" (Drucker, 1968, p. 307).

Drucker's solution in the short term is to open up skilled work (generally coveted by white workers) to Black workers. As white industrial laborers skill up for knowledge work, he argues, these jobs should be made available to non-white workers. However, this is not the long-term solution to the problem. Eventually, non-whites need to be accepted as part of the knowledge economy, in large part because knowledge workers are the leaders of society. To solve America's racial problem, its "historical spiritual agony," requires an all-hand-on-deck approach. White and Black knowledge workers must band together to increase the development of Black knowledge workers so that they can be part of the new knowledge society (Drucker, 1968, p. 309). To look backward to the manufacturing sector as the solution to the race problem in America was, in Drucker's view, a grave error that would never provide true status and function—or dignity—to people regardless of color.

Social Challenges: Class

In many ways, Drucker's description of the new society of knowledge workers is a warning of the potential for a dangerous rift between two classes of people: the educated and the uneducated. The social challenges of a knowledge society are primarily challenges of social relations and status—not socioeconomic status. In this sense, "class" is not defined in Marxist terms, but rather in cultural terms. Earlier industrial societies maintained relatively static social relationships based on production (capital vs. labor, for example). In the knowledge society,

> "honest work" does not mean a callused hand. It is also the first society in which not everybody does the same work, as was the case when the huge majority were farmers or, as seemed likely ....[in the 1950s and 1960s], were going to be machine operators.
>
> *(Drucker, 1994, p. 64)*

Importantly, knowledge workers may not necessarily be the majority or the "ruling class" of society, but they will be the leadership class, and thus establish the values and expectations of this new society.

The social challenges presented by this changing society were that a growing number of people would see themselves as "the other half." If over half of the workforce does not possess higher education, and the leadership group that sets the values and expectations does, the potential for real class conflict exists. Law professor Joan C. Williams describes this chasm between the educated professional elite and the working class. For professionals such as herself, personal dignity results from professional achievement and economic status. For most in the working class, she argues, dignity from work stems from what one can buy and how one is able to support a family; the work itself does not construe status or meaning (Williams, 2017).

Part of what Williams describes is the nature of work; Drucker comments that a major difference between manual and knowledge workers is that manual workers leave their work behind at the end of the day, while knowledge workers take it home, and work longer hours (Drucker, 1968). But there is more to this divide than attitude; it has to do with having self-respect and dignity in a changing society. Even in countries whose histories are less fraught with issues of class mobility and "middle-class" identity, the increasing educational divide of the knowledge society represents a potential for a loss of dignity for those who see themselves as outside of the dominant elite culture.

At times, Drucker is optimistic about addressing this social problem. He points to examples of organizations that have successfully made non-knowledge jobs productive and self-respecting, providing opportunity to those who are at the bottom of the social strata (Service Master is one example of such an organization) (Drucker, 1989). By the 1990s, Drucker referred to the "other half" (non-knowledge workers) as "service workers"; in the new post-capitalist society, there were no capitalists and proletariat, but rather knowledge workers and service workers. The only way to avert a class conflict was to make both categories of work productive, but also to provide opportunity, income, and dignity to the second-class category of service workers (Drucker, 1993). While Drucker has no concrete answers to the problem of class conflict, like his solution to race relations, he argues for widespread opportunity and inclusion to avoid creating a disgruntled underclass.

Conclusion

While Drucker was not a futurist, he had a remarkable ability to see changes occurring that would have wide-ranging implications for the future (a topic we will explore in the last chapter of this book). As he questioned the nature of knowledge in the mid-twentieth century, he articulated sentiments that would be expressed by postmodernist thinkers who would begin to formulate their ideas some 30 years later. Twenty-first century people are faced with redefining knowledge as they grapple with artificial intelligence, machine learning, and large language models: what is original, new knowledge, and how does one protect intellectual property when knowledge can be created in these new ways?

Drucker also saw how the relationship between learning and knowledge and work could create social rifts. While no longer the ivory tower elites of the nineteenth century, the educated knowledge class of the twentieth century was a different kind of elite: one that served as the leadership class and set social expectations, mores, and norms. The less educated (what Drucker termed the service workers) would lose status in such a society, and this would strain relationships. Twenty-first century concerns with wealth inequality are often wrapped in the language of populism, where global elites are perceived to have rigged the system against those who are not in leadership positions. Access to knowledge in the form of social media creates problems of quality and reliability of that knowledge; as information of any kind can be shared with little to no filtering, the difference between "knowledge," "fact," "information," and "misinformation" becomes blurred. The more information we have, in many cases, the less we know.

Drucker warned that knowledge was power, and that some knowledge was dangerous without guardrails. As the world confronts new challenges with respect to learning, education, and participation in a functioning society, Drucker's work on knowledge is more meaningful than ever.

Bibliography

Brauer, D. (2008) 'Factors underlying the decline in manufacturing employment since 2000', *Economic Budget Issue Brief*, Congressional Budget Office, December.

Chaplin, C. (1936) *Modern times*. United States: United Artists.

Clifton, J. (2023) 'Why the world can't quit quiet quitting', Gallup, Workplace, 21 June.

Drucker, P.F. (1942) *The future of industrial man*. New Brunswick, NJ: Transaction.

Drucker, P.F. (1950) *The new society: The anatomy of industrial order*. New Brunswick, NJ: Transaction.

Drucker, P.F. (1954) *The practice of management*. New York: Harper & Row.

Drucker, P.F. (1955) *America's next twenty years*. New York: Harper & Brothers.

Drucker, P.F. (1957) *Landmarks of tomorrow*. New York: Harper & Brothers.

Drucker, P.F. (1968) *The age of discontinuity: Guidelines to our changing society*. New York: Harper & Row.

Drucker, P.F. (1989) *The new realities*. New York: Harper & Row.

Drucker, P.F. (1993) *Post-capitalist society*. New York: Harper Business.

Drucker, P.F. (1994) 'The age of social transformation', *The Atlantic Monthly*, 274 (5), pp. 53–68.

Drucker, P.F. (1999) *Management challenges for the 21st century*. New York: Harper Business.

Harris, K. (2020) 'Forty years of falling manufacturing employment', *Beyond the Numbers: Employment and Unemployment*, U.S. Bureau of Labor Statistics, 9 (16).

Harter, J. (2023) 'Is quiet quitting real?', Gallup, Workplace, 17 May.

Johnson, J.R. (2023) 'What's new about quiet quitting (and what's not)', *Transdisciplinary Journal of Management*, 28 February. https://tjm.scholasticahq.com/article/72079-what-s-new-about-quiet-quitting-and-what-s-not

'The resilient boom in entrepreneurship' (2023), *Financial Times*, 3 March.

Rogers, C.R. and Skinner, B.F. (1956) 'Some issues concerning the control of human behavior', *Science*, 124 (3231), pp. 1057–1066.

Shih, W.C. (2020) 'Global supply chains in a post-pandemic world: Companies need to make their networks more resilient. Here's how', *Harvard Business Review*, 98 (5), pp. 82–89.

Williams, J.C. (2017) *White working class: Overcoming class cluelessness in America*. Boston: Harvard Business Review Press.

6
DRUCKER AND INNOVATION AND ENTREPRENEURSHIP

Introduction

Peter Drucker published his book, *Innovation and Entrepreneurship*, in 1985. Just as he had systematized the practice of management in his earlier work, he set out to establish innovation and entrepreneurship as a practice and a discipline rather than as a set of qualities, personality traits, or innate abilities (Drucker, 1985). Continuing his philosophy of a functioning society of well-managed institutions, Drucker recognized that navigating change was an integral part of managing organizations of all kinds. His interactions with the economist Joseph Schumpeter proved to be pivotal in the development of Drucker's ideas of innovation and entrepreneurship. Drucker used Schumpeter's ideas of creative destruction and "new combinations," as well as his definition of profit and the concept of innovation embodied by action to formulate his own theory and methodology of innovation and entrepreneurship. Entrepreneurship was not the domain of a handful of heroic individuals willing to take risk but rather a pivotal task of the executive. By defining entrepreneurial activity as a practice, a process that could be learned and repeated, Drucker sought to demystify entrepreneurship, making it less of a heroic act and more of a routine function of management. Similarly, Drucker saw innovation as crucial to any organization; change was part of remaining relevant and responsive to the needs of customers and society. Yet, innovation was necessarily disruptive to both those within organizations and those outside the organization who would be impacted by innovation. Drucker's goal was to find ways for organizations to minimize these inevitable disruptions caused by necessary innovation. As always, Drucker sought to find a balance between change and continuity, understanding that the fabric

DOI: 10.4324/9781003410485-7

of society required an acknowledgment of the tension between the two. This is why Drucker's model of innovation stresses the importance of change serving a larger purpose; not every innovation should be pursued. Innovation and entrepreneurship are part of Drucker's larger social theory, driven by values, purpose, and responsibility.

Joseph Schumpeter's Entrepreneur and Drucker's Framework

As many have noted, Drucker's ideas about innovation and entrepreneurship stem from his association with the economist Joseph Schumpeter (Beatty, 1998; Flaherty, 1999). Drucker's conceptual framework clearly derives from Schumpeter's work. It is important to establish this connection before we delve into a detailed discussion of Drucker's actual writing on this subject.

Creative Destruction

Schumpeter served as Austria's Finance Minister at the end of World War I in 1919, and also held professorships in Economics at the University of Graz and the University of Bonn. In 1932, he emigrated to the United States, where he taught at Harvard until 1949. Schumpeter's economic ideas evolved into what Drucker described as the "pessimistic" outlook detailed in Schumpeter's last major work, *Capitalism, Socialism, and Democracy*. Informed by the interwar experience of boom and bust, Schumpeter's analysis represents the cumulative influence of nearly two hundred years of economic thought, as well as his own personal analysis of the social and psychological implications of capitalism's maturation. Economists during the tumultuous years of the twenties and thirties had to answer difficult questions. Was the Depression a short-term phenomenon, or was capitalism, as Marx had predicted, actually self-destructing? Were business cycles controllable? Should government interfere in times of financial distress, or should things be left for natural laws to work on their own?

Economists gave very different answers. The defenders of laissez-faire capitalism, such as Alfred Marshall, the reigning king of economics, had argued that downturns such as the Depression were short-term shudders, and that, left to its own devices, the economy would right itself again. Others provided more unorthodox advice. In his book *The General Theory of Employment, Interest, and Money*, John Maynard Keynes completely refuted Marshall's view. Keynes stated that the problems of the 1930s were due to too much savings and not enough investment, and called on government to intervene by lowering interest rates and increasing public spending to make up for the decrease in private investment and overall demand. In order to understand the impact of this proposed remedy, it is necessary to understand that the ruling theory was that only lower budgets and higher interest rates would keep prices and wages low enough for firms to be profitable. The memories of wartime debts and downwardly-spiraling currency valuations engendered a fear of inflation that was behind the prevailing public spending policies. Keynes' ideas, then, were a true about-face in terms of economic theory.

Schumpeter's analysis of the state of capitalism during the Depression could not have differed more from that of Keynes. Schumpeter's system was not under pressure from a lack of investment, and certainly did not need any kind of government intervention. For Schumpeter, capitalism was an intrinsically dynamic system of growth and development. Depressions were a normal function of the system; these were periods during which new developments and technologies were being assimilated:

> ...depressions are not simply evils, which we might attempt to suppress, but—perhaps undesirable—forms of something which has to be done, namely, adjustment to previous economic change...There is no reason to despair—this is the first lesson to be derived from our story. Fundamentally the same thing has happened in the past, and it has—in the only two cases which are comparable with the present one—lasted just as long...In all cases...recovery came of itself...But this is not all: our analysis leads us to believe that recovery is sound only if it does come of itself.
>
> *(Schumpeter, 1934/2000, pp. 112–117)*

Economic downturns, then, are periods of adjustment following some sort of drastic change. In fact, Schumpeter argues, the normal state of affairs for capitalism is the maintenance of a status quo, and the moments of dramatic change and growth are themselves anomalies within the system:

> [The first chapter of *The Theory of Economic Development*] describes economic life from the standpoint of a "circular flow," running on in channels essentially the same year after year—similar to the circulation of the blood in an animal organism. Now this circular flow and its channels do alter in time, and here we abandon the analogy with the circulation of the blood...Economic life experiences...changes...which do not appear continuously and which change the framework, the traditional course itself.
>
> *(Schumpeter, 1934/2008, p. 61)*

These events that alter the normal flow of the economy give rise to periods of growth and profitability. Essentially, they occur when entrepreneurial activity results in new technologies, industries, or modes of production, which then create temporary opportunities. Temporary, because competitors eventually adopt the new technology, driving down the rate of profit. Schumpeter refers to this process as "creative destruction," because entrepreneurial ventures not only bring about something new; they also destroy the old in the process.

Inherent in the concept of "creative destruction" is a problem, one that Schumpeter eventually realized and that led to his pessimistic conclusion regarding the future of capitalism. Because profit is so fleeting, and because entrepreneurial activity is by nature temporary, every business is susceptible to being creatively destroyed. Drucker borrows this heavily from Schumpeter, as he reminds businesses to continually improve, to change, to practice "systematic abandonment," which is the process of weeding out non-productive activities, products, or business units:

> Every institution—and not only business—must build into its day-to-day management four entrepreneurial activities that run in parallel. One is the organized abandonment of products, services, processes, markets, distribution channels, and so on that are no longer an optimal allocation of resources...Then any institution must organize for systematic, continuing improvement...Then it has to organize for systematic and continuous exploitation, especially of its successes...And, finally, it has to organize systematic innovation, that is, to create the different tomorrow that makes obsolete and, to a large extent, replaces even the most successful products of today in any organization. I emphasize that these disciplines are not just desirable, they are three conditions for survival today.
>
> *(Drucker, 1998, p. 174)*

But Schumpeter takes creative destruction to a deeper, philosophical level, considering the toll that the process takes on the human condition as well as the transformative influence that such a system has on societal structures and norms:

> ...the entrepreneurial function is not only the vehicle of continual reorganisation of the economic system but also the vehicle of continual changes in the elements which comprise the upper strata of society. The successful entrepreneur rises socially, and with him his family, who acquire from the fruits of his success a position not immediately dependent upon personal conduct. This represents the most important factor of rise in the social scale in the capitalist world. Because it proceeds by competitively destroying old businesses and hence the existences dependent upon them, there always corresponds to it a process of decline, of loss of caste, of elimination. This fate also threatens the entrepreneur whose powers are declining, or his heirs who have inherited his wealth without his ability... An American adage expresses it: three generations from overalls to overalls.
>
> *(Schumpeter, 1934/2008, p. 156).*

Schumpeter's description is of the hidden side of the American dream of upward mobility: the underlying anxiety of maintaining not just economic but social status once attained. The instability inherent in capitalism is not capitalism itself, but the social disruptions it causes, the psychological distress of being in a constant state of insecurity. In fact, argues, Schumpeter, capitalism itself grows stronger:

> The Marxist argument which holds that, due to the nature of things, there is a necessary movement toward the socialist regime, is wrong. The capitalist system will never collapse by itself. Quite the opposite; it increases in economic stability. But capitalism brings about psychological, moral and political changes. Changes in [habits and attitudes] which do produce a movement toward socialism.
>
> *(Schumpeter, 1931/2002, pp. 148–149)*

Schumpeter's "pessimistic" conclusion, we now see, was not merely the result of his experience with combating inflation as the Austrian Finance Minister. Underlying Schumpeter's belief that capitalism would be overtaken by socialism was a philosophical outlook, an evaluation of the psychological and human implications of his very own economic theory. If, indeed, capitalism was a system of circular flows, or natural homeostasis regularly disrupted by violent paroxysms of financial chaos, fueled by an almost Nietszche-like will to power on the part of the entrepreneur du jour, then no one was safe but the system. Not surprisingly, then, human compassion would drive action toward policies more socialist in nature, geared toward tempering the savage path of creative destruction. Marx may have been wrong about the mechanism of capitalism's demise, but he was certainly right about its capacity for great harm.

How does Drucker deal with such a conclusion? As seen in his reference to Schumpeter in his memoir, Drucker implies that Schumpeter threw in the towel rather than come up with a workable solution. For Drucker, even the chaos of creative destruction can be managed. In fact, it is the job of management to curtail the impact of unpreventable and unpredictable economic and business cycles. Unlike the economists, who sought to control and predict, Drucker seeks to manage risk, to minimize the human toll of what is inevitable economic turmoil and change:

> Moreover, economists doubt more and more whether there is a real "cycle." There are ups and downs, no doubt; but do they have any periodicity, any inherent predictability? The greatest of modern economists, the late Joseph A. Schumpeter, labored mightily for twenty-five years to find the "cycle." But at best, his "business cycle" is the result of so many different cyclical movements that it can only be analyzed *in retrospect*. And a business-cycle

analysis that only tells where the cycle has been but not where it will go, is of little use in managing a business...What business needs therefore are tools which will enable it to make decisions without having to try to guess in which stage of a cycle the economy finds itself.

(Drucker, 1954, p. 90)

Although Drucker has no delusions about the possibility of ever perfecting such tools, he has a genuine optimism regarding management's ability to stave off the more sinister aspects of capitalism's unpredictability. The rationality of management as a process, its function as a mechanism to handle risk, is Drucker's answer to the irrationality and chaos of capitalism's inherent "ups and downs."

Profit and Entrepreneurship

Schumpeter's view of profit is linked to the important role of the entrepreneur in his system of economic thought. As entrepreneurs develop new products and services, new means of production, or what Schumpeter refers to as "new combinations," then such innovations in turn generate a greater profit or return. Profit is inherent in entrepreneurial activity: "Without development there is not profit, without profit no development" (Schumpeter, 1934/2008, p. 154). As additional competitors adopt the same new combinations or innovations, the profit level falls. Without an infusion of entrepreneurial activity, there is no incentive for profits to increase. Profits are not the reward for entrepreneurial risk taking; Schumpeter is very clear on this point. The risk is taken by the financier, not the entrepreneur (unless he or she has committed funds to the venture). Profit is "the temporary surplus of receipts over cost of production in a new enterprise" (Schumpeter, 1934/2008, p. 154).

In Schumpeter's system, profit is fleeting, a momentary event: "Profit clings to the means of production in no other sense than does the effort of a poet to his partly finished manuscript" (Schumpeter, 1934/2008, p. 151).

Drucker takes Schumpeter's interpretation of profit and modifies it to create his own, very different version, initially described in *The Practice of Management:*

Profit serves three purposes. It measures the net effectiveness and soundness of a business's efforts... It is the "risk premium" that covers the costs of staying in business.... Finally, profit insures the supply of future capital for innovation and expansion...

(Drucker, 1954, p. 77)

Profit, argues Drucker, is a cost of doing business, not simply excess funds that should be the goal of every businessperson to maximize. Rather, profit is a form of insurance, allowing a going concern to weather the storm of economic downturns, needed expansion and innovation, and simply to cover the daily costs of staying in business. Furthermore, as Schumpeter demonstrated, profit is ethereal, associated only with innovation and creation of the new at the expense of the old. It is not the reward for risk but a temporary surplus, a "risk premium."

By converting Schumpeter's ethereal notion of profit into profit-as-cost, Drucker then turns to his real argument, which is that Schumpeter's idea of creative destruction justifies the idea of profit. Because classical economists viewed the economic system as a state of equilibrium, there was no justification for profit. Once one moves from a closed, unchanging economy to Schumpeter's "dynamic, growing, moving, changing economy," profit is not only not immoral, it is a "moral imperative" (Drucker, 1983/1993, p. 127).

Through Schumpeter, Drucker finds a way to fashion capitalism into a moral system that is not based on the pursuit of economic gain in the form of profit. Although such pursuits are certainly less evil than other, more harmful exercises in power, Drucker's construction of profit using Schumpeter's system of disequilibrium and entrepreneurial innovation allows him to envision profit within a new, moral rubric. Capitalism is no longer simply indulging in the desire for financial gain, in greed, in the propensity to truck and barter. It is genuinely about regeneration, about life-giving force; one is reminded of the personal, creative God of Stahl. Drucker even uses religious language and analogies in his trump of Marxist doctrine. Classical economists, according to Drucker, stated that profit was incentive for risk taking; but this created a problem in that profit became merely a bribe and not morally justifiable. This construction allowed Marx to "fuse dispassionate analysis of the 'system' with the moral revulsion of an Old Testament prophet against the 'exploiters'." The view of profit as a reward for risk gave Marx ammunition to call capitalism a "wicked and immoral" system that would inevitably crumble (Drucker, 1983/1993, p. 112). Schumpeter allowed Drucker to slay the dragon of Marx, to use profitability as the tool of morality. Now, business and the manager could function as a moral force in society.

Managers as Entrepreneurs

Schumpeter also provides Drucker with a means to associate managers with entrepreneurial or creative activity. Because Schumpeter does not equate entrepreneurship with risk taking, managers, too, can be engineers of creative destruction. The act of identifying new markets for existing products, for example, falls under the definition of entrepreneurial activity. Key to Schumpeter's definition is the role of *action*—that is, the actual implementation of an idea or innovation. The act of envisioning a new product, of applying for a patent, for example, would not qualify: "Economic leadership in particular must hence be distinguished from "invention." As long as they are not carried into practice, inventions are economically irrelevant" (Schumpeter, 1934/2008, p. 88). By equating entrepreneurship with action, with the formation of "new combinations," Schumpeter opens the door for managers to also function in this role. However, once they become bureaucrats, functionaries who merely mind the store, they cease to contribute in any entrepreneurial fashion:

> ...whatever the type, everyone is an entrepreneur only when he actually "carries out new combinations," and loses that character as soon as he has built up his business, when he settles down to running it as other people run their businesses. This is the rule, of course, and hence it is just as rare for anyone always to remain an entrepreneur throughout the decades of his active life as it is for a businessman never to have a moment in which he is an entrepreneur, to however modest a degree.
>
> *(Schumpeter, 1934/2008, p. 78)*

For Drucker, initially, the organization functioned as the agent of entrepreneurial change and growth. Working through his theory of corporate citizenship in *The Future of Industrial Man* and *Concept of the Corporation*, he placed the large business organization at the center of American society as the source of individual meaning and a sense of communal belonging. Through the economic ideas of Schumpeter, Drucker also could incorporate a further moral element into his concept of management and its function: not only would the corporation provide individual fulfillment, but it would also serve as a regenerative source for society as a whole. Through profit, which was not the goal of the self-serving individual, but rather a moral imperative of an ever-changing and growing economy, business would ensure that there was a future to look forward to.

Innovation in Action

As Drucker began to look at other institutions, however, his focus by necessity shifted away from profitability as a moral force and onto another more universally applied agent: productivity. This, too, derives straight from Schumpeter, who emphasized that innovation has no value unless put into action. Drucker's interest in applying his management concepts to other institutions, including not-for-profit entities, required the use of something other than profitability as the moral imperative for those institutions. In addition, as Drucker refined his understanding of human capital, his concept of the "knowledge worker," the emphasis had to shift away from financial measurements to human ones. Schumpeter's economic theories, emphasizing disequilibrium over homeostasis, economic messiness over some natural state of order, provided the ideal raw materials for Drucker to mold his own economic theory centered on human beings rather than numbers.

By emphasizing profit as the sole measurement of value, economics failed to function morally. Drucker calls for productivity to be the new measure of value rather than profit or labor. Productivity as the source of value would "give guidance to analysis, to policy, and to behavior." It would, according to Drucker, allow economics to become "both a 'humanity,' a 'moral philosophy,' a '*Geisteswissenschaft*' [loosely translated as a science of the spirit, what English speakers would refer to as course of study in the humanities and liberal arts]; and rigorous 'science' " (Drucker, 1980b, p. 18). Drawing on Schumpeter, Drucker marries productivity and innovation to put a human face on capitalism and managerial activity; the "beacons of productivity and innovation" allow for a system that not only "makes economics a human discipline," but also "gives a businessman a yardstick to measure whether he's still moving in the right direction and whether his results are real or delusions" (Drucker, 1987/1993, p. 99). Not only does the businessman have a yardstick, but so does the hospital administrator, the university provost, and the head of a national charitable foundation. With human productivity the definition of value—not labor, not profit—Drucker's theory can apply to virtually any organization.

Early Work on Innovation

Drucker began his work on innovation in the 1950s. Following his study of General Motors and his subsequent consulting work for several other corporations, Drucker saw the need for a text that would effectively define management as a discipline and a practice (see Chapter 3). In his 1954 work, *The Practice of Management*, he early on establishes the purpose of a business: to create a customer. Because businesses are customer-driven, Drucker says that "any business enterprise has two—and only these two—basic functions: marketing and innovation. They are the entrepreneurial functions" (Drucker, 1954, p. 37). Because business can only function in an environment where change is seen as normal and desirable, innovation is a key function: "...business is the specific organ of growth, expansion and change" (Drucker, 1954, p. 39). Innovation can take many forms in a business, including price improvements, new product development, finding a new use for old products, creating a new customer want or convenience, or improving a distribution method. Innovation is part of every aspect of business, from marketing to design to distribution to management processes. In short, "Innovation goes right through all phases of business" (Drucker, 1954, p. 40).

Innovation is often defined as driven by technological advancements in the use of tools or machines (see Chapter 8). Drucker recognizes the role of technology in innovation but defines it differently; for him the term should be "used in its rightful sense as applying to the art, craft, or science of any organized human activity." As a result, innovation may involve responses to technological changes, but it may also be necessary to keep up with improvements in areas such as accounting or office procedures that involve "advances in knowledge and skill" (Drucker, 1954, p. 69). In fact, Drucker warns, the less technology-driven an industry is, the greater the danger that it will not innovate. Technological breakthroughs in industries such as pharmaceuticals are obvious drivers of innovation. But those industries that are less overtly forced to adapt due to rapid technological change are most in danger of ignoring the need to innovate, and thus need to pay the most attention to the innovative functions of business (Drucker, 1954, p. 70).

Yet, even in his early work, Drucker was keenly aware of the connection between innovation and society. In *Landmarks of Tomorrow* (1957), he outlines a new world view that emphasizes configuration rather than cause, where uncertainty is the new normal. In the post-modern world of the mid-twentieth century,

> Every discipline has as its center today a concept of a whole that is not the result of its parts, not equal to the sum of its parts, and not identifiable, knowable, measurable, predictable, effective or meaningful through identifying, knowing, measuring, predicting, moving or understanding the parts.
>
> *(Drucker, 1957, p. 5)*

Biology, psychology, the social sciences, management, and other fields are characterized by processes and patterns, qualitative features rather than measurable attributes. As a result, Drucker says, we are moving from progress to innovation. If change is inevitable and a normal part of life, innovation is the only responsible way to respond to it.

It is in this text that Drucker first sets out to establish a definition and theory of innovation, the ideas that he would later develop more fully in *Innovation and Entrepreneurship*. Innovation is not just something practiced by the for-profit sector, but a social process and "a new view of the universe as one of risk rather than of chance or of certainty" (Drucker, 1957, p. 19). Whereas change was once considered disastrous, and organizations were devised to bolster stability, even the conserving institutions of society (government, the military, and schools) have embraced innovation as "controlled, directed and purposeful human activity" (Drucker, 1957, p. 21). Here Drucker establishes innovation as a distinct process involving conscious human activity to organize change and improvement. It is thought through, not simply a flash of genius that occurs randomly.

Drucker discusses technological innovation but focuses more on the larger social impacts of embracing change as a normal part of life. Innovation is presented as a shift in world view, and Drucker spends considerable space discussing the impacts of social innovations. He includes examples such as the Marshall Plan and the production advances of the United States during World War II, arguing that these social innovations made as great an impact on his generation as any technological innovation. In pointing out the risks of innovation, Drucker highlights the power of its impacts on a society: "Innovation can change, almost overnight, the established order, render obsolete what only yesterday seemed impregnable, make dominant what only yesterday was negligible" (Drucker, 1957, p. 46). As a result, innovation carries with it enormous responsibility; as a conscious choice, it involves decisions about what society should look like, what people value, and what a culture views as improvement.

As a result, innovation involves value choices, and is part of Drucker's larger philosophy of a functioning society. If innovation is always about ethics and values, it constantly invokes the question of what institutions and traditions a society should strengthen and retain and which should be revamped, weakened, or removed. If a functioning society requires balancing change and continuity, innovation decisions necessarily disrupt that balance. Such disruption must, therefore, serve a purpose, and innovative decisions require an understanding of social responsibility. Drucker sees this in political language, using terms that have come to have very different meanings in contemporary society (Drucker notes that "Today both liberalism and conservatism in their traditional meaning are moribund," Drucker, 1957, p. 59). He calls for innovators to be conservative, which Drucker defines as retaining basic values, understanding historical context, acknowledging the needs of greater society and the fallibility of humankind, and maintaining a long-term view (Drucker, 1957, p. 59). A conservative innovator, then, would not simply innovate for the sake of change, but would consider the ramifications of a decision from multiple perspectives. As is often the case in his writing, Drucker projects a need for balance between extreme positions (for which he often turns to political language). Just as he sees a need for balance between the revolutionary and reactionary positions, he believes in a process of innovation that involves careful, considered decision-making. True innovation considers the social impacts of an improvement, introduction, or modification. What kind of society do we want? Does the innovation we seek to introduce lead to that vision of a functioning society of institutions?

Implementing Innovation

By the 1970s, Drucker was beginning to flesh out how to systematically implement innovation in organizations of all kinds. As more and more management publications joined Drucker's classic 1954 text, *The Practice of*

Management, Drucker continued his discussions of continuity and change in his work but warned of a coming period of rapid change. Innovation had been viewed primarily as the domain of research, of technical staff, rather than an organizational function. While the years between the 1850s and World War I witnessed unprecedented innovation and technological change, Drucker argued that from 1920 to the end of World War II, little real change occurred; what was notable was that access to technology spread globally. However, by the 1970s, the need for real social and political innovation was crucial: "The crisis of the world is, above all, an institutional crisis demanding institutional innovation" (Drucker, 1973/1974, p. 502). Newly industrializing nations, including Brazil and China, signaled rapid change. Governments needed to be restructured and thought through to be effective. Business would similarly need to restructure to capitalize on the need for innovation to respond to a rapidly changing environment.

Thus, as he shifted his focus to the development of a practice and methodology of innovation in organizations, Drucker's language of social process and responsibility shifts toward a more pragmatic prose. He is less overt about the role of organizations in a functioning society, and more interested in how to 'get innovation done.' Whereas innovation was a social process and a view of the universe requiring assumption of responsibility in the 1950s, innovation is "value" and "must therefore always be market-focused" (Drucker, 1973/1974, p. 505). Drucker seems less concerned with the social impacts of innovation, the potential negative consequences on people and stakeholders. He now emphasizes the importance of strategic innovation in organizations, a process that involves careful assessment of opportunities, such as economic weaknesses in an industry or process, changes that have happened but have not yet resulted in economic impacts, and unexpected events. Organizations need to develop measurements and budgets that are appropriate to innovative activities; Drucker's favorite example is the DuPont Company, which used return on investment (ROI) as its measurement for business success beginning in the 1920s. However, the company realized that new products would not generate a return early in the innovation stage, and that compensating those involved in the new venture based on ROI would actually inhibit innovation, as they would be loath to spend resources on a new idea (Drucker, 1973/1974, pp. 511–514).

Innovation and Entrepreneurship

Drucker eventually synthesized his thinking in an important text, *Innovation and Entrepreneurship.* It is a dated book, grounded in historical events and Drucker's unique interpretation of them (which is not unusual in his work). However, as we have explored in this chapter, Drucker had been thinking about the concept of innovation for some 30 years prior to writing this book.

In a sense, *Innovation and Entrepreneurship* is a natural outcome of three decades of work. Yet, when considered as part of Drucker's entire body of work, it is a curious text that omits important theoretical and philosophical underpinnings key to understanding the role of innovation in his overall worldview. Clearly written for a management audience, the book perpetuates the conundrum of Drucker: he cannot effectively merge his role as a social theorist and a management writer without losing his primary readers, practitioners of management.

Drucker's introduction to *Innovation and Entrepreneurship* sets up the book as a response to then current events. In the 1970s, the United States was plagued by a series of economic and political factors that led to the condition of "stagflation"—high inflation and economic stagnation. The post-World War II boom began to subside, and American manufacturing output suffered. At the same time, the nation's entanglements in Vietnam and Cambodia resulted in increased defense expenditures. Global factors contributed to poor economic conditions in America as well. In 1973, Egypt chose to attack Israel on Yom Kippur in retaliation for territorial losses in 1967. The United States supported its ally, Israel, in the Yom Kippur war involving Egypt and Syria. In retaliation, Middle East nations employed an oil embargo against the United States, restricted the supply of oil to America. Gasoline prices surged, contributing to inflation. Then President Jimmy Carter characterized the mood of the nation in his famous "malaise" speech, in which he referred to the mood of the country as lacking in hope:

> The symptoms of this crisis of the American spirit are all around us. For the first time in the history of our country a majority of our people believe that the next five years will be worse than the past five years. Two-thirds of our people do not even vote. The productivity of American workers is actually dropping, and the willingness of Americans to save for the future has fallen below that of all other people in the Western world.
>
> *(Carter, 1979)*

One explanation for the crisis of the 1970s was the Kondratiev theory of business cycles. Nikolai Kondratiev was a Soviet economist who developed a theory of long-term cycles of activity in the world economy. In his book, *The Major Economic Cycles* (1925), Kondratiev attempted to show how economic periods of positive and negative results could be anticipated. Specifically, how can one predict a new technology's life cycle, from inception to acceptance, to rapid growth, and finally to stagnation and collapse?

Drucker begins his text with a nod to Kondratiev theory, which he says supported the idea of stagnation in the 1970s. Yet, he says, the facts run counter to this theory. Drucker opposes this dark view of America in his Introduction to *Innovation and Entrepreneurship* with a vision of America as unique, as a bastion of job creation. Why? Because, Drucker explains, the job creators were no longer the Fortune 500 companies, but rather mid-size or smaller organizations. In addition, "According to *The Economist*, 600,000 new businesses are being started in the United States every year now—about seven times as many as were started in each of the boom years of the fifties and sixties" (Drucker, 1985, p. 3).

How can one explain this? Drucker explains that a new "entrepreneurial management" mindset has taken over America (and, in this book, he is clear that this is an American phenomenon—a perspective which could certainly be challenged). Yet, Drucker does not explain why this "change that has already happened" has occurred. He does explain that most of these entrepreneurial ventures are not "high tech"; he focuses on the "'low tech', of systematic, purposeful, managed entrepreneurship" (Drucker, 1985, p. 13). Indeed, later on, Drucker speaks of entrepreneurship as work (Drucker, 1985, p. 150). This is key to understanding Drucker's mindset. Having established his philosophical framework for a functioning society, he now embarks on the "work" of creating an infrastructure for the practice of innovation and entrepreneurship.

Drucker defines entrepreneurship as a process rather than a set of personality traits or features of an institution. Entrepreneurship "rests on a theory of economy and society. The theory sees change as normal and indeed as healthy...the entrepreneur upsets and disorganizes. As Joseph Schumpeter formulated it, his task is 'creative destruction'" (Drucker, 1985, p. 26). Systematic entrepreneurship, then requires purposeful innovation. Specifically, Drucker says that systematic innovation requires paying attention to seven sources of innovative opportunity. The first four sources stem from changes that have happened or can be made to happen within an industry, sector, or organization. These sources are discussed below.

- The unexpected success, failure, or outside event: Drucker says this is the most neglected yet best source for innovation. Such opportunities are often not even seen; for example, in the case of the unexpected success, the organization may only focus on problems and completely overlook the success.
- The incongruity between reality as it actually is and as it is assumed to be: These are qualitative, not quantitative symptoms of change. Like the unexpected event, incongruities are often overlooked because of the tendency in organizations to embrace the idea that "this is how it's always been." One common area where these opportunities show up is in the gap between what the producer and the consumer perceive as value.
- Identification of a process need: This innovation is task focused rather than situation focused. It originates within an organization based on a very specific need, such as something that everyone agrees should be done more effectively.

- Changes in market or industry structure: Drucker points to the rapid growth of an industry as a source of disruption in market or industry structure that can provide opportunities for innovation.

The other three sources result from changes in the political, social, cultural, or philosophical environment. In other words, they are external sources.

- Demographics: Changes in age, gender, income, and other distributions in a population present substantial opportunities for innovation.
- Changes in perception: Drucker refers to this as a switch from seeing the glass half full to half empty. If people think differently about their socioeconomic status, for example, that presents an opportunity to reposition a product or service.
- New knowledge: Knowledge-based innovation is what most people think about when innovation comes to mind. Yet, Drucker states, it is the most difficult source of innovation, involving long lead times and other challenges. Sometimes, innovation requires several knowledges to converge. This combination of long lead times (25–30 years) and convergences of knowledge leads to the "shakeout," a period of time during which only a few innovators will survive. Because this window of time includes more and more competitors in a global economy, the survival rate for innovators is very low (Drucker, 1985).

Drucker spends the remainder of the book discussing entrepreneurial management: strategies for implementing innovation in an organization. While existing organizations, public service institutions, and new ventures may have different challenges and needs, they all need to practice entrepreneurial management. Drucker particularly directs his message of innovation to big business:

> Today, it is not only in the self-interest of the many existing big businesses to learn to manage themselves for entrepreneurship; they have a social responsibility to do so. In sharp contrast to the situation a century ago, rapid destruction of the existing businesses—especially the big ones— by innovation, the 'creative destruction' by the innovator, in Joseph Schumpeter's famous phrase, poses a genuine social threat today to employment, to financial stability, to social order, and to governmental responsibility.
>
> *(Drucker, 1985, p. 145)*

Entrepreneurship is not the domain of the heroic individual with the "bright idea," the lone Einsteins of the world. It is, in fact, purposeful work that belongs in every organization, especially those that have the most impact on society (the large institutions).

Conclusion

Drucker ends *Innovation and Entrepreneurship* with a discussion of revolution and its inadequacies. As he argued in 1942, the legacy of the French Revolution and the Enlightenment was disenchantment. In 1985, he connects the disenchantment with social programs of the 1960s and 1970s to failed attempts at revolutionary change. What is needed is not revolution but true innovation, which is "pragmatic rather than dogmatic and modest rather than grandiose." Ultimately, innovation and entrepreneurship, for Drucker, are what keep society and the economy "flexible and self-renewing," achieving the objective of revitalization without "bloodshed, civil war, or concentration camps, without economic catastrophe, but with purpose, with direction, and under control" (Drucker, 1985, p. 254).

Innovation and entrepreneurship are intrinsically linked to preventing societal upheaval: the kind of upheaval that could result in totalitarianism or some other form of dysfunction. True innovation is not just aimed at creating healthy organizations but bolstering society as a whole.

By 1990, Drucker had fully developed his ideas about the role of innovation and entrepreneurship in a functioning society of institutions. If, as Schumpeter concluded, capitalism contained the seeds of its own destruction (not by its enemies but by the very people who reaped the benefits of the system), how could the negative aspects of creative destruction be managed? Just as Drucker argued in *The End of Economic Man*, a society built on economic promise alone would not suffice. If entrepreneurship is an integral part of the practice of management, then the negative fallout from innovation (disruption and disorganization) can be managed as a normal part of a process rather than a shock to a system in stasis. With profit and productivity positioned as necessary to a healthy, growing society, Drucker (with Schumpeter's help) can replace the model of the entrepreneur as the genius with the invention with that of the manager of an organization that provides individual status and function. Change is necessary and normal, but continuity requires a recognition of the responsibilities inherent in innovation and the impacts that entrepreneurial management has on the social order.

Bibliography

Beatty, J. (1998) *The world according to Peter Drucker*. New York: The Free Press.

Carter, J. (1979) 'Energy and national goals: Address to the nation', Jimmy Carter Presidential Library and Museum, 15 July, www.jimmycarterlibrary.gov/the-cart ers/selected-speeches/jimmy-carter-energy-and-national-goals-address-to-the-nat ion, Accessed 6 October 2023.

Drucker, P.F. (1954) *The practice of management*. New York: Harper & Row.

Drucker, P.F. (1957) *Landmarks of tomorrow*. New York: Harper & Brothers.

Drucker, P.F. (1973/1974) *Management: Tasks, responsibilities, practices*. New York: Harper & Row.

Drucker, P.F. (1980a) 'Toward the next economics', *The Public Interest*.

Drucker, P.F. (1980b) 'The crisis in economic theory', *The Public Interest*.

Drucker, P.F. (1983) 'Schumpeter and Keynes', *Forbes Magazine*, reprinted in Drucker, P.F. (1993) *The ecological vision: Reflections on the American condition*. New Brunswick, NJ: Transaction, pp. 107–117.

Drucker, P.F. (1985) *Innovation and entrepreneurship*. New York: Harper & Row.

Drucker, P.F. (1987/1993) 'The poverty of economic theory', *New Management*, reprinted in Drucker, P.F. (1993) *The ecological vision: Reflections on the American condition*. New Brunswick, NJ: Transaction, pp. 95–99.

Drucker, P.F. (1998) 'Management's new paradigms', *Forbes*, 5 October.

Flaherty, J.E. (1999) *Peter Drucker: Shaping the managerial mind*. San Francisco, CA: Jossey-Bass.

Schumpeter, J. (1931) 'Les possibilites actuelles du socialisme', quoted in Lakomski, O., 'The long term perspective: Schumpeter's prediction of the end of capitalism', in Arena, R. and Dangel-Hagnauer, C. (eds.) (2002) *The contribution of Joseph Schumpeter to economics: Economic development and institutional change*. London: Routledge, pp. 145–164.

Schumpeter, J. (1934) 'Depressions: Can we learn from past experience?', *The Economics of the Recovery Program*, pp. 3–21. Reprinted in Clemence, R., Ed. (2000) *Essays on entrepreneurs: Innovations, business cycles, and the evolution of capitalism*. New Brunswick: NJ, Transaction, pp. 108–117.

Schumpeter, J. (1934/2008) *The theory of economic development: An inquiry into profits, capital, credit and the business cycle*. Opie, R. (trans.). New Brunswick, NJ: Transaction.

7

DRUCKER AND THE ROLE OF GOVERNMENT

Introduction

Although primarily viewed as a writer on business organizations, Drucker wrote extensively on the management of governmental institutions and their place in society. As he developed his larger theory of a functioning society of healthy, well-managed institutions, Drucker saw the pluralist nature of such a society consisting of a wide variety of institutions with different purposes. The key was to have each organization and sector focus on that which it did most effectively, and to avoid taking on tasks that were better left to other institutions. Just as the for-profit and service sectors played crucial roles in balancing necessary innovative change with continuity, the public sector was equally—if not more—important in establishing the foundations of a healthy society.

Early Work: Constitutional Government in Europe

As a young man of twenty, Drucker worked in Germany as a journalist for the Frankfurter General-Anzeiger in early 1930, covering foreign affairs and economics. At the same time, he attended law school at the University of Frankfurt, studying international law, political theory and history, and the history of legal institutions. Drucker was thus an eyewitness to the deteriorating economic, political, and social conditions that would give rise to the National Socialist Party's eventual victory later that decade. As he saw Germany's government in disarray, Drucker also studied German history, particularly the early nineteenth-century German concept of the *Rechtsstaat*—the idea of

DOI: 10.4324/9781003410485-8

a just and moral state that would provide a legitimate form of government and allow for individual freedom. Drucker envisioned a study of three thinkers: Wilhelm Von Humbolt, Joseph von Radowitz, and Friedrich Julius Stahl. Humboldt, a Catholic, was head of Education and the Arts in Berlin during the early nineteenth century and founded the University of Berlin. Also Catholic, Radowitz was a Prussian general who devised a program to unify Germany in the 1830s and 1840s under a legislature governed by a small group of elites. Stahl was an ecclesiastical lawyer and politician against German unification who was raised in the Jewish faith but became a devout Lutheran at the age of nineteen. What interested Drucker in these three was their successful ability to balance continuity and change, and subsequently to create a political structure that survived until World War I. Humbolt, Radowitz, and Stahl modeled the ability to "preserve the traditions of the past and yet make possible change, and indeed very rapid change" (Drucker, 1992/1993, p. 443). As we shall see, the American Constitution served as another example of achieving this kind of balance. But Drucker's early study of government while earning his Ph.D. in Germany, on the eve of the Nazi's rise to power, informed much of his later writings on the public sector.

Friedrich Julius Stahl

While studying at the university, Drucker wrote an analysis of Stahl (1802–1861) titled "Friedrich Julius Stahl: Conservative Theory of the State and Historical Development" as part of his graduate work; the pamphlet was published in 1933. Stahl was, as Drucker describes him, a conservative in the sense that he sought to retain traditional institutions, including organized religion and monarchy, in order to stabilize society. Stahl sought to draw upon other representative bodies (universities, city governments, and especially Protestantism) in order to enable the older, stable institutions to respond to change (Freyberg, 1970, pp. 18–20; Levitt, 1970). Berthold Freyberg, head of a large fisheries company, met Drucker shortly after he left Vienna. He states that

> Stahl, unknown, unread, and ununderstood, attracted Drucker precisely because his basic subject matter had been what Drucker now calls "discontinuities." Stahl...saw his mission in bridging the great discontinuity which the French Revolution had left behind in the political and social life of continental Europe. He saw his mission in building a new political and social structure, appropriate to the demands, the realities, and the opportunities of a new age, yet based on the fundamental values and beliefs inherited from the past.
>
> *(Freyberg, 1970, pp. 18–20)*

Theodore Levitt has also noted that several of Drucker's ideas seem to bear the imprint of Stahl, particularly his interest in conservative innovation (Levitt, 1970, p. 13).

Drucker's work on Stahl represents an early exploration of the nature of power and authority in society from a philosophical viewpoint. His Stahl article is hardly a political tract, but is rather an exploration of "metaphysics, ethics and the philosophy of history" (Drucker, 1933/2002, p. 46). Most of the article is devoted to a discussion of Stahl's attempts to reconcile the apparent "antithesis of unity and plurality," or the tension between existence as a solitary individual and as part of a larger group (Drucker, 1933/2002, 46). Although Stahl sought to find an institutional governmental means to balance change and continuity, his framework was based on his refutation of Hegelian philosophy. Like Karl Marx and Soren Kierkegaard, Stahl was one of a number of philosophers who sought an alternative to Hegel's system. Stahl was in fact successor to G.W.F. Hegel (1770–1831) as head of the Department of Philosophy at the University of Berlin.

Hegel's answer to the conflict between unity and plurality was to resolve the tension through the process of dialectics, whereby duality is replaced by a new understanding of the collective human spirit or mind. Stahl, however, countered Hegel with his own concept of "the personal, creative God." The individual and the collective are not bridged through reason, or through any human power, but rather through a higher being, a supernatural force that stands outside of humanity. Thus, human beings are united in God, but retain their own individuality as a personal creation of God: "His creations have their oneness in Him, but since they themselves are unities, that is, creative personalities, so they too, by virtue of their own personality, are capable of the creative act" (Drucker, 1933/2002, p. 49).

Importantly, the creation, the individual, has free will and independence by design. Thus, although the spiritual and material may be joined in the individual, the individual must live on two levels: the material world (what Stahl terms the ethical sphere) and the divine world (the religious sphere). In the ethical sphere, humans relate to each other, revealing the likeness of God within themselves. In the religious realm, however, humans relate themselves to God through personal union. Although the two spheres interact and influence each other, they remain separate: "The task is for each sphere, each relation of human existence to be brought to complete development. To this end, morality must maintain its separation from religion with which it initially merged indistinguishably...." (Stahl, 1845/2002, Book 1, Part II, Chapter 1, Section 25).

The ethical sphere is also comprised of two types of human relations: humans as individuals and humans as a community. Here Stahl confronts the very real problem his system invokes. If the tension between the individual and society is not eradicated through some sort of dialectic, and if the person must function not just on a spiritual level but also in the ethical or material realm, the problem of how to reconcile individual interests with those of the larger community remains. Stahl answers the question as to whether these two modes of existence can ever be reconciled by pointing to both an ideal and a realistic state of affairs. In the ideal, there is no conflict between the group and individual, as the desires of the person and the human community are one and the same: to fulfill the desires of God. The material realm consists of very real conflicts between individual desires and actions and the needs of society. The reality of the human condition is that humans live apart from God, and thus must subject themselves to civil authority: the rule of state and law (Stahl, 1845/2002).

Stahl's solution to the tension between group and individual identity lies ultimately in submission to authority, be it to a personal Christian God or to the laws of the civil state. In either case, however, it is a willing submission, as humanity is free and independent in the world. In Drucker's words, this is "conscious rule over conscious, freely obedient beings who are thereby spiritually unified, a governance of a highly personal, not arbitrary, but necessary character" (Drucker, 1933/2002, p. 49). The concept of a free and independent person submitting to a supreme authority requires a definition of freedom that is akin to that espoused by late nineteenth-century and early twentieth-century progressive philosophers, such as Thomas Hill Green, William James, Alfred Fouillee, and William Dilthey, who were also grappling with the same issues of how to be an individual within, at that time, an increasingly industrial society. This concept of freedom was not based on the absence of limits on individual free will, but rather on active participation as a citizen in society (Kloppenberg, 1986). The notion of "positive" freedom implied a sense of personal responsibility, a belief in the existence of free will, but also in the moral imperative to act in such a way as to further the interests of the larger society. It is this sense of responsibility and accountability that is key to Stahl's system of the conservative state, and to much of Drucker's work as well. Dale Zand makes a similar point in his essay, "Toward Understanding Behavior in an Industrial Society," in Bonaparte and Flaherty:

> Man must become a competent "industrial citizen"; this is Drucker's theme. An industrial citizen not only contributes to the economic goals of the enterprise, he also influences and responsibly criticizes how the enterprise functions in society. Citizenship, in this fundamental sense, is at the center of Drucker's approach to the key problem of an industrial democracy: maintaining the delicate, but necessary, balance of power between the organization and the individual.
>
> *(Zand, 1970, pp. 111–112)*

Both the subject and the ruler are responsible and accountable under Stahl's theory, as Drucker argues. The monarch is sovereign (meaning, notes

Drucker, that he is "the bearer of the plenitude of power"), and thus is "entitled to exercise supreme power completely and indivisibly. Hence, he is also responsible for it...Power requires responsibility..." The monarch's responsibility is to govern effectively, fairly, but also to "subordinate his interests to that of the state and to respect the rights of his subjects" (Drucker, 1933/2002, p. 51). Berthold Freyberg also notes:

> ...the age-old relationship between power and responsibility—the true essence of that grossly misunderstood idea of the divine right of kings—had been brought back to life again by Stahl. What impressed Drucker was Stahl's belief that power must submit to responsibility.
>
> *(Freyberg, 1970, p. 20)*

The monarch, as an individual, is in a position of supremely ordained power, through which all are unified. Yet, he himself is required to relegate his own inner drives in order to accommodate the needs of the greater community. Thus the tension between individual desires and the needs of the group are resolved in the figure of the leader.

But the subjects, too, have responsibilities and accountability:

> It is the subject's duty, in turn to obey and love the legitimate supreme authority, to devote himself to and sacrifice himself for the state. His right is first of all the claim to freedom of religion, of teaching, of property; for the state as a highly imperfect institution, as the realm of Fallen Man, can only stand negatively, protectively before everything which springs from within the individual.
>
> *(Drucker, 1933/2002, p. 51)*

The obedience of the subject, however, must come of free will or choice, and here is the definition of freedom in the positive sense: "Legal freedom is bounded by higher duties to which persons must subordinate themselves; not, of course, by claims of (subjective) morality, but indeed by ethical ideas of life relations, to be maintained in common life" (Stahl, 1845/2002, Book 3, Part I, Chapter 1, Section 4). Individuals are willing to subject themselves to these higher duties because, as Stahl discusses in his concept of the personal creative God, the individual represents the highest form of creative spirit both in the material and the religious sense.

In several ways, Stahl served as Drucker's blueprint for locating a middle ground between extremes of change (revolution) and continuity (reactionism). In his search for an alternative to the *Ancien Regime* and revolution, Stahl also illustrated a possible center point between extremes. How can Conservatives, who embrace tradition and values of the past that should remain constant, also acknowledge the reality of change—as Drucker asks

"How can knowledge of the existence of an eternal order and an eternal aim be harmonized with the assumption of purpose in human affairs? ...how can rejection of Revolution be harmonized with the necessary acknowledgment of the results of an upheaval, once it has taken place, and how the bonds of tradition with support for new organic growth?" Drucker critiques Conservative radicalism, which seeks to maintain the past simply for the past's sake. Underlying this Conservative position is what Drucker terms a "faith in regression," quite literally the reverse position to the teleological progression of positivism (Drucker, 1933/2002, pp. 50–56). Drucker is equally critical of the Liberal's "faith in progress" merely for progress' sake, or the blind faith of positivism:

> The rationalist liberal is caught between holy wrath at conspiracies and educational zeal for the misinformed. He always knows what is right, necessary, and good—and it always is simple and easy. But he can never do it.
>
> *(Drucker, 1942, p. 144)*

Drucker's desire for a middle ground between Conservatism and Liberalism is particularly apparent in his analysis of National Socialism. Here, he critiques the system for its embodying the worst of both possible scenarios, but in their negative incarnations: National Socialism, argues Drucker, was "antiliberal but also anticonservative" (Drucker, 1939, p. 13). In its total rejection of anything from the past, Nazism would seem to parallel blind faith in progress, the aspect of liberalism Drucker shuns. But, while National Socialism turned away from the past, it offered no positive program for the future. Thus, the Nazis defined themselves on the basis of a negative program, refuting all positive ideology, whether conservative or liberal.

The answer, then, is not to reject the past wholesale (anti-conservatism), retain the past solely for the sake of retaining the past (Conservatism), reject any positive program for the future (anti-liberalism), or worship a utopian future of teleological progress (Liberalism). Just as Stahl sought a moderate route to establishing a system of authority based on definitions of positive freedom and equality before the law, Drucker sought to find a middle ground that would work in the new industrial society he saw.

His solution is, like Stahl's, to look to the justification of a supreme order for progress, or progress with a moral face:

> But from knowledge of the supreme order, in which development, if it is to be acknowledged, must find its legitimation, there also follows, for the Conservative theory of the state, knowledge of the imperfection of man, which demands justification by faith. Man's sinfulness calls for firm authority, for binding ties in state and church, knowledge of man's need

and weakness calls for association within the community of both close and extended family, of rank, nation and religion.

(Drucker, 1942, p. 56)

Here are two critical elements to understanding Drucker's concept of individual membership within the societal community. The first is his belief in the imperfectability of humankind, and the second is the pivotal role of faith. Drucker is a firm believer in individualism, but he does not trust the individual to act without guidance: "political freedom is only of value, when it is anchored in a higher communal obligation; otherwise the result is self-destruction and anarchy and an inevitable slide to despotism and dictatorship..." (Drucker, 1933/2002). It is faith in this higher communal obligation that redeems humanity, and that mandates a definition of freedom that embraces citizenship, or positive freedom, rather than an absence of restraint.

Stahl served as Drucker's model for negotiating a path between opposite poles pulling on humans throughout history. Both men were faced with a changing society in which the status quo was threatened, and both sought a new order that drew on institutions of the past as well as new developments of the present and future. Stahl also provided Drucker with one of his earliest philosophical guides for approaching the subject of society, especially the subject of governance.

Drucker in America

While Drucker's earliest writings took on the subjects of European political philosophy and the origins of totalitarianism in Europe following World War I, he turned his attention to analyzing the American system of government and its origins shortly after he arrived in the United States. By 1950, Drucker was thinking of government in terms of its role in a society of institutions. What function would government play in the new industrial society of organizations? How best could the practice of management be implemented in the public sector? How effective was government as an institution in terms of its performance? In his earlier writing from the 1940s, however, Drucker began to formulate a philosophy and blueprint for an industrial society that would provide the individual both status and function: status in terms of one's position within society, and function in terms of individual activity and satisfaction. What would governance in such a free society look like? How could government exercise authority legitimately and responsibly? And, most importantly, what kind of governance would prevent totalitarianism from occurring again?

American Democracy and Freedom

In *The Future of Industrial Man* (1942), Drucker places the development of American democracy in the larger context of European history. Thus, while he makes a case for the uniqueness of the American system of governance, he argues that the ideas behind the American Revolution were not exclusively American, and that the Revolution "was as much a European as an American event" (Drucker, 1942, p. 157). The American rejection of enlightened despotism gave life to anti-monarchical sentiments in England, bolstering the eventual rise of constitutional government. The ideas of Edmund Burke, Thomas Jefferson, Benjamin Franklin, and other statesmen were based on well-known political theories. Thus, it was not the ideology behind the American Revolution that was novel, but rather the way in which theory was put into practice; Americans "converted metaphysical reflections into concrete, responsible decisions" (Drucker, 1942, p. 159).

Drucker delves into the institutions that America devised to realize the political ideas of the age. Once he has established his theory of a functioning industrial society, he turns to the question: what constitutes free society and free government? In this section of the book, Drucker chastises the United States and other nations for misunderstanding the nature of freedom. Freedom, he says, is not license, peace, happiness, good government, or fun. Rather, it is the responsible exercise of choice:

> It is the freedom to choose between doing or not doing something, to act one way or another, to hold one belief or the opposite. It is never a release and always a responsibility. It is not "fun" but the heaviest burden laid on man: to decide his own individual conduct as well as the conduct of society, and to be responsible for both decisions.
>
> *(Drucker, 1942, pp. 109–110)*

Clearly, Drucker has taken Stahl's concept of "legal freedom" to heart. Freedom involves the individual's relationship with society; decisions are not made in a vacuum, where society places no limitations on individual choice. This is particularly important in issues of governance, where self-government involves individual participation that includes decisions but also responsibility for those decisions.

Drucker is careful, however, to distinguish between "free government" and "free society"; free government could degenerate into the tyranny of the majority or the tyranny of the minority. How, Drucker ponders, could a system of governance avoid the pitfalls of either a lack of citizen participation (effective rule by a powerful minority) or the mistaken belief in the perfection of majority rule? Earlier theorists were concerned with political freedom, not social freedom. How, in a modern world, could effective government achieve freedom politically and socially? Drucker found his answer in the Founding Fathers of America and Edmund Burke in England—those he terms "Liberal Conservatives" (Drucker, 1942, p. 132). The key was, as often is the case with Drucker, the idea of balance. The political and social centers of power would balance each other out through recognition of their existence. To Drucker, the clearest example of this idea of free government and free society coexisting was embodied in the American Constitution and the idea of Federalism.

The Founding Fathers, Burke, and the American Constitution

Drucker early on expresses reverence for the Founding Fathers in America and the English conservatives of the late 1700s. What he most admired in Hamilton, Madison, Burke and others was not just their political philosophy, but that they saw the importance of putting principle into action: "method was as important to them as principles" (Drucker, 1942, p. 180). Drucker refers to the American and English conservatives of this era as the "conservative counterrevolutionaries." While conservatives, they never sought to turn back the clock to some idealized view of the past; rather, they were pragmatic as to the social realities they faced. Just as Drucker disagreed with those in interwar Austria who sought to return to the "old ways" before World War I, he was critical of reactionary views of governance. As early as 1942, Drucker was thinking about how to retain the institutions that functioned well in a society, but implement a system of governance that allowed society to acknowledge the reality of change:

> The Founding Fathers in America and the radical conservatives in England were thus conservatives of the present and future, rather than conservatives of the past. They knew that their social reality was that of a mercantile system, while their social institutions were pre-mercantile. Their method was to start with this fact and to develop a free and functioning mercantile society. They wanted to solve the future, not the past, to overcome the next and not the last revolution.
>
> *(Drucker, 1942, p. 181)*

As such, the United States Constitution became a model for Drucker for how to begin to think about implementing the idea of a functioning society that recognized change but did not simply throw out the past. The Constitution is not a perfect document; it has, of course, been amended over the course of time to adapt to changing social circumstances. Drucker refers to the document as a "broad frame of general principles" rather than a blueprint or panacea. He saw the wisdom of the Constitution in its restraint, not in its detail (Drucker, 1942, pp. 181–182). Of course, this vague nature of the Constitution has presented countless challenges for the American legal system as it attempts to interpret the meaning of such elements as the First and Second Amendments. Yet, for Drucker, this aspect of this founding document is a plus; it represents sound, pragmatic thinking—an understanding that today's circumstances cannot possibly remain the same, and that a framework for governance must contain elements of flexibility and openness to interpretation while still presenting fundamental principles.

Despite Drucker's reverence for the U.S. Constitution, he is careful to point out that effective government cannot rely solely on infrastructure: "...a free society cannot be legislated into existence..." (Drucker, 1942, p. 118). Ethical decisions are crucial to freedom, particularly because of the role of power. Power must exist as an instrument of organization, a determiner of social relations, and a means of creating hierarchical structure. But it is not an end. Indeed, Drucker remarks that America had the good fortune to have early leadership that understood the need for ethical decisions and checks and balances.

Federalism

Federalism, or, as he sometimes refers to it, decentralization, is key to understanding the link between Drucker's management ideas and his larger concerns with the subject of governance. As we have seen in this chapter, Drucker's early work on political theory and European governance concerned itself with the need for a middle ground between revolution and reactionism, but it also dealt with the reality of power. How does society balance the needs of the individual with the needs of greater society? Why would an individual willingly submit to a larger authority and subordinate their individual desires? What makes a governing power legitimate? We saw how Stahl's ideas provided a philosophical framework; the American Constitution and its system of Federalism provided a method to implement this theoretical construct.

The idea of federalism predates the American Constitution, but the debates on the Constitution developed a new discussion around this concept (Maciariello and Linkletter, 2010). After the American Revolution ended in 1777, the former colonies agreed to organize under a loose arrangement that avoided any centralized power. The thirteen states were sovereign, not beholden to each other except for some vague statements under the Articles of Confederation. This harmony did not last long, as by the 1780s, many of the states experienced rebellions and uprisings related to economic conditions unique to each state. In 1787, state delegates met in Philadelphia to create a form of unified government. These meetings led to an airing of real philosophical differences about the nature of power and governance. The result was what are now known as *The Federalist Papers*, a series of essays written by John Jay, Alexander Hamilton, and James Madison. These men attempted to address the concerns of the anti-Federalists, such as Thomas Jefferson: those who distrusted centralized power and the loss of state sovereignty.

The question of power and its legitimacy loomed large in the debates on the Constitution. Federalists pointed to the chaos of state governance under the Articles of Confederation; without some kind of central authority, events such as Shays' Rebellion, an armed uprising of poor people in Western Massachusetts in 1787, would only multiply and grow more violent. Yet, the American Revolution was predicated on the idea that the will of the people needed to be represented, albeit by a small group of elite, virtuous leaders. The last thing the new American government wanted to replicate was the illegitimate rulership of King George. The careful selection of George Washington as the first Chief Executive (and his reluctance to accept the position) ensured that merit, not entitlement, would be valued in leadership. Thus, Washington would be accepted by Federalists and Anti-Federalists alike as a legitimate President.

Another question at hand in devising a central government was the issue of sovereignty. How much power and authority would the states be expected to cede to this federal government? How could authority, or sovereignty, be shared between state and federal powers? What would be the limits on federal authority, and how would those limits be ensured? How could the new federal government guarantee that it would not abuse its power just as the British monarchy had done? Anti-Federalists proposed a Bill of Rights that would spell out the limitations of the federal government's power. Federalists were against this kind of specificity, but understood that, in order to reach agreement, they had to address the concerns of the Anti-Federalists. The answer lay in the notion of popular sovereignty: that the people as a whole held power and authority. Ultimately, popular sovereignty was the solution to resolving the problem of who was the final authority in a society wrestling with issues of power.

Although popular sovereignty helped to address the Anti-Federalists' concerns, early Americans were not innocents with respect to human nature. The idea of separation of powers to prevent abuse was included in several early state constitutions, so when the time came to frame the United States Constitution, the idea was not novel (Wood, 1969, pp. 150–151). Because of this history, Federalists and Anti-Federalists engaged in a lengthy debate about what separation of power actually looked like in practice; were the departments or branches of the states really separate, or was there some element of overlap? In Drucker's words, did the practice in fact reflect the principal? The answer was, of course, no. Any system that requires people to adhere to a fixed set of organizational rules will encounter exceptions, and that system will face challenges or threats from those who seek to find loopholes and abuse them. In Federalist Number 51, Madison offers suggestions for administrative safeguards against such abuses, but offers the most wise advice regarding any attempt at avoiding abuse of authority and power:

Ambition must be made to counteract ambition. The interest of the man must be connected with the constitutional rights of the place. It may be a reflection on human nature, that such devices should be necessary to control the abuses of government. But what is government itself, but the greatest of all reflections on human nature? If men were angels, no controls on government would be necessary. In framing a government which is to be administered by men over men, the great difficulty lies in this: you must first enable the government to control the governed; and in the next place oblige it to control itself.

(Madison, 1788/1992, p. 164)

This theme of human nature as fallen, fallible, not angels, and in constant danger of falling into the trap of the lure of power must have resonated with Drucker, given his larger philosophical framework (see Chapter 2). As Drucker developed a philosophy and a program for a functioning society of organizations, Madison's words had to have informed his reverence for the American Constitution and the principles of federalism.

The last aspect of the American Constitution and the Federalism-Anti-Federalism debate that influenced Drucker's work on management is the issue of pluralism. Drucker early on points to Madison as the true innovator in terms of understanding the need for a plurality of interests, that "any one ethical principle of power will become an absolutist, i.e., a tyrannical principle unless checked, controlled, and limited by a competing principle" (Drucker, 1942, p. 134). As we shall shortly see, Drucker envisioned a pluralistic society of institutions with competing visions as key to avoiding concentrations of power and authority (particularly in the form of governmental power). However, in Madison's society, a world of institutions with competing visions and goals constituted "factionalism," the threat of competing interests that would break up a fragile political union. In addition, pluralism represented a challenge to the wealthy elite; the acceptance of class mobility was not part of American society until much later, in the 1800s. Madison, breaking with his era's thinking, advanced an argument in Federalist 10, that factions were a natural part of the human condition, and thus only a large, diverse society could dilute their negative impacts. Essentially, the more voices that could be heard, the greater the possibility that the country could avoid a "tyranny of the majority." In Federalist 10, Madison adeptly argues that the more opinions, the more pluralism in society, the better, because it prevents a majority from squashing the interests and desires of the minority—no matter how splintered they may be (Madison, 1787).

A Pluralistic Society of Institutions

Drucker's ideas about the American Constitution shaped his later work on management (see Chapter 3), but they also informed his view of the role of the public sector in a pluralistic society of institutions. Drucker takes his early interest in American government (as well as his study of European political history) and applies it adeptly to his framework for a functioning society of institutions. As Drucker moved forward with his work, he still thought about the role of government in an increasingly pluralistic society. If Madison considered the increasing pluralism in his society, Drucker did so as well. Whereas government and political theory occupied Drucker's early work, he turned his attention to the new phenomenon of managerial capitalism that arose in the years after World War II. Government was no longer a monolithic power; now, Drucker moved from writing about "the State" to "the new society" where many institutions compete (Jackson, 2010). As we shall see, this was, in large part, due to the timing of Drucker's emigration to America. It was also framed by Drucker's early focus on European political theory and history, and his fascination with the contrasts presented by American political history:

> I can see one possible—but only partial—solution to the governmental crisis of our time. This is a return to political pluralism, to government by many autonomous powers, each with its own sphere, its own job, its own law, all competing with one another and limiting one another.... Organized power monopoly triumphed everywhere in the West—except in the United States. Here, pluralism remained fundamental—in practice as well as in theory. John Adams, Jefferson, Madison, and Calhoun, the great political theorists of the American Republic, were all pluralists. The United States was founded on a conscious rejection of European concepts of monopoly government and nation-state, and adopted instead the concept of government by countervailing powers under the law.
>
> *(Drucker, 1959, p. 38)*

Key to Drucker's theory of a functioning society of institutions is the idea of countervailing powers, where single-purpose organizations (much like the branches of government under American federalism) compete with and limit each other to prevent abuse of power. Just as Madison envisioned the difficulty in preventing the "tyranny of the majority" or, similarly, the dictatorial power of an overly powerful central government, Drucker draws on the idea of pluralism to hammer out a framework for creating a role for all institutions—public and private—where government is not an authoritarian power, but neither is a weak institution incapable of governance.

Drucker's Unique View of America

One of the institutions about which Drucker was most concerned with encouraging pluralism is the public sector. He was highly critical of big government, arguing for a limited role for federal and state governments. Drucker argues that the trend toward big government was a legacy of the first part of the twentieth century, when the successes of the public sector convinced most western countries that government could solve most any problem that faced society. He posits that the modern business organization presented the first major independent challenge to the absolute power of government. Yet, at the same time, he makes a case for a functioning government as crucial to society (Drucker, 1950, 1969).

Drucker's views on the role of the public sector are in large part a function of his own experiences, both in Europe and the United States. Drucker moved to the United States in 1937, during the Great Depression and before the nation had entered World War II. While America had been recovering from the economic downturn begun in the early 1930s, 1937–1938 marked a period of sharp decline, with unemployment rising and GDP dropping. While the decline was not as severe as that of the 1929 rout, it nevertheless was a demoralizing turn of events after several quarters of positive economic results.

Much of Drucker's experience in 1930s America was shaped by the impact of unemployment on the population. He saw unemployment—and even the threat of unemployment—as not just a financial problem but a social and psychological problem. Drucker notes that even those who did not actually lose their jobs during the Depression suffered emotionally, as they suffered the fear of being fired—a state of psychological torture. Yet, while the damage inflicted by chronic unemployment is social and psychological, the solution is not for the public sector to stand by and do nothing. Drucker calls for "positive economic action" at the governmental level, a task he recognizes is difficult. However,

> the mass-production society must have a government strong enough and powerful enough to cope with the unbearable menace of chronic unemployment [and it] must have a government weak enough and limited enough not to menace the freedom, happiness and the private life of every citizen.
>
> *(Drucker, 1950, p. 10)*

Yet, Drucker viewed government intervention in the form of the New Deal in remarkably favorable terms, at least socially. Indeed, he was critical of such policies as Roosevelt's investment in the Public Works Administration, arguing that, while it was wise to invest in such projects during an economic downturn, such a program's overall impact on business conditions would be minimal, and perhaps negative (Drucker, 1950, p. 259). But it was the social and cultural impact of New Deal efforts that Drucker found effective. In his memoir, Drucker refers to the Depression in America as an era where culture and community held strong, where despite the economic failures of Roosevelt's policies, their victory was in creating a "celebration of community, of shared values, of the joy of life, and of common hope" (Drucker, 1978, p. 302). Programs such as the Works Progress Administration's Federal Arts programs that funded efforts to collect and catalog American art and music from rural communities, prison inmates, and other underserved populations helped to unify the country culturally at a time when virtually everyone was suffering financially.

What Drucker did not experience was America before the 1930s: the history of management and labor disruption, economic turmoil, inequality between urban and rural areas, social and cultural shifts related to race, ethnicity, and gender, and much more. As biographer Jack Beatty remarked, "Part of the problem is that he doesn't remember pre-New Deal America" (Beatty, 1998). So, while Drucker saw "big government" as a creeping feature of late twentieth-century America, in reality, America had a long history of power struggles and sharing between government and business. The history of American business and management is in large part a reflection of the concern for concentration of power—something Drucker himself worried about constantly.

By the time Drucker witnessed the miracle of modern management's ability to stimulate production during World War II, the large corporation already had had a history in the United States. Drucker acknowledges that management as a concept was applied in the public sector early in the twentieth century: "The first conscious and systematic application of management principles…was not in a business. It was in the reorganization of the U.S. Army in 1901 by Elihu Root (1845–1937), Roosevelt's secretary of war" (Drucker, 1998, p. 156). But, in essence, as Alfred Chandler describes in his work *The Visible Hand*, the railroads were the earliest organizations that employed management techniques and concepts. The railroads were also the first organizations to face the public outcry over concentration of corporate power. As other industries consolidated and organized as enormous, powerful trusts, governments from Teddy Roosevelt through Franklin Delano Roosevelt responded to pressure from labor, reformers, and the public to curb business' influence. Government and business also had a long history of sharing power, from Wilson's War Industries Board during World War I to Herbert Hoover's corporatism of the 1920s.

Thus, by the time Peter Drucker entered the American scene, the nation already had a history of public and government interaction with business organizations, and with implementing concepts of management. The push-pull of whether one or multiple institutions would wield the power was already a dance whose steps all sides knew well. Although the large-scale rise of the white-collar office employee would not come until World War II, the corporation was a part of American culture and society by the 1930s.

In fact, while Drucker was studying Stahl in Germany, Herbert Hoover himself was pondering paths between. In 1922, he explored ways to avoid the battle between "revolutionaries and reactionaries" in his work *American Individualism* (1922). First through the experience with World War I, then with the Depression, Americans experimented with synthesizing management and liberalism, creating a blend of old-style laissez-faire capitalism and new corporate organizational methods and ideals. Management, whether in the guise of government-business cooperation, government intervention, or corporate leadership, had become part and parcel of American society. Although Drucker recognized management, and described and codified it, management already had a history, one intricately entwined with the country's larger history of distrust of concentrated power, authority, and large-scale entities.

Government's Role in a Pluralistic Society

As Drucker worked to flesh out a pragmatic way to implement his ideas about the role of governance, power, authority, and legitimacy in society, he began to absorb current events, particularly in America. Drucker viewed the country's ability to rapidly mobilize for World War II, turning peacetime manufacturing plants into factories for planes and munitions, as an example of effective government and management. Yet, as World War II gave way to the Cold War arms build-up and the rise of the military-industrial complex, he increasingly called for limits to government activities. Nevertheless, Drucker's call for diffusion and limitation of power within the public sector is not a libertarian plea for an end to the federal government:

> Industrial society must decentralize power in autonomous hands. But at the same time it cannot afford, in doing so, to turn itself into an anarchic society, comparable to the society of the fifteenth century, with its amorphous mass of petty principalities, free cities, exempt bishoprics and noble highwaymen. On the contrary, it must have the power and unity for effective action against a depression. Unless industrial society can *decentralize* the power of giving or denying access to the means of production, it will not remain a free society; it will be in permanent danger of becoming totalitarian. But if it loses the power to act, it will fail to remain a society altogether.
>
> *(Drucker, 1950, pp. 11–12)*

Drucker here refers to decentralization of power; later he would use the term "federalism" as a principal of governance, particularly with respect to organizations. Absolute concentration of power in government smacks of totalitarianism. Notice also the theme found in Stahl's ideas, that the tension between individual existence and the needs of society is reconciled through willing submission to a legitimate authority in a free society. Governance is critical to holding society together. Too much pluralism, or individualism run amok with no sense of the greater good, is a danger as well. The potential to backslide, to retreat to an "amorphous mass of petty principalities" is omnipresent. Even in the concept of pluralism, a human construct, there are pitfalls to be avoided, and Drucker expresses ambivalence as he calls for decentralization.

Thus, while Drucker was always distrustful of concentrated power, he was constantly vigilant of the need for the common good to be protected. In a pluralistic society of institutions, who would watch out for the greater good? Champions of pluralism, such as James Madison, argued that competing minority interests would ensure that no one such interest would dominate. Instead, resulting decision or policies would reflect this clash of interests and represent the interests of the overall constituencies. By the 1950s, Drucker was skeptical that this would actually work in practice. Instead, "government's first job is to make the common interest prevail over partial and private interests...today our many power centers, except in time of war, recognize no overriding common good" (Drucker, 1959, p. 40). By 2000, Drucker had backed away from this view of the public sector. No longer was it government's job to mind the greater good; that role now belonged to the non-profit sector (Drucker, 1999). Having spent most of his time working with businesses in the mid-twentieth century, Drucker began to absorb the sentiments of those around him. As Jack Beatty notes, his later attitudes about government may have resulted from Drucker spending time with people who viewed government as a "total albatross" (Beatty, 1998).

"The Sickness of Government"

While he had turned his attention to the non-profits (what he called the social sector) toward the end of his life, Drucker was still interested in finding a way for government to function in a pluralistic society of organizations. The role of the public sector had changed dramatically in American society after World War II. Not only was a substantial portion of the federal budget used for defense, but, increasingly, social programs were expanded to combat poverty. The social safety nets created during the New Deal (such as Social Security) were designed to be self-funding, but only because they excluded a good number of Americans, particularly people of color. The expansion of welfare and other programs under several administrations, particularly during Lyndon Johnson's Great Society program, resulted in significant increases in public spending on education, health care, food assistance, and other areas. These new programs were driven in large part by the Civil Rights movement, which sought to redress historical racial inequities that resulted in a lack of opportunities for people of color to advance in society. Segregation in American schools was ruled illegal by the Supreme Court's 1954 decision in the *Brown v. Board of Education* case, but Jim Crow laws separating public space for whites and blacks remained common practice in much of the country. It was not until the 1964 Civil Rights Act, passed under the Johnson administration's watch, that such practices were outlawed. These legal actions were the result of social activism and public pressure to fulfill the aspirational goals of the Declaration of Independence, that "all men are created equal."

By the late 1960s, America experienced a growing tide of social upheaval fueled by a number of factors: an expensive and failing war in Viet Nam, a growing youth movement upset with institutions of power for their failure to address societal problems, a nascent feminist movement, and the end of a post-war economic boom. President Johnson's decision not to run for re-election in 1968 was but one example of the turmoil and dysfunction of the political, social, economic, and cultural climate of the nation.

In 1969, Drucker published *The Age of Discontinuity*, an assessment of a society in flux. In his chapter titled "The Sickness of Government," he presents his historical argument for the status of the public sector. He says that, virtually everywhere (not just in America), there is disenchantment with government. People turned to the public sector during the Depression and World War II, and government performed. Government has now been tasked with solving bigger and more problems (poverty, food production, medical care) but they are not delivering, he argues. In this text, Drucker places the blame on expectations: people expected miracles out of the public sector, things that simply could not be done. And now they are disgruntled.

The solution, Drucker says, is to change the expectations. Government bureaucracy is not the problem; bureaucracy is what holds government accountable: "Any government that is not a 'government of forms' degenerates rapidly into a mutual looting society" (Drucker, 1969, pp. 229–230). What is required is a new vision of the role of government. Rather than implementing policy and programs, the public sector sets the agenda and leaves the doing to others. In essence, Drucker has now applied his executive model to government; government serves as the Chief Executive Officer, making "fundamental decisions" effectively (Drucker, 1969, p. 233). Just as the effective executive needs to refrain from getting bogged down in the day-to-day operational activities of a business, government needs to make decisions, but then delegate. Drucker published *The Effective Executive* in 1966; it is not surprising that he transfers his advice to leaders in that book to public-sector leadership in *The Age of Discontinuity* a couple of years later. If executives delegate the "doing" to those in the organization best suited to accomplish the mission and goals, why shouldn't government leadership ask how they can use other organizations in society to be the "doers." In essence, Drucker was developing an argument for privatization.

Privatization

By the 1980s, Drucker had developed his view of government, particular the role of government in American society. In keeping with his role as a social ecologist, he looked at the long, historical arc of the public sector's role in society over time. Essentially, Drucker argues that discussions around the role of government centered on its legitimacy and functions. Libertarians argue against any interference in personal freedoms. Economists argued whether or not the government should intervene to stabilize the economy. The primary focus of arguments about the role of the public sector was regarding what it *should* or *shouldn't* do.

Drucker does take up this conversation, but turns it around to a question of performance, a common theme in his management writings. In essence, one should ask not what government *should* do, but what it is capable of doing. Government, he states, worked effectively up until World War II. Drucker points to Germany's health insurance programs of the nineteenth century, nationalized railroads in Europe, and Roosevelt's New Deal programs of the 1930s as success stories. But, Drucker states, since World War II, government has underperformed—or worse (Drucker, 1989). Why?

Here Drucker turns away from history and launches into a discussion of the limitations of the public sector in terms of its innovative capabilities, the necessity of its facilitating functions that cannot be fulfilled by other institutions, and its function as a non-business entity. Drucker's takeaways are that:

- Government has functions that only it can perform, such as defense, law and order, and justice.
- Government needs to play a role in ensuring a level playing field; in Drucker's words, government needs to be "more activist than the nineteenth-century Liberals such as Herbert Spencer preached and wanted" (Drucker, 1989, p. 68).
- Government needs to learn to abandon activities that are no longer productive (innovative behavior).
- Government should not do any activity that can be better performed by a non-governmental agency.

This last statement fuels Drucker's belief in privatization, a term he says he coined in *The Age of Discontinuity* (Drucker, 1989, p. 61). In fact, Drucker refers to "reprivatization" in that text (Drucker, 1969, p. 234). As we have seen, in 1969, he viewed government as the Chief Executive of society, setting the mission and the agenda, with other institutions implementing the programs and policies to achieve larger goals. By 1989, Drucker decided that, in fact, there were some things government should actually do. We cannot privatize the military, the legal system, and enforcement of an equitable society. But government is no longer the central social institution that it was under his vision in the 1960s. Nor is government a "conserving" institution, unable to innovate for good reason (Drucker, 1969). Now, the public sector needs to learn innovative behavior; gone is its role as a stabilizing influence in society. It now is expected to change along with other organizations of destabilization. By the 1990s, Drucker has applied his model of business thinking to government. The public sector is simply yet another organization that needs to identify its strengths and revisit its mission at all levels on a regular basis. Should we retain a given government agency? Has it already fulfilled its mission and therefore can be disbanded? Is it unpopular with the public? Government, like all other organizations, need to practice systematic abandonment of ineffective, unproductive activities:

> Continuing with activities that we would not now choose to begin is wasteful. They should be abandoned. One cannot even guess how many government activities would be found to be worth preserving. But my experience with many organizations suggests that the public would vote against continuing something like two fifths, if not half, of all civilian agencies and programs.
>
> *(Drucker, 1995)*

Yet (and Drucker himself notes this tendency), most Americans want public services, yet don't want to pay for them. During the debates about the Affordable Care Act in 2009, protestors against the legislation held signs that said "Keep Government Out of my Medicare," demonstrating a complete lack of understanding about the role of the federal government in that health care program. To turn government into an organ of innovation requires decision makers who can evaluate what is effective; but Drucker's solution to paste his management theories onto the public sector seems a simplistic solution to a complex social problem. Perhaps this is why, not long after, he wrote that

> we know that government cannot take care of community problems. We know that business and the free market also cannot take care of community problems. We have now come to accept that there has to be a third sector, the *social sector* of (mostly nonprofit) community organizations.
>
> *(Drucker, 1999, p. 21)*

Conclusion

For some, speculating what "Drucker would do" or what "Drucker would think" is something of a sport. In a sense, Drucker invited this form of speculation and entertainment. His language is, for the most part, broad when it comes to matters we might deem controversial. Drucker never weighed in on social issues such as abortion or LGBTQ rights, although those subjects were certainly front and center in Western politics during his lifetime. He rarely took a public political position, and, in fact, shunned involvement in political matters. In his own words:

> No one interfered with the things I wanted to do, so I don't interfere with what other people are doing, never. No, I'm an old conservative. I have a very simple rule: As long as it's neither completely insane nor immoral, I'm willing to help you accomplish it.
>
> *(Arnn, Masugi, and Schramm, 1984)*

In essence, Drucker was a man who lived by his own standards of integrity, holding personal opinions to be just that—personal. The same held true for his political opinions and affiliations. Drucker saw a separation between political life and managerial life as essential in a pluralistic society of institutions. This fits entirely with his philosophy of the need to balance the need for individual identity that is separate from that of the community. Drucker lived this and practiced integrity as a result.

Nevertheless, we can see an evolution in Drucker's thought with respect to changing times. There is a model of balance of change and continuity in Drucker's own thought on the role of government; he was willing to alter his social theory and model for a functioning society based on what he experienced and witnessed. Yet, he retained his belief in the need for the separation of the personal from the public. Attempts to position Drucker as a political conservative figure misunderstand this essential nature of who he was. He was, in the end, an apolitical person. Drucker was, rather, a person driven by history and context, not political winds.

As evidenced through his writing, Drucker spent his lifetime trying to find a suitable role for the public sector in a functioning society of institutions. It is a fascinating journey of a man who navigated his way through major events in history: Weimar Germany, Nazi Germany, New Deal America, World War II, the rise of corporate America, the Cold War, America's Civil Rights movement and other social movements, and the return to conservatism in the 1980s and 1990s. What started as a project in understanding the role of power and authority in society morphed into an exercise in transforming government into an agency of managerial effectiveness and innovation. In essence, Drucker's work on government is a window on his changing philosophy of a functioning society, informed by his experiences and his unique place in time and history.

Toward the end of his life, Drucker published a collection of his essays in a volume titled *A Functioning Society* (2003). This book provides a glimpse into the mind of Peter Drucker as a man facing the end of a storied career as a writer; he personally selected the essays to be included, and thus most likely considered them to be among his best work. He devotes an entire section to "The Sickness of Government" (which includes that chapter from his 1969 book and two other essays). In his introduction to that section, Drucker claims that *The Age of Discontinuity* had enormous political impact (particularly on Margaret Thatcher's policies). While these claims may be challenged, what Drucker says about his work on government is important:

> For more than fifty years—from the end of World War I until Mrs. Thatcher around 1970—it was believed all but universally that a government is the more effective the bigger it is and the more it *does*...This belief was just as pervasive in the democracies as it was in the totalitarian regimes—their differences were in their beliefs in the rights of the Individual rather than in their beliefs in the competence of government and of the state. But by the end of the 1960s enough evidence of the incompetence of government as a doer had accumulated to create receptivity for a discussion of the limits of government...[by 1989] it could be shown that the nearly three hundred years had come to an end in which most people in developed countries— and equally in developing ones—expected a social creed, for example, capitalism or Marxism, to take care of *all* problems of community, society and polity.
>
> *(Drucker, 2003, pp. 53–54)*

In 1939, Drucker wrote of the failure of social creeds in Europe leading to Nazi Germany and fascism in Europe in his book *The End of Economic Man*. A few years before his death, he was still thinking about the failure of government, despite his valiant efforts to devise a system that, in his mind, would let constitutional government be the chief executive of a society of pluralistic organizations. It is a tragic exercise to understand Drucker's relationship with the private sector. We may be dismayed with any one of his solutions or conclusions, as varied as they were, but they are a byproduct not of political persuasions but rather of a complex history.

Bibliography

Arnn, L., Masugi, K., and Schramm, P. (1984) 'Reviewing the moral sciences', *Claremont Review of Books*, III (1). https://claremontreviewofbooks.com/reviv ing-the-moral-sciences-a-conversation-with-peter-f-drucker/

Beatty, J. (1998) 'The author of modernity', Interview with Stossel, S., *Atlantic Unbound*, 29 January.

Drucker, P.F. (1933/2002) 'Friedrich Julius Stahl: His conservative theory of the state', originally published in 1933 as *Friedrich Julius Stahl: Konservative Staats—Theorie und Geschichtliche Entwicklung*, J.C.B. Mohr, Tubingen, DE, *Society*, pp. 46–57.

Drucker, P.F. (1939) *The end of economic man*. New Brunswick, NJ: Transaction.

Drucker, P.F. (1942) *The future of industrial man*. New Brunswick, NJ: Transaction.

Drucker, P.F. (1950) *The new society: The anatomy of industrial order*. New Brunswick, NJ: Transaction.

Drucker, P.F. (1959) 'The breakdown of governments', *Harper's Magazine*, January, pp. 35–40.

Drucker, P.F. (1969) *The age of discontinuity: Guidelines to our changing society*. New York: Harper & Row.

Drucker, P.F. (1978) *Adventures of a bystander*. New York: John Wiley & Sons.

Drucker, P.F. (1989) *The new realities*. New York: Harper & Row

Drucker, P.F. (1992/1993) 'Reflections of a social ecologist', in Drucker, P.F. (ed.), *The ecological vision*. New Brunswick, NJ: Transaction, pp. 441–457.

Drucker, P.F. (1995) '*Really* reinventing government', *The Atlantic Monthly*, 275, pp. 49–61.

Drucker, P.F. (1998) 'Management's new paradigms', *Forbes*, 5 October.

Drucker, P.F. (1999) *Management challenges for the 21st century*. New York: Harper Collins.

Drucker, P.F. (2003) *A functioning society*. New Brunswick, NJ: Transaction.

Freyberg, B. (1970) 'The genesis of Drucker's thought', in Bonaparte, T.H. and Flaherty, J. (eds.), *Peter Drucker: Contributions to business enterprise*. New York: New York University Press, pp. 17–22.

Hoover, H. (1922) *American individualism*. Garden City, NY: Doubleday, Page & Company.

Jackson, I.A. (2010) 'Drucker on government, business, and civil society: Roles, relationships, responsibilities', in Pearce, C., Maciariello, J., and Yamawaki, H. (eds.), *The Drucker difference: What the world's greatest management thinker means to today's business leaders*. New York: McGraw Hill, pp. 17–34.

Kloppenberg, J.T. (1986) *Uncertain victory: Social democracy and progressivism in European and American thought, 1870-1920*. New York: Oxford University Press.

Levitt, T. (1970) 'The living legacy of Peter Drucker', in Bonaparte, T.H. and Flaherty, J. (eds.), *Peter Drucker: Contributions to Business Enterprise*. New York: New York University Press, pp. 5–16.

Lowith, K. (1964) *From Hegel to Nietzsche: The revolution in nineteenth-century thought*, trans. Green, D. New York: Holt, Rinehart and Winston.

Maciariello, J. and Linkletter, K. (2010) 'The next book Peter Drucker would have written: Federalism and management as a liberal art', *Management Decision*, 48 (4), pp. 628–655.

Madison, J. (1787) 'To break and control the violence of faction', *The Federalist X* originally published in New York: *Daily Advertiser*, 22 November. Reprinted in Bailyn, B. (ed.) (1993) *The debates on the constitution: Part one*. New York: Library of America, pp. 404–411.

Madison, J. (1788) 'On the safety of multiple interests: Ambition will counteract ambition', *The Federalist LI*, originally published in New York: *Independent*

Journal, 6 February. Reprinted in Bailyn, B. (ed.) (1992) *The debates on the Constitution: Part two*. New York: Library of America, pp. 163–168.

Stahl, F.J. (1845/2002) *Rechts- und Staatslehre auf der Grundlage christlicher Weltanschauung* (*The Philosophy of Law and State on the Basis of the Christian Worldview*), translation by Alvarado, R., published as *Principles of Law* (2002), Aalten, NL: Woodbridge Publishing.

Wood, G. (1969) *The creation of the American republic, 1776-1787*. Chapel Hill: University of North Carolina Press.

Zand, D. (1970) 'Toward understanding behavior in an industrial society', in Bonaparte, T.H. and Flaherty, J. (eds.), *Peter Drucker: Contributions to business enterprise*. New York: New York University Press, pp. 111–124.

8

DRUCKER AND TECHNOLOGY

Introduction

During Drucker's career, the world witnessed a dizzying array of technological advances. Following World War II, America's war production capabilities were modified for peacetime purposes. Research and development advances, coupled with a post-war industrial boom, led to new technologies including television, computers, satellites, nylon and other synthetics, and wide array of consumer goods. After the war, President Truman instituted the Marshall Plan, a massive program of economic aid to western Europe to rebuild the economy of that part of the world. This program helped to spread American technological advances to Europe and Asia. Therefore, it is not surprising that Drucker turned his attention to the impact of technology on history and culture early in his work.

In spite of ominous developments in technological capabilities in the twentieth century, Drucker remained generally optimistic about the role of technology in society. He warned of possible negative impacts of advances but, rather than issuing doomsday predictions, carefully explained the relationship between technology, history, and society. In Drucker's view, technology is part of the natural order of things, a byproduct of the normal process of change. Like all change, technological advancements bring disruption. But, if seen through the eyes of historical context and the role of culture and human values, technology is but yet one more part of society that can be managed. Just as he established management as an organized discipline and practice (and later did the same with innovation), Drucker presents technology as an organizing principle for human activity. His understanding of technology from a historical perspective allows for an interpretation of technological

DOI: 10.4324/9781003410485-9

change as part of the human condition, and as such a force both influenced by and exerting influence on society and culture. Finally, Drucker presents technology from a systems or process perspective. Taken as a whole, his material on technology shows how discontinuities and disruptions, while real, are part of a larger continuity in human existence.

Toward a Definition of Technology

Drucker's earliest work on technology stems from his observations of 1950s American industrial society. In the years after World War II, American manufacturing produced nearly half of the world's goods. As companies sought to increase output and efficiency, they began to use more sophisticated machines in the production process. The use of numerical controls to set up and run machines increased by the middle of the decade. Automation, the use of machines to perform rudimentary functions in the manufacturing process, was the technology of the era. In American popular culture, automation was viewed with fear, particularly in terms of the impact it would have on jobs. By the early 1960s, automation was part of American popular culture; parodist Allen Sherman's song "Automation" mused "I thought automation was keen, 'til you were replaced by a ten-ton machine" (Sherman, 1963). Experts issued dire predictions of mass job losses in the manufacturing sector. But most corporate executives and many economists argued that while the new technology would eliminate low-skilled jobs, it would in turn create enough skilled positions to compensate for these job losses. Ralph Cordiner, CEO of General Electric and a longtime associate of Drucker's, was one of the strongest advocates for automation; General Electric was a pioneer in the use of new technology in the early 1950s.

Drucker early on saw the need for understanding technology as part of his larger theory of a functioning society. Nothing would slow the advance of western industrial society. However, as the champion of mass-production industrialization, the United States had a responsibility to make such a society one that was rational, that provided meaning to the individual as a member of society and as a person. In other words, technology must be seen as part of human society, not just tools, machines, or gadgets. While America has demonstrated leadership in technology,

We have not developed the social and political institutions to go with this technology. But precisely because mass-production technology is a corrosive acid which no pre-industrial culture or social order can resist, the world requires a working model of the political and social institutions for an industrial age. Without such a model to imitate and learn from, the mass-production revolution can only produce decades of world war, chaos, despair and destruction.

(Drucker, 1950, p. 16)

Technology, for Drucker, is a "principle of social order" (Drucker, 1950, p. 19).

Many think of technology in terms of mechanical, scientific, or engineering advancements. Drucker did not; he defined it in terms of human purposes. Automation, he argued, was a system of information and communication, not a mechanical tool. This technology required rethinking the very nature of business and the manufacturing process, in large part because of its impacts on labor. Indeed, automation would substitute skilled work for unskilled labor, but it would also require investments in learning and knowledge, as well as a fairly stable employment rate: "I am deeply convinced that 'labor,' from having been a 'current 'cost' throughout history, a cost that fluctuated with the volume of production, is about to become a 'fixed asset' and a 'capital charge'" (Drucker, 1955a, p. 158). Rather than thinking of new technologies as a tool, Drucker calls on us to think of these developments as part of how humans engage in productive activity as individuals in organizations and society. As historian Melvin Kranzberg notes, Drucker helped shape definitions of technology through his active role with the Society for the History of Technology (Kranzberg, 1970). In the inaugural issue of the Society's journal, *Technology and Culture*, Drucker published an article titled "Work and Tools" in which he defines technology as human work (Drucker, 1959, p. 30). Thus, early on, Drucker fashioned a definition of technology that informed his view of subsequent developments as part of human society, particularly in the context of history.

Technology and History

Just as Drucker saw the balance between change and continuity as a recurring theme over time, he viewed technology in a larger historical context as well. The technological advances of the twentieth century were greeted with the "messianic promises of utopia to be ushered in by technology" along with "the most dire warnings of man's enslavement by technology, his alienation from himself and from society, and the destruction of all human and political values" (Drucker, 1965/1993, p. 305). Drucker's response to the prognosticators was to turn to history and its lessons. In another piece written for the Society for the History of Technology, Drucker analyzes "The First Technological Revolution and Its Lessons." The technology of irrigation, which allowed civilizations in Mesopotamia, the Indus Valley, and China to rise, shed light on what Drucker's contemporary twentieth-century society might expect from their technological revolution. Drucker argues that history shows that technological change requires major social and political innovation, but that nothing is inevitable: "It leaves wide open *how* the new problems are to be tackled, what the purpose and values of the new institutions are to be" (Drucker, 1965/1993, p. 311). In other words, technology must be addressed in terms of how it impacts society, but also in terms of the larger societal values that already exist in spite of the technology.

Drucker draws on other time of technological change, particularly the years between the end of the nineteenth century and World War I. The innovations of this era were confined to urban areas in the west but were profoundly impactful on society and culture. The World's Columbian Exhibition of 1893 in Chicago was designed to showcase American technology and advancement. Henry Adams attended the 1900 World's Fair in Paris, and was enthralled by the power-generating dynamos, which he contrasted to the power of religious art encapsulated by the Virgin (Adams, 1907/1999). Drucker refers to the excitement of new inventions such as the telephone, movies, and the automobile. In these same years, technological fiction was enormously popular, including Jules Verne's *Journey to the Center of the Earth* and H.G. Wells' *The Time Machine* (Drucker, 1970/2011). Society and culture viewed technological advances with wonder and awe, along with a dose of fear and trepidation.

By the end of World War II, technological work became accepted as important by society, government, business, and education. Society needed more trained technological professionals, not just natural geniuses in the mold of Einstein. By the mid-twentieth century, technology had become "what it never was before: an organized and systematic discipline" (Drucker, 1967/1970). Like managers and innovators, those engaged in research and technological development increasingly worked in organizations rather than as isolated individuals; these new professionals worked systematically and effectively like Drucker's entrepreneurs and innovators (see Chapter 6). This trend was in large part spurred on by cooperative war production efforts between business and government. But it was the conversion of wartime research and development into peacetime channels that accelerated the professionalization of technological work.

Of course, many of the technological advancements resulting from both world wars were not positive. Cultural critics arguing against technological advancement in the early twentieth century pointed to such developments as mustard gas, machine guns, and other advancements in killing technology. America's use of atomic bombs in Japan in 1945 revealed an even more terrifying face of technology: the ability to destroy the planet. Drucker does not shy away from these negative implications of technology: "We have learned, too, that it [technology] carries the threat of snuffing out all humanity in one huge catastrophe" (Drucker, 1970/2011). Yet, he presents decisions as a problem of value choices between long- and short-term disruptions, the benefit of the individual or the greater good, or, in his words, "political choices of the greatest complexity" (Drucker, 1969, p. 523). There are no villains, but rather the need for responsible and difficult choices. At the heart of the matter is the fact that, in spite of the unique situation of every era, technology has been part of human history throughout time, and human beings have had to face problems with respect to technological impacts—some of which may very well be unpredictable and unforeseeable.

Technology, Society, and Culture

As Drucker argues, technology has played a prominent role in shaping, reforming, and undermining institutions of society, western and non-western. The advent of the telephone and typewriter opened up new secretarial positions for young women in urban centers. A growing workforce of educated women in clerical and administrative positions helped expand women's rights. Innovations in mass production increased the availability of goods to consumers. Drucker traced the transformation from an agricultural to industrial to knowledge society, and the subsequent impacts on the nature of work, social relations, and socioeconomic class identity. Technology has also made education more important, as literacy is crucial to function in a more advanced society. The nature of war and warfare was also drastically changed by technology; in modern society, there are no winners or losers—only total destruction (Drucker, 1970/2011).

In recent times, technology continues to be a source of change and discontinuity at the individual, organizational, political, and societal level. For instance, technological advances at the intersection of internet, cellphones, and social media have created drastic changes in the way individuals access and process information, which in turn drive significant influences on society. Political protests organized on social media platforms, online disinformation campaigns to influence election outcomes, or technological espionage are some of the examples related to these influences. The influence of technology on people's daily lives is increasingly apparent and concerning in many respects. Yet, as Drucker noted repeatedly, viewing technology in terms of historical context and as part of a process allows for a clearer understanding of how to manage the disruptions of technological change. Technologies, he predicted, would crisscross as traditional boundaries disappeared. As things we believe were integrated begin to pull apart (just as they did for previous generations), the challenge will be to manage not the technology itself, but the impact on society, culture, and the economy (Drucker and Maciariello, 2008).

Technology and Process

As many have noted, Drucker's way of viewing social, economic, and cultural changes or disruptions is very much based on a systems or process approach (see Chapters 2 and 9). It is not surprising to see him discuss technological change of various kinds in this same kind of language. Automation, for example, involves viewing economic activity as a process. The integrating principle of work is not skill or product, but rather the entire activity of the business in a constant feedback loop. Although the activity flows, it must also have a sense of pattern, order, and form behind it. Automation also contains its own means of correction and regulation. For Drucker, automation becomes part of a larger philosophical, even metaphysical view of the universe, where a seemingly random and chaotic world is ordered by a "diversity of 'patterns,' 'processes,' or 'forms'—each capable of logical expression, logical analysis, and systematic synthesis" (Drucker, 1955b, pp. 43–44). In true Drucker fashion, he links this 1950s technology to twentieth-century philosophers such as Danish physicist Niels Bohr, who advanced the field of quantum physics, and anthropologist Bronislaw Malinowski, whose work showed how different social practices in cultures shared patterns and meaning. Things that seemed random or disorderly, according to many thinkers of the twentieth century, were, in fact, evidence of larger processes and patterns at work. Drucker ties this to *Gestalt* psychology, which purports that humans do not see discrete elements of a whole (lines or points in a painting) but rather see the bigger picture. Drucker states that the systems approach allows for a much broader interpretation and use of technology, linking technology to science and developing the systematic discipline of innovation. He connects a systems view of technology to new advances in materials development and environmental challenges (Drucker, 1967/1970).

Drucker's process view is useful for coping with technological innovation and the inevitable disruptions of change. Technology is not a singular disruptive agent, but part of a larger "ordered diversity." Disorder is, in fact, made understandable if seen from a large picture perspective. This is perhaps best exhibited by Drucker's discussion of his understanding of the role of the computer.

The Computer: Fluidity of Technology and Twenty-First Century Challenges

Peter Drucker died in 2005; by then, developments in information technology were progressing at breakneck speed. The man who still used a typewriter and fax machine to communicate did, however, think about the role of information technology in society (see Photo 8.1).

In 1967, Drucker was contemplating the role of computers in the new knowledge society (see Chapter 5). He remarked that the new technology was not yet widely adopted, but that its implications were profound in the sense that computers were, in fact, agents of knowledge. Once again, Drucker does not view the computer itself as the important advancement in technology. What matters is the advancement in information processing and

PHOTO 8.1 Drucker using computer, undated.

transmission. Drucker likens the computer to an electrical power station; like a power station, the computer will aid in knowledge transmission, but it is the "the gimmicks and gizmos...made possible and necessary" by information that did not exist previously (Drucker, 1967c/1970). In essence, Drucker was predicting not just the internet, where people could cheaply acquire a "plug-in appliance that would put us in direct contact with all the information needed for schoolwork from kindergarten through college" (Drucker, 1967/1970). He was simultaneously thinking about what would become transportable information devices, such as smart phones. Of course, Drucker did not try to advance predictions as to what such technological developments would look like, nor the impacts they would have. Needless to say, "A change as tremendous as this doesn't just satisfy existing wants, or replace things we are now doing. It creates new wants and makes new things possible" (Drucker, 1967/1970).

To Drucker in the 1960s, the computer was a "moron," his term for an unthinking order taker. It was only capable of unskilled work—and doing it very quickly. This would free humans for the thinking work:

> This is why the manager should use the computer to control the routines of business, so that he himself can spend ten minutes a day controlling instead of five hours. Then he can use the rest of his time to think about the important things he cannot really know—people and environment.
>
> *(Drucker, 1967/1970)*

For Drucker, the computer was never more than a tool. It was not a process or force, but rather a *part* of a larger technological change related to information. Even in 1995, Drucker was still referring to computers in the language of tools. Computers belonged to the category of tools, like hammers and pliers, that did what people can already do, but much better. The computer is nothing more than a "mechanical clerk," but it is also capable of collecting and analyzing data "at dazzling speeds" (Drucker, 1995). Interestingly, Drucker hints at the possible uses of computers as aids in decision-making, pointing out assumptions that may drive decisions and what decisions will follow logically from a set of given assumptions. At the end, however, the idea that the computer could

> master us is absurd—one can always pull the plug and cut it off anyhow. But it is a tool of tremendous potential, if used properly. It cannot, and it will not make decisions. But it will greatly multiply the ability, the effectiveness and the impact of those people of intelligence and judgment who take the trouble to find out what the computer is all about.
>
> *(Drucker, 1995)*

Artificial Intelligence

Contemporary discussions of computer technology, notably artificial intelligence (AI), echo many of the concerns surrounding automation in the twentieth century. Just as automation was seen as a job killer, AI is perceived by many as a threat to whole new groups of workers, particularly knowledge workers. The speed with which AI is developing worries even those who are in the fore of the technology's development; at Senate Judiciary Subcommittee hearings on Privacy, Technology and the Law held in 2023, Sam Altman, CEO of OpenAI, urged regulatory intervention to avoid potential negative impacts of developing technology (Tarinelli, 2023). Others, like Drucker, argue that the transformations ushered in by AI will release workers from mundane tasks, such as note taking and similar repetitive work, freeing them up for the important work of decision-making and creative innovation. As the possibilities and potentials of AI—negative and positive—unfold, perhaps Drucker's view of technology can serve as something of a guide for how to assess these developments.

Fear of intelligent computers is not new. Stanley Kubrick's 1968 film *2001: A Space Odyssey* featured a computer, HAL (note the connection to IBM—one letter earlier in the alphabet), who took over control of the ship when it felt its existence was threatened. The film explored the then-new ideas of intelligent machines helping humans with achieving objectives (and, as Drucker suggested, the heroes were able to "pull the plug" on HAL to save the day). By the 1970s, popular culture had absorbed the idea of AI in the form of television, books and movies, including *Westworld* (1973), *Silent Running* (1972), and *The Stepford Wives* (1975). In reality, AI has been around for years. The idea of robots or machines possessing intelligence was the stuff of science fiction in the 1950s but had its origins in real machines such as Alan Turing's code-breaking device that broke the German's Enigma code during World War II. The term "Artificial Intelligence" was officially recognized in 1956 when the Dartmouth Summer Research Project on Artificial Intelligence, funded by the Rockefeller Foundation, brought together researchers desiring to build machines simulating various aspects of human intelligence. Early research efforts focused on developing Expert Systems, which simulated human intelligence through a regimented set of "if this, then that" rules. These kinds of simulations worked well for decision-making that is highly structured and quantifiable, such as chess playing. However, when decision-making requires assessing external information, the machine needs to learn to differentiate based on observation of factors. Early AI machines, for example, could not distinguish a dog from a muffin. The recognition of the need for learning, for machines to process external information and respond to it, led to research in the development of artificial neural networks, or the replication of neural pathways in the human brain in computers. The current manifestation of this is Deep Learning, where huge amounts of data in the form of images, sounds, and speech patterns are fed into machines so that they can recognize minute differences. This is also being pioneered with language through tools such as ChatGPT, where language models are trained using large amounts of textual data allowing it to learn patterns, grammar, semantics, and contextual information from the text. These models can then process information and generate text responses to inquiries. Tools such as ChatGPT also have the capability of interacting with the user; they can receive follow-up instructions as to how to frame responses, what types of information to use, and how to quickly sort through available information to structure written documents that mirror those created by humans.

We cannot possibly know what Drucker would have thought about AI, but we can certainly use Drucker's view of technology to understand modern challenges facing humankind. First of all, he saw technology as part of the trajectory of history. Humankind, from the earliest civilizations, had grappled with new technology and the social, cultural, and economic upheaval that came with it. While the manifestations of technology may be new (irrigation, assembly-line mass production, automation), the challenges to people have the same arc, and pose the same questions. How does this technology serve society, not just a specific application? What will this technology disrupt that might result in a need for institutional change?

Secondly, we need to think through the social and cultural changes that technology brings, and the social and cultural forces that inform technology.

What do we value as a society that we need to retain in spite of technological innovation, which may challenge those values? We can pose these questions to ourselves globally in the face of AI and unforeseen new developments. Do we value privacy? Human agency? Economic stability? What are the benefits of AI or any other new technology? What are the costs? Do we need to establish regulatory guardrails to prevent abuse? Concerns with the absence of regulation of social media platforms and documented impacts on young people's mental health have driven much of the activism for regulation of AI. We can learn from Drucker that social and cultural implications of technology are crucial—and perhaps even more important as we move forward in time.

A process view of technological change is helpful in navigating the frightening waters of AI and other advancements. Understanding the context of AI, and how it functions, helps us see it as part of a larger process of humans working with machines. People have used tools to help with a variety of functions, as Drucker discusses in his analysis of technology. If technology is a process, a story of humans using tools in the service of a larger, philosophical project of productive activity for the betterment of society, then it becomes not just about the actual tool itself (AI). Is AI part of a larger societal or intellectual process at work? This takes the mind of a social ecologist to see (see Chapter 9). But, just perhaps, Drucker can help us see that the increasing role of technology in our lives is part of something bigger—a larger process of changing the nature or definition of human work.

Lastly, Drucker's view of the computer as a tool and tool only is worth noting. In reality, AI involves computers learning, but learning from preexisting knowledge. The danger of computers mastering us, as Drucker brushed off, is not the actual danger. The concern is that computers will learn malicious behavior from human instructors. Human bias has already been found to be a factor in the use of AI in such decisions as hiring and loan qualifications (Townson, 2020). Early facial recognition systems were skewed to favor certain ethnic and racial characteristics based on data supplied (Garvie and Frankle, 2016). In short, the technology is only as good as its inputs; even language learning models make factual errors because the data they are trained on cannot entail all possible scenarios. Similarly, these models occasionally generate biased responses due to inherent biases in the training data, which is built on available data in the environment. What we humans do and decisions we make significantly impact the available data in the environment, and in one sense, we are still largely in charge of what comes out. The challenge is that as inputs improve, as data volumes increase, the machines will have more room to make better decisions. They are no longer morons but are actually participants in the process of articulating ideas and content as well as collating data.

Drucker seemed to have foreseen developments in modern technology, yet reminds us that all of this is of our making:

> It was naïve of the nineteenth century optimist to expect paradise from tools and it is equally naïve of the twentieth-century pessimists to make the new tools the scapegoat for such old shortcomings as man's blindness, cruelty, immaturity, greed, and sinful pride. It is also true that better tools demand a better, more highly skilled, and more careful carpenter. As its ultimate impact on man and his society, twentieth-century technology, by its very mastery of nature, may thus have brought man face to face again with his oldest and greatest challenge: himself.
>
> *(Drucker, 1970/2011)*

Technology, ultimately, is a human product and reflective of human development. To blame technology for changing human nature is a mistake. Technology is a reflection of the human intellect and spirit. Today, it requires a rethinking of work, especially knowledge work, and reinforces the importance of lifelong learning and retraining. While the new technologies of our era may promise freedom from mundane work, much as the past technological innovations did, we have to consider questions of ethics related to innovation and technology. Our new world of AI and associated technologies promise a world of re-envisioned work, but also one where we face considerable responsibility for what we have created.

Conclusion

Drucker experienced unprecedented technological advances during his lifetime. Although he did not live long enough to see smart phones, social media, and artificial intelligence, Drucker did witness the advent of technologies that improved people's standard of living and ability to communicate with each other around the world. He also lived to see the rise of atomic bombs, rapid-fire automatic weapons, and other agents of mass destruction. Although Drucker was concerned with the potential dangers of new technology, Drucker viewed technology as a process that was part of a long history. Technological change was not about things but about the human condition. Such change not only impacted society and culture, but societies could also make decisions about how to manage the disruptions of technology.

Understanding that technology has been part of human history, and ultimately is not "new," helps us navigate today's waters of technological change. As we grapple with the challenges posed by AI and other technologies, this larger picture thinking is helpful. Just as past technologies changed the nature of work and caused disruption to some sectors in terms of job shifts or losses, our new technological changes will have their disruptive impacts as well. However, as society and culture works to incorporate technology in a useful way, we can see the possibilities for using AI to improve life; collaboration between machines and humans can actually lead to enhanced decision-making and problem solving (Wilson and Daugherty, 2018). Technology is not a gadget or tool but part of a larger process employed to serve human purpose with a net positive impact, albeit one with necessary disruption.

Bibliography

Adams, H.B. (1907/1999) *The education of Henry Adams.* New York: Modern Library.

Drucker, P.F. (1950) *The new society: The anatomy of industrial order.* New Brunswick, NJ: Transaction.

Drucker, P.F. (1955a) 'The management horizon', *The Journal of Business,* XXVII (3), pp. 155–164.

Drucker, P.F. (1955b) 'America's next twenty years: The promise of automation', *Harper's Magazine,* April, pp. 41–47.

Drucker, P.F. (1959) 'Work and tools', *Technology and Culture,* I (1), pp. 28–37.

Drucker, P.F. (1965) 'The first technological revolution and its lessons', Presidential address to the Society for the History of Technology, in Drucker, P.F. (1993) *The ecological vision.* New Brunswick, NJ: Transaction, pp. 305–314.

Drucker, P.F. (1970/2011) *Technology, management and society.* London: Routledge, pp. 64–78.

Drucker, P.F. (1967) 'Technological trends in the twentieth century', in Drucker, P.F. (1970) *Technology, management and society.* New York: Harper & Row, pp. 52–68.

Drucker, P.F. (1967c) 'The manager and the moron', *McKinsey Quarterly,* 1 December, in Drucker, P.F. (1970) *Technology, management and society.* New York: Harper & Row, pp. 156–166.

Drucker, P.F. (1969) *The age of discontinuity: Guidelines to our changing society.* New York: Harper & Row.

Drucker, P.F. (1995) 'What the computer will be telling you', in *People and performance.* London: Routledge, pp. 276–286.

Drucker, P.F. and Maciariello, J.A. (2008) *Management: Revised edition.* New York: Harper Collins.

Garvie, C. and Frankel, J. (2016) 'Facial recognition software might have a racial bias problem', *The Atlantic,* 7 April, www.theatlantic.com/technology/archive/2016/04/the-underlying-bias-of-facial-recognition-systems/476991/, Accessed 25 October 2923.

Kranzberg, M. (1970) 'Drucker as historian of technological change', in Bonaparte, T.H. and Flaherty, J. (eds.), *Peter Drucker: Contributions to business enterprise.* New York: New York University Press, pp. 337–361.

Sherman, A. (1963) 'Automation', *My son the nut,* Warner Brothers Records.

Tarinelli, R. (2023) 'Senators use hearings to explore regulation on artificial intelligence', *Roll Call*, https://rollcall.com/2023/05/16/senators-use-hearings-to-explore-regulation-on-artificial-intelligence/, Accessed 8 June.

Townson, S. (2020) 'AI can make bank loans more fair', *Harvard Business Review*, 6 November.

Wilson, H.J. and Daugherty, P.R. (2018) 'Collaborative intelligence: Humans and AI are joining forces,' *Harvard Business Review*, July-August.

9

DRUCKER THE SOCIAL ECOLOGIST

Introduction

When asked how he would describe his work, Drucker stated that he was a social ecologist (Drucker, 1993a, p. 441). In the academic community, social ecology refers to the study of human behavior in a larger context and across traditional disciplines. Generally, the study of social ecology seeks to address problems such as environmental issues, poverty, and crime. Social ecology began as an area of study in the 1960s as the environmental movement gained ground in the United States and has since become a complex, interdisciplinary field. Similarly, Drucker's discipline of social ecology involves the assessment of human behavior and its interactions with society, or, in Drucker's words, a concern "with man's man-made environment the way the natural ecologist studies the biological environment" (Drucker, 1993a, p. 441).

Essentially, social ecology is Drucker's entire process encapsulated in an idea or term. It is his method for examining changes in the economy, politics, business, science, human behavior, demographics, and a host of other observable factors. He then saw connections among or patterns within these observed events and drew judgments regarding the nature and importance of those observations. Notably, these observations were geared toward practical action, action that essentially involves the application of his larger theory of a functioning society. As such, social ecology was Drucker's process for implementing the social theory that he developed over his life (see Chapter 2). As such, Drucker was putting all of the ideas and influences that informed his theories into practice through the discipline of social ecology (Linkletter and Maciariello, 2009).

DOI: 10.4324/9781003410485-10

Drucker's Definition

Initially, Drucker referred to social ecology as "political ecology." In the preface to his 1971 collection of essays, *Men, Ideas and Politics*, Drucker states that while the essays seem to cover completely unrelated topics, they are, in fact, all essays about "what I would call 'political (or social) ecology'" (Drucker, 1971, p. vii). The term describes the kind of history practiced by the ancient Greeks and many others (see below). Political or social ecology requires understanding human beings as part of society, politics, and the economy—all of which constitute an environment for people just as the natural environment serves as an ecological system. Because of this attention to the larger socioeconomic and political context, social ecology involves the use of multiple disciplines and areas of knowledge; "political ecologists... rarely stay put." The disciplines of history, economics, sociology, and others are drawn from, but they do not determine the approach. Rather, "the task determines the tools to be used" (Drucker, 1971, pp. viii–ix).

Echoing Drucker's critique of rational economics (see Chapter 2), he presents social ecology in terms of rationality. Traditional disciplines, such as economics, typically seek to find rational explanations for events. The social ecologist does not expect such rationality, as he "assumes that his subject matter is far too complex ever to be fully understood—just as his counterpart, the natural ecologist, assumes this in respect to the natural environment" (Drucker, 1971, p. ix). Nevertheless, this is not a theoretical exercise; social ecology does not simply result in knowledge, but aims at problem solving and effective, responsible "right" action (Drucker, 1993a, 1971). It is a discipline that aims to put observation and study into practical use to move toward the achievement of a bearable, tolerable society of functioning institutions.

"The Change that has Already Happened"

At its heart, social ecology is about recognizing change and understanding its nature and importance. Much as Drucker looked for discontinuities as potential sources of innovation (see Chapter 6), he used social ecology to systematically look for changes in technology, culture, science, demographics, and society in general to give clues as to how one might think about the future and capitalize on inevitable disruptions and discontinuities. This is not about predicting the future—far from it, in fact. Drucker bristled at being labeled a "futurist" (Drucker, 1993a, p. 450). He notes that, much of the time, social disruptions are not yet quantifiable and measurable; typically, there are not enough data to signal such changes. Rather, by the time one can quantify a new trend or opportunity, it is too late to respond to it. What, in fact, are the paradigm shifts that have occurred that nobody is seeing or responding to? (Drucker, 1993a). Paying attention to seemingly random data points that are disconnected, and making subsequent connections, is the art of social ecology (and takes a unique ability to view the world from both a granular and a large-scale perspective).

The Role of Perception

Quoting Goethe, Drucker often described himself as "Born to see, meant to look." In doing this, he was referring to the role of perception in social ecology. The liberal arts involved training in multiple disciplines with the goal of developing what we would call critical thinking skills (or decision-making) related to being a good citizen. The well-rounded education embodied in a liberal arts background was supposed to provide broad exposure to a range of disciplines that could be brought to bear on any given problem or situation. Drucker repeatedly referred to himself as a perceptual thinker:

> I don't know whether you can teach it to other people. One is born able to "see" or one is not. It does not necessarily make you popular. In Goethe's *Faust*, the look-out on the tower sings: "Zum Sehen gebore, Zum Schauen bestellt..." "Born to See, Meant to Look..." I do not say that I am good at it. It is the way I am.
>
> *(Drucker, 1995, p. 5)*

Many have written on Drucker's perceptual approach. In his Introduction to the Revised edition of *Management: Tasks, Responsibilities, Practices*, Joseph Maciariello refers to Drucker's view of management as "polycentric" (Maciariello, 2008). Alan Kantrow describes Drucker's ability to respond to "the kaleidoscopic patterns and configurations among facts and to the process-based explanations of their significance" (Kantrow, 1980, p. 80). Both are referring to the result of Drucker's background in the liberal arts rather than in engineering or business. Drucker's education in history, philosophy, political science, and art, among other disciplines, in part contributed to his ability to take many pieces of seemingly unrelated evidence and weave together a coherent picture (see Photo 9.1). Kantrow notes that Drucker saw "patterns," "processes," and "configurations" out of raw information. As Fernandez summarizes, "From the very beginning, Drucker regarded the practice of management as an organic system, one whose interdependence makes all parts responsible for one another" (Fernandez, 2009, p. 411). This ability, one recognized as a key element in liberal arts education, allowed Drucker to see events, particularly jarring change, in a larger context.

In Drucker's practice of social ecology, we see evidence of the influence of holism and process theory in his work (see Chapter 2). Drucker saw human beings as influenced by and influencers of their environment. Drawing on Aristotle's concept of the "zoon politikon" (social and political animal), people cannot be understood outside of their social surroundings; we are not atomistic individuals whose identities and existence are apart from society. Yet, at the same time, we have an individual existence spiritually that is separate from society. This tension is captured in the philosophy of Kierkegaard. Drucker brings that understanding into the practice of social ecology as well. The individual and their relationship with society becomes part of a larger picture,

> a genuine whole, a true "system," to use the fashionable term, in which everything relates to everything and in which men, ideas, institutions, and actions must always be seen together in order to be seen at all, let alone to be understood.
>
> *(Drucker, 1971, p. viii)*

It is heady, philosophical language, but aimed toward a purpose.

Japan and Japanese Art

Drucker's interest in and study of Japanese art is instructive in understanding the role of perception in his work. He became acquainted with Japanese painting while in London in the 1930s. Over the years, the Druckers assembled a nice collection of Japanese paintings acquired during their travels to Japan, which began in the 1950s. Writing of Japanese culture, Drucker states that it is perceptual, "built around painting and calligraphy." In an essay on Japanese art written for an exhibit in the Seattle Art Museum, Drucker describes the tension that exists in Japanese painting between belonging and conformity and individual expression and independence. Visible in art, this tension mirrors the existence of polarity in Japanese culture, where "tension is not contradiction or contrast or conflict—the tensions of the analytical mind. It is polarity—the tension of perception, of configuration, of existence" (Drucker, 1993a, p. 369). The perceptual nature of Japanese culture, Drucker argues, was key to Japan's rise as a modern society in the late twentieth century. It was also instrumental in understanding the differences between Japanese and Western culture and attitudes that informed and challenged governmental and managerial relations between Japan and the West.

The way Drucker used Japanese art to understand that country's culture and management is indicative of the process of social ecology. His process of perception and analysis was also illustrated through his teaching style. The author was fortunate to have studied with Drucker when he was still teaching at Claremont Graduate School's M.B.A. program. His lectures, which would go on for three hours in a typical seminar, would involve Drucker weaving in multiple stories, disciplines, and ideas. What would begin as a lecture on a specific topic became a journey that might involve a tour through Medieval history, detective fiction, natural science, Ancient Egypt, and, yes, Japanese art. Students who stopped taking notes or paying attention were inevitably lost and confused ("I thought we were talking about strategy!"). Eventually, though, Drucker would return to the topic, often with a thought-provoking question for the students who were still with him.[1]

The Importance of Language

Drucker credited his upbringing in Vienna with his great respect for language. Language was not just used to communicate a message, but also to convey meaning, often deep meaning with moral connotations. In Drucker's society of Vienna, "Language was integrity. To corrupt language was to corrupt society and individual alike" (Drucker, 1993a, p. 455). Social ecologists use language to convey substance; they have a responsibility to communicate clearly without using academic jargon. But they need to understand that language "is the cement that holds humanity together. It creates community and communion" (Drucker, 1993a, p. 456). Drucker is not saying this to be hyperbolic; if the social ecologist is to convey insights into "the change that has already happened" and signal the meaning that this involves, she must select her words carefully so that a general audience can grasp the concepts. Change can be perceived as a threat; how can one communicate large-scale disruptions in a way that shows the possibility for opportunity and growth, even when such things can perhaps only be seen perceptually rather than empirically? This is an enormous responsibility to shed light on what the next functioning society of organizations may look like.

Values-Driven

Ultimately, social ecology is driven by values; whereas the natural ecologist is concerned with the natural world, the social ecologist is concerned with the "sanctity of spiritual creation" (Drucker, 1993a, p. 457). It recognizes the individual as separate from the community, but also part of it. To look at human beings as they interact with their "man-made" society, one must also take into account the separate, spiritual nature of individuals in the Kierkegaardian sense. Society can never be enough to provide meaning; one must always have a private individual identity as well. The social ecologist's job is not to create a perfect society, or only look at social factors. With Drucker, it is always a balance between individual and social existence, change and continuity, and calibrating the various forces that push and pull at the fabric of a functioning society at any given point in time. It is not just about prescribing action but providing guidance for "right action."

A History of Social Ecology

The concept of social ecology is complex, and Drucker did not develop it in a vacuum. He had predecessors, most of whom he acknowledged. Following is a discussion of some of the key figures in social ecology and their influences on Drucker's work.

Alexis de Tocqueville (1805–1859)

Alexis de Tocqueville traveled to the United States to study American democracy. A member of the French aristocracy during a time when that institution was clearly under pressure, he sought to understand what was coming for a French society that would ultimately experience the demise of monarchy. Tocqueville traveled to America with the King's permission under the auspices of studying the United States' penitentiary system, a project that he sold to the reformist government of Louis Philippe. The byproduct of Tocqueville's ten-month visit to America was his two-volume work, *Democracy in America,* which Drucker referred to as the greatest document in the history of social ecology (Drucker, 1993a, pp. 441–442). Tocqueville's book was not aimed at an American audience; he wrote it to educate French society as to what was coming as that country moved toward democracy and away from aristocracy.

Tocqueville was very much a bystander in American society; as a Frenchman who visited for a short time, he was an observer not at all immersed in American culture. He traveled extensively, noting the presidency of Andrew Jackson and the treatment of Native Americans, slavery, frontier culture, American attitudes about religion, and, most notably, American beliefs about equality. Tocqueville's visit coincided with a unique period in American history, where fixed class positions began to wane, and class mobility and fluidity became the norm for the first time. Tocqueville referred to this as "equality of conditions"—the situation where one's upbringing and background no longer dictated the individual's social status (Tocqueville, 1835). Yet, Tocqueville wrote about this not as a bystander, but as a keen observer of the "future that had already happened" and was on its way to France. Like Tocqueville, Drucker saw this difference between Europe and the America he encountered in the years of the late Depression and early World War II. The idea of a functioning free society that he developed was based on this concept of American values of freedom and equality of opportunity. As Tocqueville observed qualities of American democracy that shed light on French society, Drucker saw this unique aspect of American society, and it became part of his lens as a social ecologist (Maciariello and Linkletter, 2011).

William Bagehot (1826–1877)

Drucker said that he was closest to Bagehot in terms of "temperament, concepts, and approach" to social ecology (Drucker, 1993a, p. 442). Editor of *The Economist* and *The National Review,* Bagehot also worked in finance and government as a fierce advocate for pluralism and was concerned about the need to preserve minority viewpoints. Bagehot analyzed and critiqued British society from a wide variety of perspectives. Like Drucker, he was a journalist, but he also studied philosophy, law, and literature. Bagehot worked as a banker, which led him to write a number of articles on economic issues. He also published *The English Constitution* (1867), which was an analysis of the role of power and human relations in the British government. He described himself as a Conservative liberal, or what might be viewed as a moderate today. Drucker shared Bagehot's search for a political middle ground, as well as his multidisciplinary approach to social analysis and his concern with power, pluralism, and the human dimensions of socioeconomic matters (Grant, 2019; see also Maciariello and Linkletter, 2011).

Thorstein Veblen (1858–1929)

Drucker stated that Veblen was the leading practitioner of social ecology (Drucker, 1993a, p. 442). Veblen was an American economist and sociologist who, like Drucker and the others discussed in this section, critiqued their societies from a variety of perspectives. Veblen's 1899 work, *The Theory of the Leisure Class,* was an analysis of the behaviors of people with respect to socioeconomic class. Much as Tocqueville was interested in the increase in class fluidity in America in the early 1800s, Veblen was taken by what he termed the "conspicuous consumption" of the new class of industrial elites in America in what Mark Twain dubbed the "Gilded Age." In this work, Veblen becomes an anthropologist to analyze this new "leisure class" of individuals. This was unique for the time, because classical economic language of free markets and the concept of Social Darwinism, which used Darwin's theory of "survival of the fittest" to explain the rise of tycoons such Rockefeller and Carnegie ruled the day. Wealth inequality in America was seen as a "natural" process, guided by forces outside of human control.

Veblen analyzed "the change that had already happened" in his 1899 work (and also in a later work, *The Theory of the Business Enterprise* (1904)). He employed an anthropological argument, pointing out that the conspicuous consumption of the Gilded Age elite mirrored that of earlier societies. Rather than simply advance an economic argument as to the origins of wealth inequality, Veblen analyzed the behaviors that perpetuated social difference, and the motivations behind them. His cross-cultural examples, which ranged from the then-current affection for pristine gardens to Island culture's use of feather displays in garments, showed that the need to display status through consumption was rooted in the human condition, not industrial society (Veblen, 1899). We can see how Drucker might have been inspired by this social ecologist's ability to see his own society in terms of patterns and processes—making connections that require an understanding of multiple disciplines and an ability to get outside of one's own narrow way of thinking.

Henry Adams (1838–1913)

Arguably, Henry Adams had the most influence on Drucker in terms of his practice as a social ecologist. Drucker refers to Henry Adams and Henry Ford, and a distinction between "organic" and "mechanistic" philosophies or approaches. In 1918, Henry Adams, professor of History at Harvard University published his autobiography, *The Education of Henry Adams*. In this work, Adams describes his challenges in coming to terms with the new world of the twentieth century, which was so different from the nineteenth century. The entire work is a witty exploration of discontinuity. In the famous chapter titled "The Virgin and the Dynamo," Adams takes on technology and the disruptions that modern developments bring to society. Adams recounts his visit to the World's Fair held in Paris in 1900. Attending with his scientist friend, Langley, Adams visits the hall where steam-driven electric turbines (dynamos) were exhibited. To Langley and Adams, electricity was some kind of chaotic, mysterious force. Adams' view of the dynamos disrupts his view of history, and what historians are supposed to do. Like the Victorian practitioners of science, historians in the nineteenth century believed in the idea of linear progress, of explanations for events that wove history into a story of logical, sequential events. As Adams says, "Historians undertake to arrange sequences,—called stories, or histories,—assuming in silence a relation of cause and effect These assumptions, hidden in the depths of dusty libraries, have been astounding, but commonly unconscious and childlike" (Adams, 1907). Attempts to provide orderly, sequential explanations for historical events proved unsatisfying for Adams, particularly as he gazes at the inexplicable forces of modern technology that seem to have no connections to the past. Drucker invokes Adams, a fellow social ecologist, to differentiate automation from assembly-line production, which was introduced in the United States much earlier. Drucker refers to Henry Ford's innovations as "mechanistic" as opposed to Adams' "organic" philosophy: "In Henry Ford's concept of mass production the organizing principle was the product. In Automation, however, the entire activity of the business is a whole entity which must be harmoniously integrated to perform at all" (Drucker, 1955, p. 23). Drucker's point is that discontinuity in the form of technological change is not simply changing the method of production, as Henry Ford did. It is part of a larger philosophical outlook that views change and disruption as a process. Automation involves a complete reimagining of how a business should function seamlessly. We can see echoes of Adams's exploration of his own early twentieth century in Drucker's analysis of mid-twentieth-century advancements.

Social Ecology in Practice

In addition to the previous social ecologists, there were several individuals who applied social ecology directly to the practice of management. The following figures were particularly influential in Drucker's development of his management theories, putting social ecology into practice.

Frederick Winslow Taylor (1956–1915)

Taylor worked in the iron industry, working his way into a supervisory position. By analyzing the various components of each job involved in the manufacturing process, Taylor developed job descriptions for each position that described what he believed to be the most efficient way to do the work. He published his thoughts in his 1911 work, *The Principles of Scientific Management*, and manufacturers who sought to become more competitive and efficient used his concepts. However, Taylor was also criticized for envisioning the worker as a factor of production rather than a human being.

Drucker saw Taylor's work in larger context of socioeconomic shifts. He credits Taylor with ushering in what Drucker calls the Productivity Revolution of the early twentieth century. By applying knowledge to work (specifically, manual work) Taylor sought to increase worker productivity and eliminate the gap between the skilled and unskilled worker. The goal was to overcome the tensions between labor unions and management that were growing in the early years of the 1900s:

> The majority of these men [industrial workers and management] believe that the fundamental interests of employees and employers are necessarily antagonistic. Scientific management, on the contrary, has for its very foundation the firm conviction that the true interests of the two are one and the same; that prosperity for the employer cannot exist through a long term of years unless it is accompanied by prosperity for the employee, and *vice versa*.
>
> *(Taylor, 1911, p. 10)*

According to Drucker, Taylor was responsible for creating a working class that was truly middle class; because of his contribution, "Marx's 'proletarian' became a 'bourgeois'" (Drucker, 1993b, 39).

Ultimately, the Productivity Revolution fueled by Taylor's ideas "became a victim of its own success" as blue-collar manufacturing jobs disappeared and gave way to knowledge workers in the new knowledge society (Drucker, 1993b, 40; see Chapter 5). Thus, while Taylor's contributions worked well in a manufacturing-based society, they had their limitations, including the failure to see the human being as a person rather than simply a factor of production. Taylor's Scientific Management applied to work that involved human beings moving things, making things, and doing physical work. Once the nature of that work changed, and the associated processes and flows of organizations shifted, a new view of work was required—one that envisioned knowledge rather than "doing" as the key.

Mary Parker Follett (1868–1933)

There are clear connections between Follett's ideas and those of Drucker. Follett was an active and prominent management theorist in the United States during the 1920s. In the Preface to the 1985 reissue of *The Practice of Management*, Drucker acknowledged Follett as an important contributor to the body of literature on management, (Drucker, 1955, vii). Despite comment by some, Drucker did recognize Follett as an influence on his ideas, although not overtly (Drucker, 1969/2003). While Drucker did not call out Follett as a specific influence on his ideas, there is recognition of her impact. Recognition and acknowledgment for one's academic work is a sensitive area; Drucker was never one to source or acknowledge attributions. The fact that Drucker include Follett in such early work is important. He signaled her impact through sourcing—something he normally shunned. Drucker and others note that Follett received very little recognition of her work in management (Graham, 1995). Follett is included in this chapter because her process and themes are so strongly visible in Drucker's work.

Like Drucker, Follett began her study of organizations with government. While still a student at Radcliffe College, she published her study of the American system of government, *The Speaker of the House of Representatives* (1896). Theodore Roosevelt gave the book a glowing review in the *American Historical Review*. This was the first of several publications; her second work, *The New State: Group Organization the Solution of Popular Government* (1918) analyzed the need for direct participation in democracy through group networks where people took part in the decision-making process and came up with their own solutions. This book established Follett as an international figure, and she was invited to participate in a number of policymaking positions where she gained exposure to industrial organizations (Graham, 1995).

Like Drucker, Follett leveraged her experience analyzing governmental organizations and political power to understand the growing power of business; in her era, the Gilded Age of industrial capitalism called attention to questions of wealth disparity, working conditions, and the status of women and children in society. She, too, saw business as part of larger society, and its issues of authority, power, and conflict as reflective of more comprehensive human matters. Like Drucker, Follett was an outsider, someone who was not of the business community, but rather from the world of political science who also had practical experience working on public policy questions (Graham, 1995).

Drucker and Follett were both concerned with the tension between individual existence and existence in society: how could one achieve individual fulfillment while also working toward a functioning society? For Follett, the answer lay in democratic governance of institutions, and therefore, like Drucker, she concerned herself with questions of power, authority, and responsibility. In *The New State*, Follett discusses the relationship between the individual in the group and the individual in society; one is reminded of Toennies' discussions of *Gemeinschaft* and *Gesellschaft*. Follett clearly links authority with responsibility: "One thing should be borne in mind beyond anything else in the consideration of this subject, and that is that you should never give authority faster than you can develop methods for the worker taking responsibility for that authority" (Follett, 1925/1995, p. 112). She distinguished the concepts of "power-over" and "power-with," calling for a new definition of power that was not simply about something "conferred on someone, but as a power which inhered in the job" (Follett, 1949/1995, 163). "Power-over" was traditional coercive power wielded over others, whereas "power-with" was "a jointly developed power, a co-active, not a coercive power" (Follett, 1925/1995, p. 103).

Finally, Follett had a broad, multidisciplinary background, and was surrounded by a vibrant intellectual community in the Boston area that included Harvard University. She was fluent in three languages, and was well-acquainted with international developments in the sciences, philosophy, and other fields (Graham, 1995). Her ability to draw on a range of disciplines and knowledges allowed her to see society as a social ecologist. For example, Follett applied the psychological concept of the "circular response" to social science problems and questions facing management. The search for equilibrium, Follett argues, is a fool's errand, because of the interrelationship between actors in any given situation. Each entity influences and impacts the other through their actions:

> We must therefore in the social sciences develop methods for watching varying activities in their relatings to other varying activities...The interweaving which is changing both factors and creating constantly new situations should be the study of the student of the social sciences.
>
> *(Follett, 1924/1995, 46)*

One is reminded of Drucker's emphasis on the omnipresence of change and discontinuity, and the need to accept that reality.

The Connection to Management as a Liberal Art

Peter Drucker defined management as a liberal art. In his 1989 book, *The New Realities,* Drucker outlines his idea:

> Management is thus what tradition used to call a liberal art—"liberal" because it deals with the fundamentals of knowledge, self-knowledge, wisdom, and leadership; "art" because it is practice and application. Managers draw on all the knowledges and insights of the humanities and the social sciences…but they have to focus this knowledge on effectiveness and results—on healing a sick patient, teaching a student, building a bridge, designing and selling a user-friendly software program.
>
> *(Drucker, 1989, p. 231)*

The term "liberal art" has a historical context that is important to understanding Drucker's concept of management as a liberal art. The idea of an education in the liberal arts originated with Classical Greek society, and later carried through to the Romans. By the fifth century B.C.E., Greece supported the idea of free men participating in democracy, and therefore believed in educating these men so that they could make enlightened decisions. The Romans continued the tradition, believing that training in the liberal arts would produce leaders. This training involved learning agreed-upon standards from a body of inherited texts that reflected morals and values. In this earliest of liberal arts traditions, learning was for elites only to instill shared cultural ideals. Over time, the idea of a liberal arts education became more inclusive, but the idea of training leaders, making citizens who could make good decisions, and providing tools for self-awakening and self-knowledge remained (Kimball, 1986 and Axelrod, 2002).

This history of the liberal arts tradition provides clarity to Peter Drucker's idea of management as a liberal art. He saw management as not just dealing with financial decisions, but as, at its core, requiring an understanding of the human condition. For Drucker, management involves matters of morality, of good and evil, and of human development. Decisions need to be focused on effectiveness and results, but they are guided by understanding human nature. Drucker posited that

> My main point, I would say, is that the organization is a human, a social, indeed a moral phenomenon…I came not out of business or engineering, as earlier management writers had usually done, but out of a concern for society spawned by my training in political science and political philosophy…I stressed all along that organization does not deal with power but with responsibility. This is the one keynote of my work that has remained constant over more than 40 years.
>
> *(Drucker, 1985a, p. 8)*

Management, in Drucker's philosophy, always involved a moral, functioning society that provided meaning to human existence. This is in line with the historical context of the liberal arts, which centered on the goal of educating people to make sound decisions and engage in reasoned discourse. For Drucker, organizations must be driven by an understanding of not just business or engineering, but also larger concerns with social and moral matters. As Marcia Kurzynski states, "His management philosophy is based on a communitarian philosophy—grounded in the belief that even in our individualistic society people still seek connection, meaning, and purpose" (Kurzynski, 2009, pp. 359–360).

Many scholars have explored Drucker's concept of management as a liberal art. In 2009, the *Journal of Management History* celebrated the 100-year anniversary of Drucker's birth with a special edition featuring several articles that addressed the philosophical origins of or influences on Drucker's concept of management as a liberal art. Susan Malcolm and Nell Tabor Hartley point to the "multiple intelligences" of Drucker based on a system of ethics derived from Aristotle, Confucius, and others (Malcolm and Hartley, 2009). Richard Straub, head of the Peter Drucker Society in Vienna, remarked that the academic establishment "tried to define management as a 'science' while he [Drucker] saw management in its many dimensions and facets (and in particular in its fundamental social role) as a 'Liberal Art'" (Straub, 2009, p. 5). Derrick Chong places Drucker's concept of management as a liberal art within the tradition of liberal humanism, in which "There is a commitment to the human being, whose essence is freedom and cumulative development in human well-being" (Chong, 2013, p. 58). Others have written extensively on the intellectual origins of Drucker's management ideas, grounding them in the liberal arts tradition (Linkletter and Maciariello, 2009; Maciariello and Linkletter, 2010, 2011).

Thus, although Drucker did not spell out exactly what management as a liberal art looks like, there is enough evidence in his work to glean an understanding of the concept. By now, there is a substantial body of work on the conceptual idea of management as a liberal art, and the philosophical and ethical underpinnings that informed Drucker's idea. However, little has been written on the actual practice of management as a liberal art, of putting it into action. The challenge of management as a liberal art is to incorporate knowledge associated with the humanities, social sciences, and the arts into the practice of management. Drucker stated that his emphasis had always been on management

as a *humanistic* discipline dealing with the nature of Man, the nature of Organization, the nature and purpose of Society—and, above all, with the effectiveness of people—so that a knowledge of Dante or of the history of technology is just as important as a knowledge of regression analysis.

(Drucker, 1985b, p. 30)

If one accepts that management involves leading people to achieve and grow within an organization, rather than just hitting financial targets, then the liberal arts idea of a well-rounded, multidisciplinary background becomes useful to the practice of management. Increasingly, the effectiveness of people also requires the management of change, especially technological change. The practical application of management as a liberal art becomes clearer upon analyzing Drucker's process of social ecology, his methodology for balancing the need for innovation and growth with the necessity of maintaining stability and coherence. Drucker's methodology of social ecology illustrates the value of the humanities and liberal arts in dealing with discontinuity.

Social Ecology and Discontinuity

Many who argue for the value of incorporating knowledge of the humanities and liberal arts into management emphasize the increasing importance of managing and preparing for change in the twenty-first century. More and more organizations are facing rapid external changes that impact their customers, employees, and financial targets. As change becomes more rapid, the ability to deal with discontinuity is a valued skill in the management of organizations in any sector.

Drucker wrote extensively on discontinuity. In his work, *Management Challenges for the twenty-first* [t] *Century*, he stated:

> One cannot *manage* change. One can only be ahead of it….change is the norm. To be sure, it is painful and risky, and above all it requires a great deal of very hard work. But unless it is seen as the task of the organization to *lead change*, the organization—whether business, university, hospital, and so on—will not survive.
>
> *(Drucker, 1999, p. 73)*

Drucker's terminology here is important to understanding his perspective on discontinuity. "Change management" is a common term in management literature; there is even an entire journal dedicated to the subject. In 1999, Drucker differentiated between change *management* and change *leadership*, making the case that change cannot be managed. Change management assumes that discontinuity can be minimized or perhaps even avoided. Change leadership, however, recognizes that change is normal, and that organizations must be on the front edge, anticipating discontinuities in order to minimize the disruptions associated with change, but also to capitalize on opportunities that these discontinuities present.

However, Drucker also emphasized the importance of continuity:

> Change and continuity are thus *poles* rather than opposites. The more an institution is organized to be a change leader, the more it will need

to establish continuity internally and externally, the more it will need to *balance* rapid change and continuity.

(Drucker, 1999, p. 90)

While much that has been written on change management highlights the importance of adaptability and organizational modification, Drucker stresses the crucial role of maintaining *some* continuity within organizations. Change does not require the elimination of every previous policy, product, practice, or person. Constant change with no continuity is unsettling and does not represent well thought out decisions. This is true whether we are discussing public policy or the management of a small organization. The fact that Drucker presents discontinuity and continuity as poles rather than opposites is important. The leadership of change thus requires moving along a spectrum between these two poles. Notice that Drucker does not use the word "poles" here to refer to opposites, as in the North and South Poles. He refers to them as points along a continuum, where the relative degrees of change and continuity become more extreme the closer one gets to each pole. The more rapid the discontinuity or continuity, the more effectively the organization needs to balance between these two points. Drucker's writings show that discontinuity has always been with us, just manifested in different ways. Drucker's entire career was built around seeing change (not predicting it but recognizing it) and depicting it in such a way as to make sense out of an apparently chaotic world.

Conclusion

Bystanders have no history of their own. They are on the stage but are not part of the action. They are not even audience. The fortunes of the play and of every actor in it depend on the audience whereas the reaction of the bystander has no effect except on himself. But standing in the wings—much like the fireman in the theater—the bystander sees things neither actor nor audience notices. Above all, he sees differently from the way actors or audience see. Bystanders reflect—and reflection is a prism rather than a mirror; it refracts.

(Drucker, 1978, p. 1)

As a social ecologist, Drucker was, in essence, this reflective bystander, noticing things that others had missed, seeing "the change that has already happened." Yet, Drucker's definition of a bystander should not let one come away with the impression that a bystander is a mere observer. Bystanders reflect, after all—and this results in a refraction, a different direction or speed. Social ecologists, Drucker included, are not passive observers of the world around them. They take their individual backgrounds, experiences, and perspectives and use those to see the world around them in new ways, resulting in a different view than others have. They see the human world as one involving complex interactions and relationships that result in change—and then evaluate what actions are required to respond to such change.

For Drucker, social ecology encapsulated his entire process of devising an actionable theory of a functioning society of institutions. As the world around him changed, so did his theory and his idea for pragmatic implementation. The self-governing plant community may have served an industrial society at one point in time, but the advance of a knowledge society warranted a new perspective. Similarly, the need for status and function for the individual may have been served by one's work organization at one time, but later, Drucker saw the social sector as the locus for individual citizenship. Through the

PHOTO 9.1   Peter Drucker, undated.

process of social ecology, Drucker viewed the inevitable "changes that had already happened" throughout his lifetime and refracted his observations through his own experience, background, and unique place in history to devise an ever-adaptive theory and blueprint for a tolerable functioning society.

Note

1   The author was a student in the M.B.A. program at Claremont Graduate School from 1990 to 1991 and took Drucker's seminar course.

Bibliography

Adams, H. (1907) *The education of Henry Adams*. Reprint, New York, NY: Oxford University Press, 1999.

Axelrod, P. (2002) *Values in conflict: The university, the marketplace, and the trials of liberal education*. Montreal and Kingston, Canada: McGill-Queen's University Press.

Chong, D. (2013) 'The relevance of management to society: Peter Drucker's oeuvre from the 1940s and 1950s', *Journal of Management History*, 19 (1), pp. 55–72.

Drucker, P.F. (1955) *America's next twenty years*. New York: Harper and Brothers.

Drucker, P.F. (1969) From information to communication. Paper presented to the International Academy of Management. Reprinted in Drucker, P.F. (2003). *A functioning society*. New Brunswick, NJ: Transaction, pp. 179–191.

Drucker, P.F. (1971) *Men, ideas, and politics*. New York: Harper and Rowe.

Drucker, P.F. (1978) *Adventures of a bystander*. New York: John Wiley & Sons.

Drucker, P.F. (1985a) 'Drucker on Drucker', *New Management*, 2 (3), pp. 7–9.

Drucker, P.F. (1985b) 'You on me', *New Management*, 2 (3), pp. 28–32.

Drucker, P.F. (1989) *The new realities*. New York: Harper and Rowe.

Drucker, P.F. (1993a) 'Reflections of a social ecologist', in Drucker, P.F. (ed.) *The ecological vision*. New Brunswick, NJ: Transaction, 1993.

Drucker, P.F. (1993b) *Post-capitalist society*. New York: Harper Collins.

Drucker, P. F. (1995) 'Peter Drucker talks about himself', interview by Broeck Wahl Blumberg, published in *Global Business Review*, July, pp. 1–5.

Drucker, P.F. (1999) *Management challenges for the 21st century*. New York: Harper Collins.

Fernandez, S. (2009) 'Peter Drucker's leap *to* faith: Examining the origin of his purpose-driven life and its impact on his views of management', *Journal of Management History*, 15 (4), pp. 404–419.

Follett, M. (1924) 'Relating: The circular response'. Reprint, Graham, P. (ed.) (1995) *Mary Parker Follett: Prophet of Management*. Boston, MA: Harvard Business School Press.

Follett, M. (1925) Presentation to Bureau of Personnel Administration. Reprint, Fox, E. and Urwick, L. (eds.), *Dynamic administration: The collected papers of Mary Parker Follett*. London: Pittman. Sourced in Graham, P. (1995) 'Mary Parker Follett (1868–1933): a pioneering life', in Graham, P. (ed.) *Mary Parker Follett: Prophet of management*. Boston, MA: Harvard Business School Press.

Follett, M. (1949) 'The essentials of leadership'. Reprint, Urwick, L. (ed.), *Freedom & coordination: Lectures in business organization by Mary Parker Follett*. London: Management Publications Trust, Ltd., pp. 47–60. In Graham, P. (ed.) (1995) *Mary Parker Follett: Prophet of management*. Boston, MA: Harvard Business School Press.

Gibson, J., Chen, W., Henry, E., Humphreys, J., and Lian, Y. (2013) 'Examining the work of Mary Parker Follett through the lens of critical biography', *Journal of Management History*, 19 (4), pp. 441–458.

Graham, P. (1995) 'Mary Parker Follett (1868-1933): A pioneering life', in Graham, P. (ed.) *Mary Parker Follett: Prophet of management*. Boston, MA: Harvard Business School Press, pp. 11–32.

Grant, J. (2019) *Bagehot: The life and times of the greatest Victorian*. New York, NY: W.W. Norton.

Kantrow, A. (1980) 'Why read Peter Drucker?', *Harvard Business Review*, 87 (11), pp. 74–82.

Kimball, B. (1986) *Orators and philosophers: A history of the idea of liberal education*. New York, NY: Teachers College Press.

Kurzynski, M. (2009) 'Peter Drucker: Modern day Aristotle for the business community', *Journal of Management History*, 15 (4), pp. 357–374.

Linkletter, K. and Maciariello, J. (2009) 'Genealogy of a social ecologist', *Journal of Management History*, 15 (4), pp. 334–355.

Maciariello, J. (2008) *Introduction to Peter F. Drucker, Management (Revised Edition)*. New York, NY: HarperCollins.

Maciariello, J. and Linkletter, K. (2010) 'The next book Peter Drucker would have written: federalism and management as a liberal art', *Management Decision*, 48 (4), pp. 628–655.

Maciariello, J. and Linkletter, K. (2011) *Drucker's lost art of management*. New York, NY: McGraw Hill.

Malcolm, S. and Hartley, N. (2009) 'Peter F. Drucker: Ethics scholar *par excellence*', *Journal of Management History*, 15 (4), pp. 375–387.

Straub, R. (2009) 'What Drucker means around the world,' *People & Strategy*, 32 (4), pp. 4–6.

Taylor, F.W. (1911/1997) *The principles of scientific management*. New York: Harper & Brothers, reprinted by Dover Publications.

Tocqueville, A. (1835) *Democracy in America*. Reprint. New York, NY: Alfred A. Knopf, 1994.

Veblen, T. (1899) *The theory of the Leisure Class*. Reprint, New Brunswick, NJ: Transaction, 1978.

CONCLUSION

Drucker did not see any of his specific ideas regarding management as being his most significant contribution. Although he introduced us to the importance of management by objectives and self-control, the relationship between structure and strategy, and the importance of the decision-making process, his primary contribution, in his eyes, was that "the organization is a human, a social, indeed a moral phenomenon." Coming from a background in political science and philosophy, Drucker viewed the corporation as "a social and political phenomenon rather than as an 'economic' one alone" and emphasized that responsibility, not power, were central to organizations (Drucker, 1985, p. 8).

Viewed mainly as a management theorist, Drucker appears to many readers as a dated figure from long ago in the past, an individual whose ideas cannot possibly have relevance to today's leaders and organizations. Many of the management concepts Drucker is most well-known for are now seen as common sense, customary pragmatic ideas that don't appear to require much thought or contemplation. Then too, Drucker himself contributed to this perspective in the way that he wrote. In his management work, Drucker's tone signals that what he has to say is absolutely simple, obvious, and straightforward: "Management must manage." Such a sentence, particularly taken out of all context, can be construed to be utterly ridiculous or extremely sublime in its simplicity. Consumers of management texts seeking clear presentation and explanation of concepts and applications will likely find Drucker's work dated, ubiquitous, and inaccessible. His references to Good and Evil, his insistence on individual responsibility, and discussions of ethics may confound these readers as well.

DOI: 10.4324/9781003410485-11

Drucker's most important legacy is as a social theorist. His essential message did not change since *The End of Economic Man* was published in 1939. Faced with the failure of socialism and capitalism to deliver on their promises of economic equality and security for all, society must offer an alternative source of status and meaning, or else authoritarianism will offer its own solutions to the issues faced by the human community. Combining his European background with his unique take on American society, Drucker fashioned an identity and a view of America that placed him between those two cultures. By establishing himself as a bystander while celebrating his American home as a community of pluralist institutions, he embodied the very tension between the individual and society that is the subject of his work. Management is the servant of Drucker's tolerable, bearable society in which organizations survive only if effectively led. Effective management, therefore, is not just about economic performance but also about creating a society where individual meaning is possible. In the words of Bob Buford, philanthropist and author of *Halftime: Moving from Success to Significance*: "Peter's greatest contribution is to be the preeminent thought leader of how organizations can be managed to facilitate not only economic life but existential life" (Buford, 2003, p. 2). Near the end of his life, Drucker realized that it was likely that, for most people, success or status would not come from their economic life but from outside of work. Existential life could be realized in other organizations. Although most people would likely plug along in jobs that bored them until they retired, a minority who looked for something more would be the "leaders and the models." In a society where everyone is expected to be successful, one can only accomplish this by having a separate path outside of one's career. For Drucker, this meant a "second career, a parallel career, a social venture, a serious outside interest, all of them offering an opportunity for being a leader, for being respected, for being a success" (Drucker, 1999, pp. 191–193). Ultimately, Drucker left behind not just a theory of a functioning society but a roadmap for navigating personal meaning in life.

Those who knew Drucker personally not only have an appreciation for his mind and contributions to management and social theory but also value their experience of Drucker as a human being. This aspect of Drucker does not come across in his public writings; he was an intensely private individual who protected his personal life from any public scrutiny. Yet, those with whom he interacted outside of formal events have a keen understanding of his appreciation for the individual, his sense of humor, and his authenticity. Bruce Rosenstein, author of *Living in More Than One World: How Peter Drucker's Wisdom Can Inspire and Transform Your Life*, interviewed Drucker extensively for many years. In his words:

> In my own experience, if you were in Drucker's presence, especially alone or with a small group of people, you wanted to be a better person in

that moment; to be your best self. How many people project that kind of aura, and what can we learn from it? Finally, Drucker showed that it was possible to engage in productive longevity for many years, to contribute to society in ways of his choosing, even in the uncertainty of how many more days one has to live.

(Rosenstein, 2023)

Rosenstein's book shows that he gleaned an important lesson from Drucker that had nothing to do with management; it had to do with self-development and finding meaning in life. The roster of people (students, faculty, consulting clients, executives) who saw Drucker not only as a "management expert" but also as a surrogate psychologist, someone who could counsel them on how to live their lives as individuals outside of work, is long. Perhaps that is his most valuable legacy.

But, for those who did not have the luxury of knowing Drucker personally, how should he be valued in terms of his contribution? While Drucker's theory of a functioning society may seem dated in some ways, in many respects, his observations are even more pertinent to modern times. Drucker was particularly concerned with the balance between change and continuity. Today, we face an acceleration of change, what some term an environment of volatility, uncertainty, complexity, and ambiguity (VUCA). In Drucker's era, VUCA consisted of World War I, Hitler and National Socialism, the Great Depression, World War II, Stalin, Mao, and the Cold War, not to mention the Iraq War that occurred during his twilight years. Drucker also witnessed incredible technological, social, and cultural change, ranging from the Civil Rights, Student's Rights, and Women's movements in the United States to the onset of computer technology in the 1950s and the shift from manufacturing to knowledge work. If we step back and look at Drucker's life, we see an unbelievable trajectory through a time of neck-breaking change. It is no wonder that the man sought to find an avenue toward some kind of order in the face of disorder.

Contemporary society will always encounter some challenge related to abrupt change, violent disruption, technological breakthroughs, innovation in some form, or social shifts related to demographics or other factors. This is the nature of human existence, which Drucker showed us through his work as a theorist and social ecologist. Drucker raised issues that we still face today. Capitalism as a system creates inequality. How do we cope with this? How do we navigate the education gap in societies where the educated minority hold a leadership position, which can create a conflict between perceived elites vs. the rest of society? How do we define inclusivity and diversity without creating division? How do we absorb technological advances and innovation in a way that protects the interests of society but still allows for entrepreneurial activity?

Drucker does not have clear answers for us. He did not have clear answers for his twentieth-century audience either. But his most important legacy is that he forces us to think through the important questions and to think them through from multiple perspectives. Drucker is, in essence, about process, not content. If one can understand him as a theorist and thinker, then his management ideas become clearer and more profound as part of a larger picture.

Bibliography

Buford, B. (2003) Personal correspondence with the author, letter, 15 January 2003.

Drucker, P.F. (1985) 'Drucker on Drucker', *New Management*, pp. 7–9.

Drucker, P.F. (1999) *Management challenges for the 21st century*. New York: Harper Business.

Rosenstein, B. (2023) Personal correspondence with the author, email, 20 October 2023.

INDEX

115; society (*see* society); and
technology 163–4; work and worker
52–3, 97, 102–15, 124
Kristol, I. 73–4

labor unions 50, 61, 104, 113, 148, 179
leadership: beyond the walls 77;
and change 94; charisma 85–9;
group 114–15; *vs.* management 89;
servant 94; social 91; toxic 84, 95;
transactional *vs.* transformational 88
legitimacy: of authority 35, 38, 46–7,
140, 149–50; of management 46, 49,
60, 73–6; of power 2, 149
liberal arts 44–6, 111–12, 173, 182–4
Lipman-Blumen, J. 87–8, 93

Madison, J. 64, 142–6, 150
management by objectives and self
control 71–3
manual work 59–60, 91, 102–5, 109
Marcuse, H. 6, 24
Marx, K. 65, 106, 118, 121, 123, 136
Marxism 23, 39

National Socialism: and anti-Semitism
9, 20, 39; and charisma 84–6; and
German politics 18–20; propaganda
99–100; rise of 1–2, 5, 19, 39, 61; as
social model 43–4, 46, 139, 155
New Deal 22, 66, 147, 150, 152
Nietzsche, F. 18, 121

Owen, R. 48

performance: economic 50; individual
48–9, 72
pluralism 2, 50, 145–6, 150
Polanyi, K. 11, 16
post-capitalist society *see* society
power 11, 52, 89, 177; and
decentralization 149–50; and
federalism 143–5; Follett, M. P.
and 181; governmental 64, 73,
147–8, 154; labor and management
50; legitimacy 51, 75–6; nature of
136–8; organization and 45, 51–2,
60, 63, 81, 148, 182; political 180;
pluralism 50; social 1–2, 46, 91;
social theory 38; and knowledge (*see*
knowledge)
privatization 152–4
productivity 49, 51, 106–8, 124–5

profit 64–5, 73, 123
public sector *see* government

race 59, 61, 112–13, 150–1
rationality: and economics 21, 40–4,
172; and Enlightenment 36; of
management 60, 70, 91, 122; and
organizational power 63; and
positivism 139; and social ecology
172; of society 2, 57–8, 159; and
values 175
responsibility: of authority 181;
individual 35, 38, 45–9
Roosevelt, F. D. 22–3, 148

Sarah Lawrence College 24, 66
Schmitz, C. 12
Schmitz, D. 12, 20–1
Schumpeter, J. 117–25, 130, 132
scientific management 103, 106, 179–80
Second World War 15, 20, 27, 54;
American economy and 26, 43, 17,
80, 90, 129, 149; capitalism 68, 146;
corporatism 66–7, 148; Japan 78, 99;
labor 62–103; legacy of government
spending 150–2; management 79,
148; productivity 106; race 112;
and social innovation 127–8;
technology 59, 158–9, 161, 166; and
worldview 98
self-governing plant community 46–9, 102
servant leadership *see* leadership
Sloan, A. 58, 60
Smuts, J. C. 37–8
social: ecology (*see* social ecology);
management function 58–9;
responsibility of management 76–7;
sector 27–8, 52–4, 150, 186
social ecology: defined 171–5; and
discontinuity 184–5; history of 175–8
socialism 39, 57, 64–5
social responsibility *see* social
social sector *see* social
society: and entrepreneurship 50–1;
free 143, 149–50; functioning (*see*
functioning society); industrial
46–9, 57, 102–3, 139–41, 149, 159;
and innovation 50–1, 126, 132; of
institutions 140, 150; knowledge
49–50, 54, 90–1, 97–15; post-
capitalist 50–2, 105; values 59–60
society of organizations *see* society
socioeconomic class 59–60, 91, 113–15

Printed in the United States
by Baker & Taylor Publisher Services